T0365099

The Investor's Code

To preserve capital and become a successful investor, the following code of conduct is highly advised:

1. I promise to get investment education on a life-long basis from a true source and keep enhancing my knowledge base regularly.

2. I promise to set an investment goal and modify it as time goes on, but always adhere to it and implement it in all of my activities.

3. I promise to use only investment strategies that support my goals, and not those that detract from it.

4. I promise to use the exact trading methodology and ideas as provided by the true source and never deviate from it.

5. I promise to stay always in communication with the markets in which I am involved.

6. I promise to find a niche market that suits my **main** idea of investment and stay in that niche until its mastery.

7. I promise to develop and establish a mental system for investment and doing it on a systematic basis, all based upon pre-calculated risks.

8. I promise to keep accurate records of the investments that I make and use the mistakes effectively, and not to blame myself, but to correct my future activities by learning from my mistakes.

9. *I promise to stay in exchange with the markets I am involved, and never assume that profits will flow without doing my initial research and homework.*

10. *I promise to use trends in my investment activities and follow the proper formula for each trend in a correct manner.*

11. *I promise to plot my investment activities on a graph and analyze it on a weekly basis for emerging patterns; use the slope of the trend line to guide me to the correct decision of what the next action should be.*

12. *I promise not to alter the exact trading methodology as prescribed in the "true source" textbook and not to combine it incorrectly with other techniques.*

13. *I promise never to use the rent money or money allocated for other purposes to do investments.*

14. *I promise to risk only the money I can afford to lose in any investment activity.*

15. *I promise never to be a patsy but through achievement of an expert knowledge, become my own consultant.*

16. *I promise to fly with the eagles and never associate with the turkeys of this world or utilize them as mentors.*

17. *I promise to Investigate before I invest.*

Advanced Principles

Of

Success

&

Prosperity

Empower the Genius Within

Matthew M. Radmanesh, Ph.D.
Professor of Electrical
& Computer Engineering,
California State University, Northridge

authorHOUSE

AuthorHouse™
1663 Liberty Drive
Bloomington, IN 47403
www.authorhouse.com
Phone: 833-262-8899

This book is a work of non-fiction. Unless otherwise noted, the author and the publisher make no explicit guarantees as to the accuracy of the information contained in this book and in some cases, names of people and places have been altered to protect their privacy.

Published by AuthorHouse 12/15/2021

ISBN: 978-1-4772-5522-3 (sc)
ISBN: 978-1-4772-5521-6 (hc)
ISBN: 978-1-4772-5520-9 (e)

Library of Congress Control Number: 2012913985

Print information available on the last page.

Any people depicted in stock imagery provided by Thinkstock are models, and such images are being used for illustrative purposes only. Certain stock imagery © *Thinkstock.*

This book is printed on acid-free paper.

Because of the dynamic nature of the Internet, any web addresses or links contained in this book may have changed since publication and may no longer be valid. The views expressed in this work are solely those of the author and do not necessarily reflect the views of the publisher, and the publisher hereby disclaims any responsibility for them.

Advanced Principles of Success & Prosperity

Matthew M. Radmanesh, Ph.D.

Why This Book?

With the publication of the first book "The Ultimate Keys to Success in Business & Science" the groundwork for understanding the management principles governing any business enterprise, whether a local supermarket or a national government, was laid down solidly.

This book takes off from that solid platform and flies off like a rocket into the wild blue yonder, exploring high speed methods of expanding one's wealth as well as zones of influence and prosperity well beyond one's wildest expectations.

This book is your high speed bullet train into the realm of prosperity and makes one an invincible and extremely intelligent force in the realm of business and investments. This is done simply by tapping into genius power dormant within any individual, which is lying in wait to be explored and uncorked.

In summary, utilizing this book in one's life will make one a recession proof individual who can withstand high destructive forces of the economy and still come out on the other side smelling like a rose!

*Dedicated to
the Infinite potential
of Man's Spirit Where
Ability is the Prosperous King
and
Matter the Mere Servant!*

Contents

PART 2
The Slant of Life Is Toward Selling 161

PART 3
Key 1: Who Do You Have to Be to Succeed? 219

PART 4
Key 2: What Is Your Knowledge Base? 231

PART 5
Key 3: What Are Your Leadership Qualities? 257

PART 6
Key 4: What Is Your Winning Edge in the Market? 267

PART 7
Key 5: How Connected Are You? 277

PART 8
Key 6: What is Your Niche Market? 291

PART 9
Key 7: What Team Are You Working With? 299

PART 10
Key 8: How Many Streams of Income Do You Have? 319

PART 11
Key 9: Do You Know The Trends in Your Marketplace? 347

PART 12
Key 10: Do You Know the Laws of Your Business? 367

PART 13
Lifelong Selling 377

PART 14
The Timeless Principles of Business 399

PART 15
Advanced Business Principles 445

PART 16
Unlimited Income Strategies 471

PART 17
The Final Summary of Thoughts 509

PART 18
The Epilogue 555

$\mathscr{P}$*reface*

Recently the author published a popular book entitled *"The Ultimate Keys to Success in Business & Science,"* which was well received by the investing community. This book clearly sets the foundation for understanding our world of business of which sciences are but a subset.

However, upon further research, more data concerning our business world with its many misconceptions and common pitfalls was obtained. This is a universe far more dynamic and crucial to one's survival than the field of sciences. The business principles even though separate from our scientific world and its laws, could not possibly come into practice without a thorough understanding of the technical side of life.

In other words, for a person to engage in business and exchange of goods and services, he needs to be technically either well versed or have that area headed by a technically able individuals.

Therefore, the need for such a further elucidation is what led to the creation of this second book and is where it takes off. It is the sequel or the second installment to the first book and intends to undercut areas that were not illuminated in the first volume.

The present work is the culmination of many years of study, observation, and pondering on the dilemmas and enigmas of the business world and their origin. The resultant understandings that were extracted from this sophisticated and at times incomprehensible arena was amply rewarded in the process and became the essence of the current work.

It is an interestingly uncommon book written primarily for the business-minded as well as the technical individual. It is intended to serve several classes of our society.

a) The business owners and investors,
b) The office managers,
c) The engineers, scientists, entrepreneurs, etc.
d) The career seekers or job hunters,
e) The common man wishing to achieve a greater level of prosperity.

This book will surely serve also an important class of our society—the technical inventors who are looking for inspirations and new ideas to imbue them with enough understanding to finalize and materialize their thoughts into reality.

It is written for the average man who may or may not be technically versed and yet desires to learn about the business world at large, or the job opportunities in his immediate surroundings. It is intended to lift the aura of "black magic" surrounding the world of business, to enlighten and demystify this subject in the minds of ordinary individuals.

The Reasons for This Work

Everyone, in today's society, is struggling with this dominant and imposing thing called the business world and strives toward a higher understanding of its inner workings. Yet most books present the basic concepts with so much complexity and filled with so many business jargons that the general public has given up on the subject, choosing to retire to the sideline by deciding to work full-time for someone else. In other words, their hopes of owning a company or a small business have been dashed aside and their dreams of a higher understanding have not been fulfilled in any of these books.

Within the confines of this book, one is given a chance for the first time to take an in-depth look and to inspect first-hand the code combination to the locks placed on the treasure vaults deeply buried within our business world. These locks, which are mostly invented false data, have created an imposing barrier to the individual's prosperity in many unsuspecting and hidden ways.

By reading this work, you have taken the first step to explore the basics of our business world and armed with the tools laid down in this book, you will soon find yourself on a higher plateau of existence.

Many of the concepts are totally new in the business world and express the powerful principles lucidly and dynamically, in simple terms with clear explanations, and thus provide an unforgettable impression in the reader's mind.

This is a new approach unmatched in any extant text today. The discovery of these fundamentals has had a huge impact on our current world and has truly made our business world a bright beacon of hope with a renewed interest in conquering our physical universe. This work has created, in very simple terms, a "unified theory" about the two distinct aspects: the business world and the mental universe.

Finally, this work lays out the major milestones, that the business-minded, the scientist as well as the non-technical individual need to know before traveling on this adventurous road. The individual will be able to formulate and develop his own business plan that would crack open the *Treasure Vault of the Business World*. This has been kept hidden and locked to the average man, and this book will begin to bring him a completely new perspective on the concept of prosperity and in fact make it within his grasp.

The Author's Goals

The author intends to bring forth a milestone achievement that can be summed up as:

a) Introducing a whole new thinking methodology in the investment arena,

b) Tapping into the hitherto hidden genius potentiality of an individual,

c) Shedding light on the concept of selling and why it is so essential in any and all aspects of life,

d) Presenting 10 golden keys that will unlock one's life and take the mental brakes off,

e) Making enormous prosperity well within the reach any individual coming from any walks of life.

Any communications in the way of a healthy criticism and/or correction are welcome. Moreover, the author considers it one of the most rewarding things to have others grasp these materials in all of their simplicity and increase their own potential survival in this universe and help others to achieve their survival goals. In this process, Man is helped to take control of his own destiny, and without being shackled by the chains of higher authority or superstition.

Therefore, in order to improve the quality of this work, the author would like to have all comments or suggestions be sent directly to:
Dr. Matthew M. Radmanesh
18111 Nordhoff Street,
Department of Electrical and Computer Engineering,
California State University, Northridge, California 91330.
Or email to: **matt@csun.edu**

Matthew M. Radmanesh, Ph.D.

Acknowledgements

The current work, as presented in this book, has been truly a journey from the realm of the unknowns into the bright sunlight, filled with many amplified business principles. These principles have been obtained through the scientific methodology filter to achieve a workable set of keys that will open many doors for the reader in science, business and ultimately life!

The author would like to further thank many of his professional colleagues, Dr. George Haddad & Dr. C. M. Chu (University of Michigan, Ann Arbor, MI), the early mentors at the University of Michigan (Ann Arbor), Dr. S. K. Ramesh (Dean of College of Engineering and Computer Science, CSUN), Dr. Ali Amini (ECE Dept. chair, CSUN), Dr. Ramin Roosta (CSUN, CA). Their support and collegiality through the years is definitely appreciated.

My gratitude also goes to Jaime Rodriguez, a highly-valued individual, who put many of the presented principles to work and gradually became a hub of overnight success through the application of these business principles.

Finally, the author's deep gratitude belongs to his lovely wife, Jane, and his brilliant son, William, for making life full of fun and happiness during this power-packed project, and to his parents, Mary and the late Dr. G. H. Radmanesh, for their true love and unconditional support.

Matthew M. Radmanesh, Ph.D.
Dept. of Electrical and Computer Engineering,
California State University, Northridge,
July 2012

The Importance of Work

This book is structured around tapping into the infinite potentiality of life, which is surrounded in a sea of finiteness of the physical universe. It is a roadmap leading the individual out of the quagmire of finiteness and limitedness into the unlimited state of prosperity and abundance.

It is not based upon, "Here are some important business concepts, so let's learn them and maybe we can improve our understanding of the business world." This is the approach most business books take and fill the reader full of business terms, jargons and terminologies, hoping that it would lead to a successful business activity down the road.

Moreover, the books written by the founders of certain business enterprises are not broad enough to expand upon. They are usually narrow in the angle of their presentation and cannot be easily generalized into other investment fields.

Therefore in this work, we have taken the high-speed road to a completely new approach in business, where we are in for the long haul, for an infinite income potential and work in eternity.

This approach is based upon simplicity of life itself, combined with a new approach of using highly novel techniques and newly minted principles, which can morph any ordinary business into a superior cash machine.

This is where we have structured this book on a top-down basis, with governing concepts at the outset and the byproducts as examples at the end. By using a simple and straight language and clarity of presentations, we enable the reader to create a new business or manage an existing business enterprise at high speeds with the wisdom of Buddha, cut through the haze with the sharpness of a diamond saw, and see problems from afar with a 20-20 vision.

What Sets This Book Apart

"Superstition sets the whole world in flames; philosophy quenches them."

— Voltaire (1694-1778)
French Philosopher

This book lays the trail map of how to energize any and all establisments that man has built through the ages and shows how to bring new resurgences into any part of it with great rapidity. The list of establishments is endless; prominent amongst them are the governments, corporations, companies, local supermarkets, family units, so on and so forth. Wherever there is life existing and trying to survive toward prosperity, this book could help out greatly to improve conditions.

Just like the abolishment of the slave trades, which was made to be archaic through a higher awareness of its negative effects upon the humanity as a whole, thus revolutionizing our world, so would this book by bringing on a new era of incredible developments for mankind!

This book is the road map leading to the discovery of great mental abilities and physical treasures and could guarantee enormous success in life or business. This is done simply through the discovery of one's hidden potential and qualities inherent but masked in any individual!

The motto is *everyone is sitting on a gold mine, but his unawareness of it causes him to look elsewhere for gold!* This book provides the tools he needs to use in order to first survey the mine and then using proper tools tap into the gold vein and create enormous wealth for self and others in the process.

You are indeed fortunate indeed to have this valuable book to help you along the path of life toward a higher plateau of existence, unobservable from our current vantage point, but surely existing beyond and above the clouds awaiting to be discovered.

Why Should I Read This Book?

"To be philosophy's slave is to be free."
—Seneca Wallace (5 - 65 AD)
Roman Philosopher

This book is structured around the infinite potentiality of life, which can deliver speed, vision and humanity to the business world. It is a roadmap leading the individual out of the problem-oriented world that he finds himself and will lead him into the sunshine of communication and the unlimited possibilities of brighter solutions to which he has never been introduced either by the academicians in the higher education system of colleges and universities or by the school of hard knocks.

This book is based upon the proven and basic principles presented in the first book, The Ultimate keys to Success in Business and Science, and takes off where the first book leaves off.

It is truly a tour-de force achievement and a ne plus ultra (highest) state of accomplishment to have a book introducing concepts that makes men into super human beings. It makes one stand in awe of one' own eternal nature and one's enormous untapped hidden capabilities.

Therefore, in this work, we have taken the high road to a whole new approach in business, where we are in for the long haul, for an infinite income potential and work in eternity.

This approach is based upon simplicity of life itself, a totally new approach, where we have structured it on a top-down basis.

By using a simple and straightforward language and with the help of the powerful principles, we enable the reader to achieve his dreams and soar like an eagle into the realm of unlimited prosperity.

Here is a book where, for the first time, we have ignored the mechanics of existence (comprised of physical limitations and quantities of things) and have focused primarily on the quality of life (comprised of ability and potentiality of things). A shift of focus from what is and how limited life is to what could be and how unlimited the potential of life is! This approach is a total shift of focus from limitedness and scarcity of things that we mostly hear about, to unlimitedness and enormous capabilities that exist in any situation and how much a slight shift in viewpoint can drastically change the outcome in any situation in life or business.

The ultimate elixir in life, which can turn any low-production, hopeless or bankrupt business back to prosperity is the positive qualities inherently resident in the life force of the individual, which has been mostly ignored by the mechanistic approach of the "authority".

Therefore, it is not with great surprise that by simple implementation of the principles laid down in this book that we can effectively turn any low-production business around and place it into health much faster and sooner than all of the mechanical approaches that are presented by business experts.

We also show him where the turkeys are so that one can stay away from and thus never mingle with them, so that their contagious bad habits never have a chance to transfer over to one's life!

The obvious reasons of staying away from turkeys are three folds:
   a) First, turkeys can't fly,
   b) Second, they have this self-created and yet erroneous notion of "how they know it all" as well as "how to best survive in life," and
   c) Third, they are usually somebody else's meal.

Therefore, this is a book written for the eagles of this world and intends to turn them into super eagles; a new specie of birds that are more intelligent and much superior than any existing breed!

PART 1

The Essence of Being a Genius

The Evolution of Knowledge

The current work is truly the result of evolution of knowledge, which has been unearthed through the years. It is the amplification and advancement of the discovered principles covered in earlier works. It is the result of combining and utilization of the many discovered principles in order to forge a more advanced technology so that the individual may reach his destination much faster. The current work owes its lineage and heritage to the following ancestors:

A. **Book 1**: The beginning of the current journey began several years ago when the book *"The Gateway to Understanding: Electrons to Waves and Beyond"* was published. This is the cornerstone book that started it all and paved the way for all future scientific developments in sciences as well as the discoveries of all fundamental and advanced principles in the field of business, and life in general. In this book the genius founders of electricity and waves were introduced and the subject of *electronic waves* was unified with an old subject—optics. This book was a new look at the hard-core science of electricity with its commanding presence in our society and how the genius minds of its founders helped to shape the technical world that is blossoming today.

B. **Book 2**: A natural sequel to Book 1 entitled, *Cracking the Code of Our Physical Universe,* followed a few years ago. This book further amplified and opened up the subject of general sciences and made a foray into the materials composing our world both on a microscopic and macroscopic scale: *from an atom to a galaxy* and beyond. It examined many aspects of our world hitherto misunderstood and brought forth the concept of scientific methodology and how it can be used in sciences or any aspect of life, to bring about workable technology. It cut a wide swath of clarity in the confusion of information and the massive false data existing and surrounding an average individual on a daily basis. It helped to fill the void of knowledge and to blaze a path to a higher plateau of understanding of life.

C. **Book 3**: From the scientific principles explored in Book 2, the author created a successful dual universe wherein the scientific methodology was employed to obtain new information concerning the business world, which dominates every aspect of our existence. Using the duality principle, the principles that were discovered and codified in this book, helped to create a firm foundation for the business world. This book expanded the scientific principles to life and the business world, thus the dual sequel (or the business sequel) entitled, *The Ultimate Keys to Success in Business & Science,* was born. In this book, eight keys to success in any life activity or business enterprise were identified and established for the first time and were treated in depth.

D. **Book 4**: In the current book, **Advanced Principles of Success & Prosperity,** we have used books 1 and 3 as the launching platform to release a set of principles and laws, which are extremely potent and irresistible in actual use. This book enables one to achieve one's goals in earnest and thus allow him to attain unlimited prosperity.

Therefore, we have come back full circle to where we started our work in Book 1, about the laws of electricity, its genius founders, and their postulates; however, there are two major distinctions worth mentioning:

1. We have isolated the fifty characteristics and traits of a genius for the first time and have provided a road map of how to achieve each trait, one by one, and thus anyone can become a genius if he stays the course. In this work, we are no longer fascinated with the bright minds of science nor do we stand in awe or embroider upon the achievements of the genius minds of the scientific community; rather we emphasize the fact that anyone can become a genius and achieve similar results if he utilizes this book cleverly!

2. We have introduced some solid encompassing principles, which when combined with the genius traits, will create magical results. It will start dispelling all ambiguities of how to engage in any activity, whether in life or business, and emerge victorious no matter what life throws at one. This ultimate factor of allowing the individual to implement his dreams confidently puts him at the positive cause point of one's own life, enabling him to see the future and enter a zone of prosperity. This is a vision, which comes into focus in one's own mind and gradually takes root in the physical universe and eventually becomes a reality well within his reach.

Following the Book 1's style of title, an alternate name for this book could have aptly been *"The Gateway to Prosperity: From Matter to Viewpoint and Beyond."*

In short, this book is your ticket for the bullet train ride to the realm of immeasurable success and incredible prosperity.

The essence of this work and its relation to its ancestors are clearly delineated in the diagram shown below.

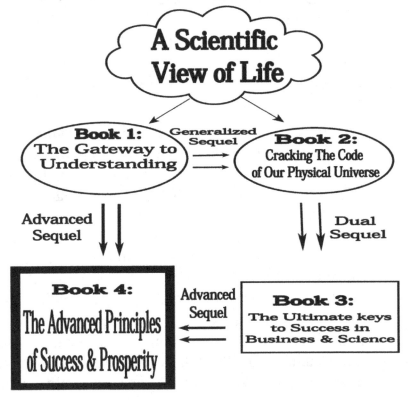

The Essence and Inter-relationship of This Work to Its Ancestors.

☙ ✳ ❀ ✿ ❀ ✳ ❧

The Misconceptions of Being a Genius

The English dictionary defines a genius as *"a person having exceptional natural capacity of intellect, especially as shown in creative and original work in fields such as business, science, music, art, etc."*

With this definition in mind, one can see that almost anyone of a sane mind can rise to the occasion and with hard work and proper mental training become a genius in a chosen field of work.

However, as simple as this concept may seem to one at first glance, one will run into a society which has an enormous prejudice and a major reservoir of false data on the subject of "being a genius."

In today's society, if you are not born with such natural abilities to think like "an Einstein," or "a James Clerk Maxwell" or "a Michael Faraday" one could never be called a genius. It is arbitrarily assumed that one has to be born a genius in order to be one. People mistakenly think that a) it is not developable, and b) no one can be made into one. Either you are born a genius and have it at birth or you don't—that is the common false data propagating around in the society.

Therein lies the answer to this enigma: the society's opinion leaders, the schoolteachers, the media, the professionals, college educators, etc., cannot grant beingness to any individual who does not have the proper diploma or college credentials and degrees. Most of these *Opinion Leaders* are below the power of perception of simple truths and are mostly tooting the horn for some vested interest somewhere, who has a great interest to ignore and discredit any that does exhibit the genius traits.

Therefore, our society has apparently run into a major dearth of geniuses and is run by mediocre to poor leaders in many subjects and fields of endeavor. Our economy is run into the ground of insolvency, decay and poverty by some very low-competence but highly credentialed leaders, who easily defy all natural laws and violate them on a constant basis. They create mayhem in our lives politically, economically and socially and yet never even have a second thought about what they have done, because they are far below the threshold of observation of their misdeeds!

There are fields of study such as mental sciences, economics, etc., which have been so dominated by a number of "ignorant" and extremely unaware people, calling themselves scientists or better yet "pseudo-scientists," that it will take untold number of man-hours to purify these fields from a complete chaos that they have caused.

These *pseudo-scientists* who are mostly funded by government appropriations and special vested interests have knowingly or unknowingly introduced a number of arbitrary and false principles that have made their subjects very unworkable and thus have put the public as a whole into a complete quandary and utter confusion of what the truth really is!

A few examples may elucidate this point further:

a) To take a flawed concept such as "communism" and force it as a principle of operation in economics and government, and then govern a country into the ground accompanied by very low public morale is beyond imagination. To be so engrossed with such an untested and impractical concept and yet fail to see that it has slid everything and everybody into the dark ground of deep insolvency is pure ignorance and shows how far the political leaders have sunk below the level of simple observation of the obvious. Yet it is a common practice and there are countries that rule the lives of people and consider it a workable method of government and economics. It also shows the depth of desperation of mankind and how astray he can be misguided into believing a false field of operation as truth and adopt it as a correct philosophy of government and economics.

b) To have a government run by and for the vested interest and then pass laws to allow the human rights of any defenseless citizen to be compromised in the name of national security (e.g. at the airports, wire-tapping of citizens, false arrests for bogus reasons, etc.) is pure ignorance of the laws of nature, showing a great lack of understanding of basics of life and fundamental principles of management. This creates a dangerous environment where the future growth of a society becomes greatly curtailed and stunted to a point where the average citizen is no longer interested in creating a future toward prosperity but is worried about the safety of self, family and close associates, let alone the society and the globe at large.

c) To allow the "pseudo-scientist" psychiatrist to have a carte blanche (i.e., full authority) with their ice picks, their shock machines and poison pills, to injure anyone at will in the name of therapy is unthinkable. To give them a playing field in the subject of mental healing and have them introduce many untested, arbitrary and baseless theories as a scientific study, such as the flawed theory of "chemical imbalance in the brain," etc., is an oxymoron to the nth power (a huge contradiction). To pass laws to empower them to become loose upon the defenseless children is a further sign of degradation of the term "scientist." Giving them power for drugging the public and enriching their own wallets and that of their masters (pharmaceutical companies) shows us that we as a race of intelligent beings have sunk to the basement of perception, way below the threshold (the minimum required) level of observation of truth!

Compounding this problem with the fact of not giving recognition of any kind to a genius, as a more intelligent being amongst us, someone who can dream up bright solutions to problems and make them vanish has created an enigma.   Instead, most geniuses and their bright solutions easily get discredited by the vested interest and the slave master who oppose it through many media channels of black propaganda. This has doomed us to a very distasteful state of affairs and a dim future.

In the final analysis, we see that there exists a public misconception that a genius is usually an eccentric and a crazy scientist. Most people believe that one is born a genius at birth and acquires the genius quality through a superior genetic hereditary. The general public has also been brought to think that they need to see credentials and university degrees before they can stamp the vote of approval on someone.

Quite to the contrary, genetic hereditary has a small role in this matter since a genius is a summation of many positive qualities in one person, which can indeed be created and brought into existence by:

a) Proper training in true data,

b) Correct training in the genius traits as discussed and presented later,

c) Adherence to strict moral principles, and

d) Proper subjective counseling to remove hidden reservoirs of harmful sources of internal false data and prejudice from the mind, thus enabling the mind to observe and be placed into a high state of alertness and vitality that can identify and receive the correct information and at the same time filter out the falsities.

Correct application of (a-d) above will enable any sane human being to tap into the enormous gold veins of precious qualities deeply buried within him, and in time emerge as a true genius!

How One Develops Genius Traits

"Life-transforming ideas have always come to me through books."

—Bell Hooks (1952-)
Distinguished Professor of English

There are a specific set of character traits that sets one apart as a head and shoulder above any average humanoid and makes one a super special being. These are called the genius traits, seldom seen but often desired.

These traits are learnable and can be mastered on a gradient scale much like anything else in life. These are exceptional human qualities that can make one a superstar in a chosen field of study.

We may occasionally run into a person displaying a genius trait in a specific field of study, but mostly in today's drug-crazed and highly materialistic society they are looked upon as abnormal, or at best odd characters.

These geniuses are the trend-setters, game-changers, franchise-players of our society and oftentimes their decency and good nature does not allow them to protect themselves from the merchants of chaos who have an avid craving for dirt, even if they have to manufacture it or sensationalize it when it does not exist.

If one must rise above the average humanoid and above the noise of the crowd, then one must be conversant and extremely familiar with the principles laid down in the first book, *The Ultimate keys to success in Business and science.* Then and only then, with the help of that text and familiarity with this one, the individual has a deep enough foundation to embark upon the road to infinite prosperity, the road to genius traits that will open many locked doors of opportunity and speed one toward the promised land!

The Character Traits of a Genius

"Ability will never catch up with the demand for it."

—Malcolm Forbes (1919 - 1990)
American Author & Publisher

In the ensuing pages, fifty genius character traits are explored in depth. If one masters each one under the correct guidance and leadership of an expert or even strive to master them on one's own power, one will in time arrive at the final destination of great skills and exceptional powers of the mind that can bring much prosperity to one's own life and the associates.

Others cannot help but to notice one's genius powers and cooperate fully, because their own life as a result gets better and becomes enriched by being around a genius.

One should heed an important false datum implanted in today's think in the society and that is "a genius is somewhat crazy, eccentric, out of kilter and uncoordinated in his life and whereabouts; thus one should be wary of these blokes!" This is purely a black PR (Public Relations) campaign run on the bright minds of the society to disenfranchise and debar them from the community, as their presence could bring about bright solutions much to the demise of the vested interest (which are running a business based upon public ignorance). Obviously, these bright solutions as offered by the genius could potentially ruin the cash flow business based upon ignorance, and thereby upset the shiny apple cart set up by the vested interest!

A true genius, quite contrary to the general belief, is very rational, an extremely friendly person, a humanitarian, and is very outgoing and helpful to others. He grants people a high degree of beingness, is benevolent and wants the best for his community and the society at large.

Given the specific attributes for a genius as described in the following pages, if one makes a sound effort to study them as a true pupil, then one would enable himself to make some very positive adjustments in his business and life upon their mastery.

With this book, one has the solid approach that would open the doors of opportunity as never before, and invigorate his lost dreams into a realm of possibility—the ones he has dreamt about all of his life but are left unfulfilled!

Don't think Big, Think Infinite

"Time is an illusion."

— Albert Einstein

This book is a roadmap toward prosperity, which is a state of existence in which one is thriving and flourishing well, and overall is very successful.

If you have ever dreamt of such a state of prosperous existence, then you are in good company as we will travel down this road with the book as your roadmap. You will find many fascinating things about your hidden assets that have never been explored but now with this book, have a chance to be developed and turned into real assets.

Many hidden treasures of one's personality can be strengthened and turned into genius traits by pure perseverance and daily practice.

One will soon rise toward an unlimited thinkingness, and the old cliché "think big" seems too small to even bother with or utilize in one's long term thinking methodology in business or life. Instead, one should now substitute this old cliché in his daily endeavors with a more modern and appropriate one: "Think infinite!"

The Fifty Genius Traits

"There are no limitations to the mind except those we acknowledge."

—Napoleon Hill (1883-1970)
American Author

Through many years of research and observation on optimum human behavior, the following fifty traits have emerged as the most valuable human virtues. These are the ones that one must master well before one can achieve a high peak of prosperity on many levels and arenas. These are:

Trait #1
Having a Great Drive

Trait #2
Having Great Courage

Trait #3
Being Highly Devoted to Goals

Trait #4
Being Immensely Knowledgeable

Trait #5
Having a High Honesty and Integrity Level

Trait #6
Having Great Optimism

Trait #7
Having a High Ability to Judge

Trait #8
Being Highly Enthusiastic

Trait #9
Being Highly Willing to Take Calculated Risks

Trait #10
Having a Dynamic Energy flow

Trait #11
Being Highly Willing to Undertake an Enterprise

Trait #12
Being Highly Able to Motivate and Close People

Trait #13
Having an Outgoing Personality

Trait #14
Being a Great Communicator

Trait #15
Being Extremely Patient

Trait #16
Having Great Perception Powers

Trait #17
Being a Great Perfectionist

Trait #18
Having a Great Sense of Humor

Trait #19
Being Highly Versatile

Trait #20
Being Highly Adaptable

Trait #21
Being Highly Curious

Trait #22
Being an Excellent Individualist

Trait #23
Being a Great Idealist

Trait #24
Being Immensely Imaginative

Trait #25
Having a High Ability to Grant Beingness

Trait #26
Having a Great Balanced Life

Trait #27
Being a Great Leader

Trait #28
Being an Intelligent Investor

Trait #29
Being an Expert Salesman

Trait #30
Being a Great Humanitarian

Trait #31
Being a Great Environmentalist

Trait #32
Having a Great Spiritual Understanding

Trait #33
Being Highly Divine

Trait #34
Being a Clever Innovator & Problem Vanisher

Trait #35
Being a Superb False Data Detector

Trait #36
Being a Master Negotiator

Trait #37
Being a Great Futurist

Trait #38
Having Unlimited Space

Trait #39
Being able to Handle Incoming Force or Motion

Trait #40
Being a Great Scientist

Trait #41
Being able to Stay Exterior Stably

Trait #42
Being Able to Select the Correct Game to Play

Trait #43
Having Great Self-Cultivated Qualities

Trait #44
Having Great Certainty

Trait #45
Being a Great Visionary

Trait #46
Being a Great Adventurer

Trait #47
Being an Excellent Decision Maker

Trait #48
Having an Excellent Awareness Level

Trait #49
Being Able to Remain Always at Positive Cause

Trait #50
Being Able to Assume Any Identity at Will

Let us now begin exploring these fifty traits in more depth, in the ensuing sections with the hope of cultivating them one by one in our own behavior.

Trait #1
Having A Great Drive

One important quality of a genius is that he has a strong desire to work hard and long. He has a great self-initiative and does not wait for orders to start working or get moving toward a future goal that he has in mind.

He is well aware of his current accomplishments and has a huge drive toward achieving a future goal. Therefore, this awareness translates into a strong driving force forward which coordinates and mobilizes people around him to share his vision and thereby help him more effectively to achieve the desired goal.

His focus is on the future and the accomplishment of the intended target. The future is where he lives and that is where he gets all of his energy and force in life.

Exercise 1: Think of a goal and put your attention on it. Now notice how much drive you can have if you just focused on that goal and forgot the present time momentarily. Write down your observations.

᚛ ౭ ✶ ❀ ❊ ❀ ✶ ౨ ᚛

Trait #2
Having Great Courage

Having courage means meeting danger without fear, which is an admirable quality of a genius.

Frankly, in this day and age it takes courage to get things done that others would consider impossible.

It takes courage and fearlessness to start a new business and take on the competitive forces of the business world as well as the economic challenges of a new environment and the balancing act of keeping ahead of the supply and demand curve.

A genius stops worrying about what others think if he thinks differently and independently than average, or if he does things that are unorthodox. It takes courage to be different and to do bold and new things. He has a high degree of courage to withstand high peer pressure or be persuaded to act and think like everybody else!

Exercise 2: Think of something new that you could take on right now. See if you can gather enough courage to go ahead and do it regardless of the odds of success. Write down your findings.

Trait #3
Being Highly Devoted to Goals

A genius has a specific and clearly defined set of goals that he has set for himself and must be accomplished. He knows what he wants, therefore he can easily create a **plan of action** to achieve it. This plan of action guides him and prevents a lot of wasted time and misguided efforts.

By generating a constant stream of goals into the future, a genius creates time; he creates positivity and a bright future to look up to and relish.

By setting goals that reach far into the future, he achieves two things:

1. He generates a daily schedules that revolves around his goals and feeds him positive thoughts constantly,

2. He puts in positive controls on the general picture of his life and thus he is guided in life with total aim at what he does. His projects all dovetail into the bigger picture of his goals and thus he does not wander aimlessly in life.

Exercise 3: Think of one goal that you would like to achieve and see if you can develop a plan of actions to achieve it in a systematic way. Write down your findings.

Trait #4
Being Immensely Knowledgeable

A genius is constantly and continually gathering accurate information related to his field of study. His search for true information and facts about his chosen field encompasses many avenues and involves several perception channels.

He is usually reading informative books in his field of study or you may find him listening to live lectures, or recorded information on CDs, tapes, etc. He also watches videos and films of how something relevant to his field of study is done or designed, in order to learn new sets of skills. He is a sponge for true and workable information.

He asks questions from people who know his field of study and wants to find the correct answers to his dilemmas. He is not dismayed by naysayers who either discourage him or do not wish him to gain more knowledge. He constantly pushes his knowledge envelope further out.

He has a good detector for false data offered to him or passed on to him by the misinformed or the individuals or groups with vested interest.

His knowledge base is such that he automatically filters out unrelated and immaterial information and quickly absorbs the needed facts and the correct workable data of operation. He has a high perception of truth in what he observes, reads, listens or sees.

His sensitivity to false data is fantastically high. This is perhaps the single most positive attribute of a genius that not only rewards him in many ways (such as guidance of self and others, personal achievements, etc.) but also saves him from much confusion. This trait protects him from active participation in poisonous activities that are purely set up as a trap by the unholy or the current culture such as drug use for joy, rumor mongering, picking fights, petty thefts, etc.

One positive aspect of increase in one's knowledge base is the inevitable increase of one's sphere of influence and zone of responsibility at home, work or in society. One would start taking on more projects and be more effective at work and quickly move into a senior position with a good increase in his paycheck, and thus gain more respect amongst his peers.

A genius, with his enormous accurate knowledge base, has a great advantage of recognizing and knowing the truth in any piece of data or information and as a result, has a high perception of truth.

Exercise 4: Pick up a newspaper and read an article or news story and then a) see if you can detect some false data printed to make you think wrongly about things, and b) Now, see if you can pick up some hidden truth in what you have just read. Write down your findings.

☙ ❧ ✴ ❀ ❁ ❀ ✴ ❧ ☙

Trait #5
Having a High Honesty and Integrity Level

Honesty refers to one's truthfulness in relation to others and one's behavior or actions, which are free of deceptions, misrepresentations and fraud. On the other hand, integrity refers to one's soundness (wholeness, health, in good condition and free of defect) of character and possession of high standards of right or wrong, which creates a warm fuzzy feeling of trust.

Honesty and integrity deal with truth and facts and is one of the main traits of a genius. A genius is truthful, frank and forthright, and free of any deception or lies.

A genius's stock in trade is facts and accurate information. He has personal integrity, that is to say, if he makes a mistake he is willing to admit it and furthermore learn from it.

He will not hide an error or a problematic area with the hope of others either not finding it or forgetting about it in time. He is the first to come forward and admit it and either present an amicable solution or ask for a remedy to eradicate the problem issue. He is forthright and sincere about it. He does not pretend imagined injuries and injustices to justify his mistake.

In short, a genius creates an atmosphere of trust and truth and thus can be trusted in business dealings or affairs. This gives one a high comfort level to deal with information, or work or actions that emanate from a genius, knowing well that he will never betray any of the parties involved!

Exercise 5: Think of a scenario in your past where your honesty helped you handle a mistake you had made more effectively and you actually came out on top smelling like a rose. You were eventually validated for having admitted it and taking responsibility for the mistake. Write down your observations and findings.

Trait #6
Having Great Optimism

By definition, optimism is one's tendency to look at the bright side of things, and the favorable or the good side of happenings and circumstances. A genius is an optimist.

A genius as a leader in his group has plenty of optimism toward what he observes as events in the environment. He would rather focus on the half of the glass filled with water rather than the empty side, a shift of focus heavily on the positive side of life and events. Therein lies his effectiveness as a genius because he is dealing with reality of things rather than the reality of missing things (which is an unreality).

Focusing primarily on the mistakes and errors of self and others, as well as the missing things in life puts one into a negative territory of thinking methodology and operation and one is apt to make quite a bit of further mistakes and wrong decisions. This is mediocrity and humanoid type thinking!

On the other hand, a genius focuses primarily on the bright side of the existing situation at hand and the positive reality of the scene, so he places himself on the positive domain of thinking methodology. He can come up with extraordinary solutions to enigmatic problems that most humans think impossible.

This is because he is being guided by the positivity and rightness of the scene thus his morale remains high. His mental state is kept at a constant optimum level as he progresses toward the solution. There may be negatives in a scene that needs to be handled but he is not focusing on them.

Due to his high mental alertness and not being shut down by focusing on the wrongnesses of the situation, his observation powers as well as his capability to propose and effectuate bright solutions is dramatically increased, well beyond that of an average human being.

A genius never doubts that he will succeed in any given project or any situation in life, and always sees what good things he can create with what he has at his disposal at the present moment. He deliberately focuses on what good he can create for self and others. In other words, he is a positive thinker no matter how negative the news or the situation is!

His optimism is also very contagious and if not interfered with, can actually lift up a whole group's morale and thinking pattern toward a much higher state of positivity and prosperous existence.

Exercise 6: Think of a problematic event that you saw or read about in the newspaper, or happened on TV, etc. See if you can see any positive aspects to it and if so, see if you can propose a bright solution for its resolution from that positive angle of observation. Write down your findings.

᭏ ℘ ✶ ❀ ✖ ❀ ✶ ℃ ᭏

Trait #7
Having a High Ability to Judge

To judge something means to consider something, and then form an opinion as regards to its merit, worth, amount, size, etc. It is a very high ability in a person to be able to consider an idea, a business proposal, a loan offer, a purchase proposal, etc., and determine its worth and validity and thus make a quick and accurate decision.

A genius has a high ability to understand the facts of a situation before he can judge on it. He first looks at the body of evidence and associated facts with an open mind, and after careful considerations then and only then he moves to the evaluation and judgment stage.

He is free of prejudiced concepts and preconceived notions and uses a great amount of logical thinking in his considerations of things and eventual formation of an opinion.

He cannot be swayed by false data, black PR (public relations), lobbying groups, vested interests, bribery or other unsavory sources to influence his final decision and judgment. He puts aside rumors and innuendos.

He is a rational "thought machine" guided by truth. He has personal integrity in what he observes as facts and holds them as the cornerstones of his decisions and judgments.

Lies, false data and rumors are not given any attention or validation and thus play no role in his considerations. This is the main reason and why he is a superior being, and is actually what separates him from the pack of the average human beings!

Exercise 7: Think of a book that you read, a movie that you saw, a person that you know, etc., and putting personal interest and emotions aside and only based on facts, make a judgment on its worth and merit. Write down your findings.

Trait #8
Being Highly Enthusiastic

Enthusiasm means being eagerly interested in an activity and showing a great amount of excited involvement in it.

Keeping this definition in mind, we can quickly see that a genius has plenty of enthusiasm in his daily activities and instills that in others. He is so excited and eager about what he is doing that others inevitably are greatly encouraged to chip in and help the ongoing activity.

A genius so truly believes in what he is doing and its positive outcome that he does not hold back anything and gives it all he has got in terms of mental fortitude or energy and physical effort.

A genius's state of mind and interest level in life's activities and his environment is so high that others get positively affected by it and actually change for the better in the presence of such a great bundle of vitality and enthusiasm.

Exercise 8: Think of something such as a situation, a project, a task, etc., and see if you can get enthusiastic about it and then observe the effect of such a mental shift in self and others. Write down your findings.

☙ ⬥ ✶ ❀ ❉ ❀ ✶ ⬥ ❧

Trait #9
Being Highly Willing to Take Calculated Risks

A genius can easily overcome his fear of failure and can take on a new enterprise or undertaking without much concern, knowing well that he can learn from his mistakes, overcome the obstacles and come out on top at the end.

A genius has such a high level of self-confidence that he is willing to experiment in new things, take on new challenges and make new waves in a new arena of activity.

He is not afraid of failure or rejection because he knows deep within that he is invincible as a being and thus does not allow small setbacks in life get in his way or discourage him from his main objectives or the bright future ahead of him!

Exercise 9: Think of a new project that you could take on or one that you have been thinking about for some time and see if you could get into the spirit of doing it, and take a calculated risk without much concern. Write up your findings.

Trait #10
Having a Dynamic Energy flow

By dynamic energy flow, we mean an active, vigorous and energetic flow of power toward life and its many activities. This is where a genius lives, that is to say, he can create plenty of clean energy to imbue life with, and thus engage self and others into a great deal of good and positive action.

He does not sit around and wait for someone to motivate him into action. He is self-motivated and is in constant action and motion, not aimless motion, but harmonized and organized action toward the accomplishment of a specific goal.

He constantly exhibits this trait of dynamic energy flow by supplying life with his own positive energy and getting things done with the least amount of harm to others.

He does not backstab "Joe Public" or betray him by an elaborate plot to steal his money in order to survive better. Instead, he gets Joe involved in a positive project and gets him to produce plenty by mutual effort and co-action toward the goal, thus earns his respect and admiration. This is where a genius thrives best!

Exercise 10: Think of a worthwhile project and mentally see if you could direct some energy toward doing it and what would happen if you could do so. Write up your findings.

Trait #11
Being Highly Willing to Undertake an Enterprise

By enterprise, we mean a bold, difficult and yet an important project that no one dares going near or approach for its high degree of impossibility.

A genius is an opportunity seeker by nature and is willing to take on jobs that others are not willing to touch. He is not afraid of taking on the unknown, new opportunities and bold undertakings.

A genius is willing to look into new things and try on new approaches to solve old problems that have remained yet unresolved.

His ability to differentiate between similar things and differentiate differences is great. Moreover, he can identify similarities in seemingly different scenarios, which makes him a superior being. He knows that he has the mental wherewithal to take on new challenges, enterprises and difficult tasks and come out ahead of the game.

This is an admirable quality in a genius leader whose group depends upon him and expects a brighter future and a more prosperous time!

Exercise 11: Think of a difficult project that no one likes to do, and then see how you can take it on and succeed in it. Write down your observations.

Trait #12
Being Highly Able to Motivate and Close People

To motivate someone is *to provide with a motive (a reason to act) or an incentive so that one moves and acts in a favored and desired direction.* On the other hand, to close means *to conclude successfully by arranging the final details of something such as a sale, a contract, negotiation, etc.*

A genius has plenty of mental power to convince anyone to do some beneficial thing and of mutual interest. A genius knows how to motivate and close people to help him do certain actions and thus attain the desired goals.

His forthrightness and powers of persuasions are such that people will do it now rather than later. It is all because he sincerely believes in what he is doing as to be the ideal solution and the best course of action for all parties involved, which also happens to provide the least degree of harm to anyone or anything. His logic and reasoning is impeccable. This is the main reason why he is so successful in the field of persuasion, motivation and closing!

Exercise 12: Think of some positive thing such as playing a game, going to a movie, going to park, etc. that you would like to do. Find a friend and see if you can persuade him to do it and then close him on it with a commitment using what you have learned so far. Write down your observations.

Hint: Make sure you believe in it and have persuaded yourself first before doing this exercise!

Trait #13
Having an Outgoing Personality

A genius is a very friendly person and has a great ability to get in communication and make mere strangers feel comfortable with him.

A genius is able to make friends easily. He is loyal to his friends and respects the friendship that has been bestowed upon him. He never puts others down nor does he play practical joke on them. Rather, he speaks favorably of his friends and associates and shuns all disparaging remarks or comments, whether self generated or created otherwise.

His mere presence and friendly gestures in many instances is a morale booster. He stays positive in the conversation and never criticizes others for "their own good." This attitude wins him many friends throughout the course of his life and people gravitate toward him as a stable friend.

He is the opposite of a vampire personality (a type of personality where the person preys ruthlessly upon others, discussed later). As a teammate, a coworker or a boss, a genius helps others to be at their best and to improve in their outlook toward life.

Overall, people at work or in life perform much better around a genius and are willing to contribute and help far beyond average to complete the desired projects. Therein lies the main reason for the successful existence of a genius.

Exercise 13: Find a friend or an associate and notice something positive about him/her, and make a complimentary remark about it. Make sure it is sincere and an honest compliment and something that is also real to that person. Observe to see if this helps to improve your friendship. Write down your observations.

Trait #14
Being a Great Communicator

Being a **communicator** refers *to an individual who is able to get his ideas across to others clearly and effectively.*

The concept of *communicator* could encompass a whole gamut of professional people who are vital to our society and can function in different capacities such as a writer, an educator, a lecturer, an artist, a musician, a singer, a philosopher, a salesman, a public speaker, etc.

A genius has a great ability to communicate well and capture the audience's attention. Therefore, because of his great communication ability he is well listened to and is highly respected as an opinion leader.

Moreover, as an opinion leader he knows the basic principles of communication so well that he can apply them with ease and confidence, persuade and motivate his group, and thus lead them toward a higher level of success and prosperity.

A genius has mastered the different aspects of communication to such a degree that he can put a command across, get a response and acknowledge it appropriately.

He listens well and does not interrupt others when they speak, so as to interject something or make a point. In other words, a) he allows others to finish their train of thoughts when they speak, and b) he grants others beingness and shows a high degree of respect and therefore does not create hostility by creating incomplete cycles of communication.

He has an excellent command of the language, pronounces each word correctly and annunciates the overall message well to the audience. This makes him a perfect candidate for public speaking circles and venues.

One of the main aspects of communicating well, much revered in the public's mind, is being a great public speaker and a genius is no stranger to this concept. He can deliver a lecture, a concept or a message effectively to a live audience and create a wave of positive motion forward toward a benevolent cause. He can grab an audience's attention with no effort, purely through his positive power of granting beingness and transference of his great enthusiasm to others.

He is always willing to hear from others and has an open door policy with regard to communication from others at all times. He can always be reached.

Exercise 14: Find a friend and say something positive about the weather or some neutral subject, and then listen to what he says to you without interruption. At the end of the conversation, give him a good acknowledgement and say farewell in a friendly way. Write down what you learned.

⊷ ᘒ ✳ ❀ ✿ ❀ ✳ ᘖ ⊶

Trait #15
Being Extremely Patient

There is an old cliché that says, "Patience is a virtue." A genius is very patient with others for their pretty foibles and errors.

A genius is very tolerant of other's viewpoints and behavior and does not try to make them wrong for something that they said or did, which would be improper in his frame of mind. This is the hallmark of a genius in being able to entertain other people's opinions, behavior and actions without necessarily accepting it or agreeing with it.

Another aspect of this genius trait is that even though he may be patient with others, but he is relentlessly impatient with self and expects far more from self than he does from anybody else. He competes with himself and his own past performance and constantly raises the bar on it. He does not tolerate mediocrity.

To sum, a genius is easy and patient with others but is tough on self and has a much higher self-expectation than from anyone else!

Exercise 15: Find a friend and see if you can exhibit patience while being around that person. See if you can listen to his views and patiently prevent self from interrupting or interjecting comments. Write down what you learned.

❧ ✻ ❀ ✾ ❀ ✻ ☙

Trait #16
Having Great Perception Powers

A genius has great perception powers. He has his perception channels alert to the environment, and keeps them highly tuned, trained and maintained to receive accurate information without any alterations.

A genius has a healthy and a well functioning body that collects information of many forms and wavelengths such as sight, audio, smells and touch of things. He perceives the world and the people in his environment with great clarity and vividness. Beyond physical perceptions, he also has his mental radar working full time, picking up all other energy forms and frequencies that the human body is incapable of perceiving.

Due to his great perception powers, life as a whole and in its many forms takes the center stage for him. He values and respects people and living things. A genius thinks highly of others and understands their needs and wants, even more than his own immediate desires.

In other words, others are important to him to such a point that he is willing to make sacrifices in his own life that others would not dare even considering it. He can grant people as a whole, particularly friends and associates, a lot of beingness and much respect for being alive. He openly acknowledges other people's presence and allows others to show their true feelings. He does not find fault or criticize them. He is very sensitive to others' feelings, needs and desires and actually helps them to achieve their various targets.

Exercise 16: Close your eyes for five seconds, then open it, look around you and see if you can notice something that you have never noticed before. Write down your findings.

Trait #17
Being a Great Perfectionist

A **perfectionist** is a person *who seeks and demands perfection, high excellence, and faultlessness in himself.* He constantly strives to do better than yesterday.

A genius is not satisfied with mediocrity and cannot tolerate being an average. He has to be above the crowd and is not easily satisfied with himself.

He has big dreams of excellence in certain chosen fields of endeavor and as a result he has developed a mental philosophy of "flying with the eagles and never hanging around the turkeys!"

A genius gets enormous pleasure in constantly working toward a better tomorrow. In other words, he never stops or rests on his laurels!

Exercise 17: Think of some project that you are currently doing, whether at home or work, and see if you can tweak it and make it one notch better in your mind. Then within the next few days take the necessary actions to carry it out in the physical universe. Write down your observations.

Trait #18
Having a Great Sense of Humor

A genius is very playful about life matters and does not take them seriously. He has a high spirit of play with things and events. He respects people's feelings and beliefs and is not interested in ridiculing or mocking others. Instead, he usually tries to make himself the butt of all humorous comments so that no one would be offended.

A genius has a rather vast sense of space around him and does not easily introvert when the joke is on him, thus he is willing to laugh at himself and be playful about himself or his characteristics. In other words, he does not take himself seriously.

He usually sees something interesting and worth laughing at even in the most serious events in life. He is light-hearted and very funny about things, and usually makes attempts to make others laugh. His lack of seriousness makes people become easily fond of him, admire him or befriend him in many ways.

Exercise 18: Think of something you have observed recently or some ongoing matters, and see if you can make a light hearted and funny comment about it. Write down the effect it created on others.

Trait #19
Being Highly Versatile

Versatility means *the ability to do many things well.* A genius has an uncanny knack for being versatile when the need arises.

A genius is extremely versatile in that he can assume many roles and identities and as a result perform things with great dexterity as the situation demands. For example, he could be a teacher, a professional businessman, an author, a volunteer minister, a scholar, and a scientist as he wishes. In sports, he can play many positions equally well!

To achieve such a versatile quality, a genius strives to learn more things everyday and does not shy away from getting into areas of learning or endeavors.

The versatility trait makes a genius very self confident, because no matter what the game of life throws at him he can assume the necessary role and identity and thus rise up to the occasion to do the correct actions to overcome any potentially unforeseen adversity. This quality alone makes a genius extremely bullet proof to economic pitfalls, which are daily faced by the average man!

Exercise 19: Think of something new and within your range of interest that you could learn. Then do a research type action to see how you could get into learning it and actually take the next step in doing so. Write down how it affected your self-confidence.

Trait #20
Being Highly Adaptable

By **adaptability,** we mean *an ability to change easily to fit different conditions, and showing flexibility in the face of changing circumstances.*

A genius is very adaptable in that he thinks with the current data in the existing situation at hand and refuses to be stuck in some past and fixed conclusion.

When things are different, he resists doing things the same old way that may be very unworkable now. He is not worried about changing his thinking pattern as conditions or technology changes and is more than willing to consider new options.

A genius welcomes new facts and truths that cause change in terms of better results and improved human conditions. He does not want to maintain a monopoly on a certain business practice just to have a healthy bottom line profit.

If new technical information reveals that old way of doing things is less practical and inefficient, he would be the first to switch over and improve his practice to include the new methodology rather than fight it ignorantly or worse, use black propaganda to discredit it. In other words, he is an enlightened individual who can see the truth in new and improved methods and is willing to embrace it full heartedly!

A simple example may add some light to this topic. There are certain health practitioners who believe so thoroughly in drug therapy and surgical procedures to help the sick patient that they are not willing to look at any other means of therapy.

The new technical research has revealed that psychosomatic ills are about 70% of our current chronic diseases. Furthermore, there are new methods of healing such as chiropractic adjustments, light therapy, heat and cold therapy, vitamin therapy, etc. and yet these still maintain the old school of germ theory and refuse to see the new technical breakthroughs in the real of bio-knowledge, and actually fight it openly. They are "playing ostrich" either by their deep ignorance or due to their own vested interest and their ties to the drug companies that are financing their lifestyles.

On the other hand, there are many adaptable and enlightened health practitioners who saw the truth in the wave of new information and incorporated them quickly in their healing methods and adapted their practice and thus improved their healing percentage dramatically, and along the way saved the lives of many patients with less drug abuse and less surgical trauma.

Exercise 20: Carefully look around your environment and see if you can find any new things that would cause you to change your old style of doing things and then do it. Write your findings.

᠆᠆ ℘ ✶ ❀ ✂ ❀ ✶ ℘ ᠆᠆

Trait #21
Being Highly Curious

Curiosity means *an eager desire to know something.* This is an important quality in a genius and keeps him active in seeking new information.

A genius with an inquisitive mind does not mind admitting that he does know it all and thus is willing to learn. This avoids a pompous and lofty position that most scholars and authoritarian get into who are so blinded by their own ignorance that they cannot dig themselves out of the camouflaged hole that they are occupying.

A genius may ask questions to broaden his point of view in order to learn new information about someone or something. He never assumes that he knows before finding out the facts either through questions, surveys, research or live communications. This is how he succeeds in life day after day (short term) or year after year (long term).

By having an open and curious mind and allowing open channels of communication to exist, he allows the information to enter and enrich him further.

An important caveat worth mentioning is that a genius has zero curiosity in the enturbulated (mangled and distorted) form of information consisting of lies, gossips, rumors, black propaganda, critical and hostile remarks, invalidation of others, and merchants of chaos type news and in reality completely shuns them.

A genius is only curious on the positive side of life and has a complete roadblock on all other types of information. This admirable quality of a genius could be called **"selective curiosity,"** which acts as a valuable filter in removing harmful information particles entering the mind.

Selective curiosity in a genius is actually a self-empowering tool that feeds him facts and positive truths, and yet is a self-protecting mechanism that prevents him from being poisoned from the dark side of life.

Exercise 21: Look around your fields of interest and find a topic in which you could get interested. Now, see what positive information you could learn about it that could broaden your zone of knowledge. Write down your findings.

᠊ᢞ*✻✕✻*᠍᠊

Trait #22
Being an Excellent Individualist

Individualism is *the concept wherein the freedom, rights and independent thought or action of the individual is important and plays an essential role in the welfare and ethical well-being of the group as a whole.*

A genius is an individualist, which means that *he is a person characterized by great independence in thought and action.* He is very self-determined and difficult to enslave by the slave master.

A genius having this trait does things the way he thinks should be done without fearing somebody's disapproval because he thinks it is the most beneficial course of action for the people involved and the right thing to do.

A genius thinks and creates independent of other mass-think ideologies, collective thought agreements or approval from the masses. You cannot force him to do something unethical and against his will just because of fear of disapproval or ostracism.

A genius is a living and breathing individualist who knows his own importance in the society and has an understanding of the positive value and worth he brings to the society in terms of ideas, presence, behavior, action, etc.

In other words, he is somebody to reckon with. One who cannot be hushed or bulldozed over into a pit of oblivion and slavery by some political system or superstitious type of religion that does not recognize the individual as the source of life and the actual building block of the society.

Therefore, here we have a stable and functioning spiritual being, a solid rock and independent thinking individual who is himself and knows he has an infinite positive potential to be and create, and no mental philosophy can tell him otherwise, much to his detriment and decay.

In a genius's world, nobody has the power to mislead him and make him think that:

a) He is a body (as done in medicine), or

b) He is a brain (as done in psychiatry), or

c) He is an action-reaction type of mind (as done in psychology), or

d) He is an evil sinner (as done in some religions), or

e) He is an animal (as done in biology), or

f) He is a conglomerate of atoms and molecules (as done in physics), or

g) He is a computerized machine (as done in engineering), etc.

An individualist genius will not accept such tainted false data coming from ignorant individuals and knows that they have an axe to grind and usually have a vested interest and serve other masters. He will not bow down to the pressure of the masses or bend before the mighty and corrupt state trying to control him. He is an emancipated being!

Exercise 22: Think of an individual characteristic that you possess and see if you can think of ways to protect it from all outside influences and thus foster individualism in self. Write down your findings.

Trait #23
Being a Great Idealist

An ideal is a *standard of perfection or excellence, which creates an ultimate model for others to follow or imitate.*

A genius is an idealist, which means that *he has high ideals and acts to achieve them. He cherishes and pursues noble principles and high goals.*

A genius is a visionary who keeps his feet on the ground but his head in the clouds. He constantly strives to achieve great things, not just for himself, but also for the betterment of mankind.

A genius just doesn't think big, he thinks in unlimited solutions benefiting all and lasting forever! He makes the world better in many ways. His high ideals constantly provide a clean form of drive to push forward and onward.

He means well and actually represents a bright world full of life and vitality. He believes in his ideals to such a degree that no one can stop him, and since he includes everyone in his plan of actions and everyone willingly helps to realize his dreams. He has an ideal scene in mind and stands for the greatest force of good that this world has ever seen!

Exercise 23: Think of an ideal that could help everyone at home or work. Write it down and see if you could think of ways you could implement it.

Trait #24
Being Immensely Imaginative

Imagination is *the power of forming pictures or images in the mind, not present to the senses at the moment.*

A genius has great powers of imagination in that a) he knows how to think in new combinations, and b) he is able to see things from different perspectives much better than the average person is.

A genius can easily unclutter his mind from mental debris and give himself the opportunity to daydream, fantasize and drift into a dreamy inner world of magic, just like the time when he was a child.

A genius can waive a magic wand and create something beautiful, new and totally fascinating in his mind. He can control his mental machinery to such a degree that the past is out of view and does not bother him a bit. He is totally in present time while commanding the future into existence by working on mental creations that would morph into physical realities shortly.

A genius, in his mind's workshop, gets a preview of what the coming attraction will be, before the physical universe presents its physical reality existence in terms of its actual mass, color, form, etc. He is thus seen to be one-step ahead of the present time. He can be considered as someone who is peaking his "mental head" out of the cloak of present-time realities and seeing the future happenings occurring at the present time. He sees the bend ahead on the road of life, far before the bend appears and this alone will guide and steer him toward his eternal prosperity.

A genius has a great ability to endow things with life and put vitality into things purely by the process of imagination and postulation.

A genius appears to be a super human being at first glance, but he is actually the positive and the bright side of life and the incredible ability of any being to breathe life into things and give it force and validation! His presence, his imaginative powers, his granting powers of life to things and his high mental power of creation gives him a mystique and sets him far apart from the pack.

Applying the concept of imagination to the field of problem solving and bringing forth practical solutions utilizing engineering, we need to coin a relatively new term: Imagineering.

Imagineering means *imagining brighter solutions to existing or new problems and bringing them down from the realm of thought to earth in order to develop and engineer practical applications that would benefit mankind.* A genius is a champion in imagineering.

In short, a genius is a very special being with very positive magical powers. He is a truly live being with a keen sense of knowing and a life-endowing power. He is a magician who has taken the joy of creation to a completely new level and one that truly personifies the ideal human being!

Exercise 24: Imagine something new in your life and get a vivid picture of it in your mind with full color. Write down what your imagination was about and draw a picture of it.

Trait #25
Having a High Ability to Grant Beingness

A genius has a great ability to grant beingness to others (imbue or bestow life to others and things) and treat them with a high level of respect and dignity. He understands that other people are important and should be communicated to in a proper way and treated with a high degree of regard for their feelings and opinions.

He must take a great degree of care not to invalidate or make others wrong for expressing their opinions or feelings. This is such an essential factor in human relationship that those who violate it are relegated to the scrap heap of total contempt and ostracism, and are usually shunned.

A genius with his positive presence alone can grant powers of life and vitality to others and even to things. His responsible handling of people and his own possessions as well as other people's is a direct index of his superior quality and thus sets him far apart from the average humanoid pack.

In short, genius has a life-endowing quality as well as a granting beingness power to others and things that is incredible. He has a high affinity for people of all walks of life and his positive presence of "allowing others to be at ease around him" can be very contagious to a point that others start becoming more capable and healthy by just contacting him.

He has a superior understanding of other human beings in terms of what they stand for and who they are, and does not find fault or criticize or demean them just to make himself look superior! He knows that his own prosperous existence directly depends upon other people's well-being and success. Therefore, his own vector of life is in the direction of pushing people up toward a higher plateau of survival in abundance.

In summary, a genius is standing on such a secure rock of solid security and a high self-confidence coupled with a granting of positivity to life and existence all around him, that he is not jealous of the other fellow gaining more power or intelligence, nor is he even vaguely envious of others becoming better than him. He admires positivity in life and shuns negativity in thought or behavior. He is truly operating on empowering life with his own life force.

Exercise 25: Think of a positive quality that you possess in your own life and get a vivid picture of it in your mind. Now see if you can recognize that positive character in others and acknowledge others when they do display that positive quality. Shun the negative aspects. Write down your observations and what you learned.

Trait #26
Having a Great Balanced Life

A genius by definition must set an example for the rest of us to follow. This means that he must have a happy and balanced life—that is to say, he should have mastered and perfected his own life before attempting to set an example for the rest of us. The following are some of the areas that a genius should master on his way to greatness:

a) A genius should be in great physical shape with a tremendous degree of health and physical prowess. He should have a pain-free body, devoid of any chronic disease or body malfunction. He habitually should eat nutritious diets, and avoid drugs and alcohol. He should develop great habits in regular exercise of the body and bathe regularly to be free of any unpleasant body odors.

b) He should have a great family life, in terms of keeping his marriage vows intact and be very faithful to his spouse. He should have a great level of interest in helping children and be genuinely comfortable around them. He should take care of his parents and respect them for what they have done for him. He should have a great relationship with his siblings and be in regular and good communication with them.

c) He should not be a recluse but have many great friends who sincerely like him and admire his sense of individuality. He should be a social personality with a great sense of humor. He should be very pleasant in social circles as he brings a whole new level of vitality and brightness to any gathering.

d) He should be well dressed at work and have a clutter-free and clean office. He should welcome visitors and be willing to talk to anyone even without prior appointment. His open door policy and warm greetings at the door should be a sure sign of his ability to grant beingness and receive guests at any time. He should be very glad to have contributed to someone's forward progress and to have been of service, without asking or expecting anything in return.

e) A genius should be a great learner and be constantly engaging his mind in learning new subjects and expanding his horizons and boundaries of knowledge. He should never assume that he knows all there is to know. Instead, he should avidly search for new viewpoints and new realms of information. He should have a never-ending quest for better and more efficient ways to perform tasks as well as improving himself and increasing his abilities and potentialities.

f) He should have an affluent financial scene, wherein he is never delinquent on any bills, keeps his debts paid, and his financial obligations all met. He should have a great sense of financial responsibility toward what he signs in paperwork or verbal promises and never intend to violate any of its terms negligently or intentionally for profit seeking motives.

In short, a genius with his great balanced life, his positive presence, his imaginative powers to teach and learn, his granting powers of life to things in the society, and his high mental power of creation in a positive direction should have the ability to solve any problem at will. He should be truly a problem solver and welcome challenges that life hands him in his endeavors. He should have an uncanny ability to perceive truth and this fact alone would set him far apart from the pack.

A genius truly should have the most balanced life amongst all of his peers and associates. A genius, having mastered this trait soundly, would provide us the most compelling and the highest remarkable example to follow!

Exercise 26: Consider your life and get a vivid picture of it in your mind. Pick one area that needs some attention and has room for improvement. Devise a short plan of action so you could bring it into a more balanced view. Write down your observations and what you learned from them.

Trait #27
Being a Great Leader

It is a well-known fact that a team is a necessary and required element in one's equation toward achievement of any worthwhile goal.

A genius has a great ability to become the leader in his own area, whether large or small. He can talk to people, get them mobilized to get the job done, and oversee it until it is done right.

A genius is actually the positive and the bright side of life who can give positive orders and exert positive control on the environment around him. This will create a cohesive group to engage their efforts in order to push the activities onward and thus create a forward motion toward the goal.

A genius has the incredible ability of ignoring the negativity and breathing positive life into things. He can envision positive programs and goals that directly relates to his vicinity and by inviting cooperation of other group members give it a positive direction, force and validation!

His presence, his imaginative powers, his positive mental attitude allows him to assume leadership rather easily and get the job done through teamwork and compliance. He knows policy well enough to organize all force vectors of the group into the intended direction and obtain a positive result. This is a fantastic level of productivity that a genius can bring about, quite contrary to what we see all around us in the work place and hear in the newspapers, mostly in the form of a torrent of mutinies, rebellions or strikes in the society.

In short, a genius is a leader in the truest sense of the word: His team likes him, the public adores him and customers praise his products. However, the competition and the enemies are very unhappy and critical of his level of success and production and even though they try to use black propaganda and false rumors to discredit him, his team and the adoring public will defend him vigorously to their last drop of blood because his team knows he is benevolent and means well.

In short, a genius is a special being with very positive magical powers of commanding and positive control of others. He is a truly live being with a keen sense of knowing, and a life-endowing power. He is a bright manager who has taken the joy of creation to a whole new level and one that truly personifies the ideal leader!

Exercise 27: Think of a project at work and see if you can first visualize a solution by inviting the cooperation of others to join you in doing it. Then see if you can actually implement it at work with your coworkers. Write down the solution to your project and the final result.

Trait #28
Being an Intelligent Investor

To invest means *to lay out or put something (e.g., time, money, energy, etc.) into an activity (e.g., education, business, stocks, etc.) with the expectation of producing a later benefit or profit.*

A genius is an intelligent investor in that he knows wherein he should invest to get the desired benefit. He invests his time and capital in things that help the society and mankind. His focus is on service and producing products that help others, thus he is paid well for his actions with high salaries and many fringe benefits.

His income is always greater than his outgo, thus he is never upside down in financial planning. He has a high income to expense ratio by planning his resources, such as time, money, intelligence, skills, etc., well and by not engage in unnecessary and off-purpose activities.

His areas of investment are:
   a) Investing in *personal resources* (e.g., abilities, perception, alertness, enthusiasm, etc.).
   b) Investing in *education.*
   c) Investing in *society services.*
   d) Investing for *financial wealth.*

These four areas are explained and further elucidated in depth below.

a) A genius never invests his resources (such as time) in actions and activities that produce zero or negative effects such as:

* Playing video games,
* Social chit-chat by the water cooler,
* Dawdling in the markets,
* Aimlessly browsing the internet,
* Laying in the sun lazily,
* Watching TV habitually,
* Reading the newspaper avidly,
* Getting drunk at the local bar,
* Filing frivolous lawsuits,
* Sending scam emails,
* Creating spy or malicious software, etc.

None of these and a thousand others will ever add up to real production and thus no real end result!

Instead, he invests his resources in productive things that can boost society's as well as own production and morale. He would do things that would give him more leverage in life, enhance his knowledge base and more resources to combat the real enemies of man such as disease, ignorance, famine, illiteracy, financial depression, housing shortage, etc.

A genius values other people's time and energy and would always act in a manner that engages people in a positive way. His respect for his fellow man is high, thus he would not engage in useless and intentionally stress-creating things such as practical jokes and pranks on others. He exudes positivity and portrays time efficiency in life!

b) A genius is an avid learner and believes in education. He would spend his time and energy to get an excellent education whether at a good university or at the school of hard knocks as a first order of sound investment practice. He would avidly read books on a life-long basis and help people by re-educating them on the correct principles of life. He would spend time on worthwhile projects that would make the world win on many levels.

A genius spearheads a renaissance on earth, not by revolution and overthrow of the governing system as it is advertised on earth today, but by evolution of thought and existence through a great emphasis on the correct education fundamentals and rehabilitation of a person's ability and vigor.

A genius has a great interest in the society's improvement, vitality and mental health because deep down he knows that he would be affected by it in his lifetime, on some level whether good or bad. After all, it is the people around him who give him a job, give him food to eat, water to drink, a house to live in or a car to drive. Granted he has to pay for it in order to get these goods and services, but it all depends upon an economy of fair exchange created by the people around him.

One is born into a society and his head is held above water, from birth onward, by the positive exchange of people all around him. Without these people, he would be living in a damp cave at the mercy of the tigers, lions and other beasts of the jungle as well as the elements. Therefore, one's existence directly depends upon other people's existence. In fact, if one violates this fact and goes against the society by committing harmful acts against any member of the society or any group, he essentially has denied himself the support of mankind and its buoyant force, which is holding him up above water. The moment this positive force from under his feet is removed, he will quickly sink underwater. In fact, in a short order of time he will find himself in the modern equivalent of a damp cave, a jail cell, and at the mercy of the prison warden with his trained team of jail guards, who are all equipped with modern weapons much deadlier than a tiger's tooth and claw!

Moreover, a genius knows that no man is an island and that a sick and unhealthy society will eventually cause him much harm and grief unless he helps it to undo the decay and damage afflicted upon it by the ignorant and the unholy!

A genius would not tolerate modern methods of slavery thrown into the midst of people camouflaged with media's faulty explanations and justifications, such as: economic meltdown, financial crises by design, psychiatrist's gift of drug to mankind, psychology's mental screening, government's welfare program (that prohibits the person to work), so on and so forth. He knows these are poison pills designed to disable and disarm the public and lull them into a walking zombie status, an unthinking vegetable.

d) A genius also knows that to achieve his goals and to survive in abundance he needs to have his finances in affluence. Thus, he masters all financial investment fundamentals and advanced concepts early in his life. He does not focus upon a constant and relentless wealth accumulation or valuable goods collection program, but devotes most of his energy to worthwhile goals that would benefit many people. These are activities such as: writing books, speaking to groups to motivate them toward a brighter future, counseling those downtrodden individuals who really need assistance, enlightening people on the human virtues, teaching people about real prosperity and how to attain it, so on and so forth.

He never engages in high risk investments such that he could potentially lose everything if things do not go his way. He knows that this style of investment (high-risk investments with no insurance or protection) is the gambler's mentality and completely wrong in the modern era of investing. He calculates his risk in advance and knows exactly what it is before putting his hard-earned money at the mercy of the markets foolishly. He is his own counselor and avoids the normal pitfalls in investing such as following the crowd on a hot stock tip, or buying into a hyped up real estate deal, or listening to the latest news on gold or oil from some vested interest, which could cause him to commit his investing capital to it.

He knows the "math of investment" and "reward to risk ratio" well enough to apply it intelligently in any investment opportunity such that the end result is a profitable activity.

He cuts his losses short (i.e., unloads poor deals that have a negative cash flow) and lets his winners run successfully (holds onto good investments that have a positive cash flow). His financial investment philosophy breaks down into the following principles:

1) The Cookie-Cutter Principle: He has developed an exact recipe or formula for purchase (or sale) of a specific asset (such as a single-family house, a commercial building or a stock or option) such that when an exact series of parameters align and meet certain values he instantly pulls the trigger and procures the asset. This is called a cookie-cutter principle that allows him to procure successful assets and by repeating it (like a cookie cutter) he keeps adding to his wealth and further expanding his operations. Moreover, he does not cap his profits by selling too early or putting imaginary restrictions on the earning potentials of a good investment. He keeps it until the proper indicators signify the correct selling action.

2) The Adjustment Principle: If an asset is underperforming and appears to be a bad investment but has a great future and a good potential for positive income, he may try to adjust his position and improve the asset into a positive cash flow territory before completely unloading it.

3) The Unload Principle: He lets go of losing investments very quickly and early on before too much time is wasted and before things change from bad to worse, thereby ruining his self-confidence and damaging his decision power, and

4) The Insurance Principle: One great aspect of correct investment methodology is to have proper insurance for all aspects of operations and a genius employs this principle in all of his investment activities.

A genius is not motivated by greed or fear in investment, because he is using long-term problem solving methods with proper planning and good reasoning power, rather than desiring quick and overnight riches advertised and exaggerated by some con men from whom he should know better to stay away.

He knows that to invest properly, he needs to:
a) Buy an asset in an uptrending market,
b) Protect it fully in a clever way and then
c) Gather and build a team around him to manage it well for monthly income,
d) He sells before he buys the asset, that is to say, before he buys the asset he already knows at what price it could be sold in the market. Therefore, he is one step ahead of the crowd and sees the bend in the road far in advance of anyone else!

Concluding Remarks:
A genius does not seek to obtain off-line advice from people or make decisions based upon unreliable sources that truly are not in that field but are somehow connected to it. Such off-line people will include brokers, telemarketers, receptionists, cold callers, financial software makers and their associated sales force, newspapers, TV broadcasters, media, etc.

You will never find a genius in the food-stamp line or in the government welfare program. Quite the contrary, he is the one providing charity and assistance to the needy and the downtrodden members of the society.

He has a great ability to detect and bypass the embedded false data in any information concerning what and where to invest in (buy or sell). He has his basic education in this field to guide him through the mirror maze of financial data. He knows how to analyze data and how to discard the unwanted and misleading data. His understanding is superior to the head-fakes or tricks in the market and he neither freezes nor falls for the shortcut methods offered by the unscrupulous promoters who want to make a patsy out of him.

In short, a genius knows his basics so well that he becomes his own counselor, provides his own advice and makes his own decisions. He avoids *time wasters* and frivolous or negative actions, and instead invests his resources (time energy, ability, etc.) intelligently into education, into service to society and into building financial wealth and a recession-proof stream of income.

Exercise 28: Identify an uptrending market through personal research, whether real estate, stocks, commodities, etc. and then see at what price and when you could sell it if you bought it at the current price. Make up your mind to do a mock investment by buying it (paper trading). Over a period of time, check to see if your investment did pan out the way you had intended it. Write down your findings.

Trait #29
Being an Expert Salesman

A genius has a great ability to sell a large gamut of things ranging from ideas, projects, to goods and services. He has a great ability to convince others to do what he wants them to do not out of self-interest but what truly is good for the customer.

He can be very convincing to others about the product, because he is convinced on the product himself. He has used the product and in fact has one in his own household and believes in the product genuinely. Therefore, it is easy for him to transfer his feelings to others and convince them to do the same as he did it: buy it!

Most of the time the image of a salesman conjures up images of a shady and tricky con man talking about the exaggerated features and imaginary benefits of a product all peppered with great lies in between just to get into the wallet of the customer. This is dishonest and lacks a great deal of integrity. This is not salesmanship but chicanery and fraud, and as result has given the sales profession a very bad reputation!

However, truth be told, everyone has to sell to survive on a daily basis. We sell our ideas to our spouses, to our boss, to our workers, to the merchant, etc. Selling is part and parcel to life and no one can live without it in one form or another. Those who engage in dishonest selling actions soon get caught and do not survive well, and forever lose the trust of their public. Dishonesty and no integrity in selling is the poor man's road to poverty and doom!

A true salesman never cheats or tricks the customer, in fact just the opposite, he honestly informs the customer about the merits and pitfalls of the product and helps them to make the correct decision so that the product truly is what they desire.

A good salesman does not pressure-sell the customer to force a quick decision because it could backfire on him and completely turn away a bona fide customer. It is a completely wrong-headed approach to arm twist or trick, swindle, hoodwink, cheat, threaten and other dishonest methods to make a sale. Such a person is not truly a sales person as he is engaging in some reprehensible crimes against the customer and humanity as a whole. This is not a sales process.

A sales process is a happy event, with the following steps:
a) First, a true enlightenment based upon facts takes place and the reasons why the customer should have the product,
b) A discussion of what truly is good for the customer should follow.
c) Next, any objections of the customer should be handled with utmost sincerity and cordiality with no added false impressions,
d) At this stage the price and suitable financial terms should be discussed. The salesman is selling a tangible physical product and an intangible feeling of trust and integrity and great customer support to the customer.

e) At the end of the process, the customer is delighted to have the product and is happy to part with his money and go home with the product as a true benefit to his life.

Anything less than these five steps is not a sales process but a misrepresentation or a deviation from a process that could ultimately empower both parties if done honestly.

A genius recognizes that selling is a quality that everyone must possess to survive and to become successful. This is true regardless of one's position in life or in his company. A genius is trained to be a super salesman at whatever he takes on. His great imaginative powers, his high level of enthusiasm, his granting powers of life to things and his high mental power of creation gives him a great ability to convince and close the sale.

He understands the general concept of sale so well that he not only can sell products but also any idea to anyone and command any audience. Therefore, as such he could be a great teacher if he chooses to do so, because he recognizes that to teach is to sell ideas and to learn is to buy them!

In short, a genius is a very special being with very positive magical powers of convincing, persuasion and closing. He is a truly live being with a keen sensitivity for the customer's needs and wants. He is a magician who has taken the joy of creation to a whole new level of helping and empowering others through the sales process, and one that truly personifies the ideal human being!

Exercise 29: Imagine something new that you have seen around and want it in your life. Get a vivid picture of it in your mind with full color. Now sell yourself in wanting to procure it and use some persuasive techniques to close yourself on it. Finally see yourself using it. Write a short essay about the product and the sales technique you used. Draw a diagram of the steps.

Trait #30
Being a Great Humanitarian

A genius has a great ability to understand and love mankind and respect other human beings regardless of their creed, gender, nationality or race.

He devotes his time and energy to better the conditions of living for mankind, whether directly by engaging in philanthropic activities or through inventing, research and developing helpful products that puts man on a higher plateau of existence.

You do not see a genius in any way or form associated with activities that:
a) Deal with making bombs or weapons,
b) Promote racism, or slavery,
c) Disgrace the religions of the world,
d) Use his authority for vested interest to enrich own pocket,
e) Drug the children and the ignorant,
f) Advocate torture as a therapy (e.g., electric shock therapy, lobotomy, deep sleep therapy, etc.),
g) Betray man by spreading false data (e.g. "war is good for economy," "To die for your country is your duty," "be a martyr for your religion," etc.),
h) Promote all illegal activities such as drug dealing, prostitution, robbery, white collar crime, artfully lying,
i) Lead to fabricating false news, black propaganda, rumors, and making others suffer, so on and so forth.

Quite the opposite, a genius is engaged on a constant basis in:

* Promoting peace,
* Pushing for more religious tolerance,
* Enlightenment of the masses (e.g., writing books, educating others, spreading truth, etc.),
* Establishing groups that help educate and salvage the masses,
* Developing methods of education that can increase people's personal ability and intelligence,
* Developing instruments that increase man's productivity (e.g., farming, power generation, manufacturing, communication, etc.),
* Exposing the lies and false data propounded by the vested-interest authority,

Thus, he brings a whole new level of freedom by rehabilitating and removing the parasites of the society such as the child slave master, computer virus producer, security hacker, warmonger, etc., and freeing mankind from the yoke of modern slavery guised in various ways.

A genius is actually the positive and the bright side of humanity and has a great level of empathy for the feelings and sufferings of others, and intends to make this world a better place than how he found it at birth. His intentions are extremely good and he wants to create a brighter future for self as well as others.

He solves daily problems in such a way that the least number of people get hurt and the most benefit from his actions. Therein lies his benevolence and good intentions that reside deep within him.

A genius is beloved by the majority of people who support him wholeheartedly and want to pitch in and put their shoulders to the wheel and expand his humanitarian purposes even further. The only opposition he gets is from a few unholy corrupt individuals who have deep vested interest and serve evil masters. It is interesting to note that even this unholy bunch, deep down, respect the genius, despite their showy protests and surface hates.

Exercise 30: Identify a person of good will or a humanitarian group (on the internet, by phone or in person) and find out how they are helping mankind. Ask them the benefits that they receive as a result. Write down your findings and observations.

Trait #31
Being a Great Environmentalist

By *environmentalist,* we mean someone who has good intentions toward the environment and surroundings, and wants to safeguard it against harm and wishes to improve it through enhancements by:

a) Not polluting or littering it through the discard of waste and poisonous materials into the air, water supply or the grounds as a cost cutting measure. For example, there are companies that dump all of their chemical toxins into the local river to cut their shipping costs and not send it to a safe location.

b) Striving to increase the awareness of the public toward the dangers of environmental pollution and toxins that can harm the living conditions for humans as well as the other elements and inhabitants, such as animals, plants, air quality and oceans.

c) Setting a great example of his own by keeping his own areas clean and kempt, whether it is work office, living quarters, neighborhood streets, city grounds, state parks, so on and so forth.

A genius has a great ability to keep things in great working conditions and even often upgrades them by adding positive factors that contribute to their quality and enhances their longevity.

A genius by nature is a great environmentalist who actively supports all endeavors that add to the environment such as:

a) Planting trees,

b) Creating more parks,

c) Building dams that create clean electricity and irrigate the neighboring plantations,

d) Turning useless land into public parks,

e) Stop deforestation of earth,

f) Substituting polluting forms of energy with cleaner ones,

g) Organizing "earth day" events where he arranges people of all walks of life to go to parks and beaches to clean up debris and trash, etc.

A genius wants to save the earth from the negative influences and unethical business enterprises that try to rape, plunder and abuse it without taking proper responsible actions, or giving anything back in return to mend the ravages that they leave behind.

There are such irresponsible profit-motivated operations such as tree loggers who can deforest an area very quickly chemical drug manufacturers who can dump all of their toxins in the nearby river, mining companies that can deface an area in a short order of time, nuclear power plants that can dump their nuclear waste in open areas, etc. These if left to their own devices can raise havoc and threaten the survival of all of us, thus a genius as an environmentalist has a high interest to raise awareness of others to these issues. His presence becomes an extremely positive and necessary factor in our society.

In short, a genius is a very special being with a very alert and aware identity that is well tuned toward survival not just for self but also for all life forms including other human beings, animals and plants and the beauty of our home planet!

Exercise 31: Examine your area and find a messy area at home, office or back yard that raises a red flag or an outpoint, which needs proper handling. Now take the necessary actions that could bring order and cleanliness to the area. Then take an extra step of upgrading it to a higher state of existence. Write down what you learned from doing this.

Trait #32
Having a Great Spiritual Understanding

A genius has a great understanding about the source and essence of life, which happens to be non-material. He knows that the material aspects of life are secondary to human values and the spiritual qualities of life.

A genius has a high level of knowledge and understanding about the mind and the spiritual side of life. Therefore, his actions at any moment of time and on any level are such that his personal integrity and values are never jeopardized. He does not lie, cheat, steal, betray, do illegal things, file frivolous lawsuits for easy money, bear false witness, act as a victim, or commit any kind of harmful acts.

A genius knows well that every time he does one of the harmful acts cited above, his psyche, his consciousness or his personality becomes poisoned and impacted for worse, and actually causes him to start descending down the chute toward the abyss of darkness and misery. His main redeeming feature is his clean hands and extreme honesty and truth with which he surrounds himself everyday.

A genius knows that to be the positive and the bright side of life and the incredible ability to breathe life into things, requires a spiritual presence and a mind free of secrets, hatred, vengeance, hidden evil intentions, grief, bitter anger, hypocrisy, angry arguments, disagreements, deceits, past pains, and trickery.

A genius knows that in order to maintain his high state of high core values he has to keep the spiritual side of life always in mind and act with kindness, even in the most unholy places or dealing with the most corrupt people. He knows that to maintain his high level of spirituality, he needs to increase his knowledge base constantly by correct education and get proper counseling when he goes astray.

A genius is a truly live being with a keen sense of knowing, and a life-endowing power. He knows that to preserve his joy of creation and maintain positive powers of existence, which are the envy of any humanoid, he needs to rise above the average and never value mediocrity as a way of life. By striving to reach this pinnacle of excellence and actually succeeding to the top, he should set an example for the rest of us to follow!

Exercise 32: Imagine a quality in your life that you would like to improve. Close your eyes and visualize what you need to do to achieve that quality, and get a vivid picture of it in your mind with full color and see how it would feel to have that quality. Write down what your imagination was about and what you learned from this exercise.

Trait #33
Being Highly Divine

By being divine, we mean having qualities that are godlike, heavenly and much superior to anything observable on earth today.

There are qualities such as kindness, admiration, graciousness, respect, love, tolerance, vitality, enthusiasm, fairness, good will (free of vested interest), honor, high level of truth, faith, help, trust, and competence that are seldom found today in our highly technical and mechanized world. These qualities when at high levels are all attributable to gods and divine beings. A genius has all of these great qualities at the core of his personality and in his make-up.

Although he is wide open to help anyone in trouble and considers it one of his greatest virtues, nevertheless he never tries to go near the dark side or negative part of life or try to understand it, duplicate it or mingle with it. He deeply knows there is no understanding or knowledge on the negative side but entrapment, enturbulation, disorder, poison, miscommunication, discord, sickness and misery. His superior knowledge is such that he knows the dark side is an extremely elaborate trap designed to submerge one into it unwittingly, much like a quicksand that swallows one, with no escape possible!

A genius has a great ability to endow things with life and put vitality into things purely by his positive presence free of criticism, granting of beingness to others, a high level of admiration for people in general and his clean and healthy level of communication to the environment.

These qualities puts a genius at a level unrivaled by any human being, attributed only to gods and godlike characters throughout history, far above any human being who is riddled with much envy, enormous false data and many hidden evil intentions toward life and existence.

The divine qualities of a genius may not be apparent at first glance, but when one looks at his behavior, reactions and overall track record of his existence, one cannot help but to notice that a genius is existing on a much higher plateau of immortality occupied only by a handful of deities and supernatural beings.

A genius is actually the positive and the bright side of life to such an extent that no present time negative event, or past misfortune could ever detract or make him forego his positive future, which has a great base of optimism at its core. He does not hold grudges or dwell in the past.

In short, a genius is a very special person with extreme positive powers of analysis and understanding, which enable him to love despite all invitations to hate, and build rather than destroy. His life-endowing powers are based upon his high knowingness and understanding of life itself.

Exercise 33: Consider a divine quality that you would like to see in yourself. Get a vivid picture of it in your mind with full color. Write down what your imagination was and describe your findings.

⊷ ℘ ✷ ❀ �֍ ❀ ✷ ℘ ⊷

Trait #34
Being a Clever Innovator & Problem Vanisher

By **innovate** we mean *to introduce new methods, technologies, or devices in order to improve the existing conditions in life, business or some arena.* This really means bringing in new solutions to old and established ways of doing things, or introducing new changes to improve things.

A genius is a very clever innovator and can see how to improve upon life by coming up with new solutions. He is not just a problem solver, but far beyond that he has a great ability to make problems vanish for good.

Most of us are engaged in solving problems on a daily basis and we are successful to some degree but never achieve a 100% solution. Most of traditional methods of "problem solving" done by most humans are faulty, since it creates other forms of problems somewhere else.

For example, one is short in money, so he solves it by pilfering at the job by tapping into office resources. Obviously, this creates problems at the office. Another example, is a salesman who wants to sell "product x," so conjures up a lot of slick and hyped-up advertisement to attract people. His business may pick up and he may sell quite a bit, but now the customer is upset since he is stuck with a product, which performs below par. Another example is one who has to get up early morning everyday to go to work but feels tired. To solve this problem, he starts taking uppers or coffee to keep him alert on the job. Over a few years, he will find himself addicted to the drug or caffeine and cannot stop it because doing so creates headaches and drowsiness.

When a genius innovates or solves a problem, he solves it in the following way:

a) He uses a scientific approach to get a superior technical result.

b) He uses a long-term approach and not a band-aid or short-term potpourri of untried methods.

c) He uses a systematic methodology that encompasses all aspects of the problem.

d) He solves it in such a way that all parties involved benefit with the least amount of suffering or damage to anyone.

A genius appears to be a super human being at first glance because he has this outstanding ability to solve problems in such a way that everyone wins and benefits from it. He finds new ways to doing old things that no one even questions or sees anything wrong with, let alone innovate or improve upon them.

A genius is at the core of all successful and expanding business operations, because he is genuinely interested to help others and does not wish to create conflicts or new problems down the road, so he solves it for good!

A genius has great powers of perception for truth in any problem or conflict; therefore, he can quickly solve it in the best interest of all involved, without favoring his own party more than the rest or putting it first in line.

A genius is such a bright and positive side of life that problems or conflicts vanish in his vicinity and won't last very long; problems disintegrate in his presence just like a snowball on a hot summer day that melts rapidly!

He has a high mental power of observation and rationality, so he can outcreate any problem. This factor alone gives him a mystique and sets him far apart from the average humanoid thinking, which goes something like "eye for an eye and tooth for a tooth," or "get them before they get you," or "men are evil so should be punished to become moral."

A genius solves the problem from everybody's viewpoint, that is to say, gets everyone involved, and comes up with a solution where everyone benefits from it, thus the solution sticks and becomes workable. He oversees the execution of the final solution as a definite part of his task and makes sure all parties adhere to what was agreed upon, thus ensures the vanishment of the problem forever.

In short, a genius is a very special being with very positive powers of innovation and solution-ability. He is a truly live being with a keen sense of knowing and a genuine magical power of improving things, much better than how he found them and vanishing undesirable conditions for good. This is very much like a magician who would vanish a rabbit, except with a major difference of using no sleight of hands or any hidden trickeries!

Exercise 34: Imagine something as a problem and get a vivid picture of it in your mind with full color. See if you can vanish or innovate upon it by first viewing it from all angles in order to get a good idea what to do. Then solving it by coming up with a new solution or an amicable and positive method of resolving it. Write down about your imagined problem and what you learned from this exercise.

Trait #35
Being a Superb False Data Detector

A genius has a great ability to detect false data in the information sources he encounters daily whether at work, in the media, from textbooks, from medical authorities, government centers, latest drug breakthrough, etc.

He can see through the barrage of misleading information that is being flooded into business marts, schools, universities and our lives by the merchants of chaos. Even when the source is the "authority," he can still see through the lies. For example, he may hear from the medico that the source of "common cold" is germs, which is caused by damp and cold weather. However, he knows that the germ theory is only 30% of the reason; the other 70% is psychosomatic.

The reason he can detect false data in the external environment is that the stored internal false data has been stripped and removed from his consciousness. Therefore, he can use self as the knowledge basin from which the validity of all other data can be ascertained.

Of course, we know the genius by his high rationality and positive method of thinking. He has such a certainty of self as a source of certainty and positive data that all the false data of the world does not shake or throw him a bit from his perceptive power of truth!

In short, a genius is a well of truth, which can never run dry. His keen sense of knowing is the beacon and torch of light that shines the light on the false data and exposes it for all to see! Even though he constantly seeks to expand his horizons of knowledge, however, he filters out the false data in any field and stops it dead in its tracks from further encroachment into his thoughts and core personality, lest it poisons the well!

Exercise 35: Pick up a newspaper and see if you can detect a false datum in one of the news stories. Write down what your observation was and how it affected you and what you learned from it.

Trait #36
Being a Master Negotiator

By definition to negotiate means to discuss and settle the terms of an agreement in an amicable way. The reason we need to learn the skills of negotiation is because almost anything one desires to have is owned by another party and one must enter a negotiation process to obtain it. Most of us have some familiarity with this process but a genius is a master negotiator.

A genius possesses two essential requirements much needed in any discussion or negotiation process: a) a great command of communication process, and b) a great ability to grant beingness to others.

A genius's skill in negotiation enables him to act in many instances as a neutral party in command of any conflict or scene of contention. He does not blow up or make hasty remarks in a meeting to regret later. He is a calm, aware and calculating navigator who listens intently to find points of agreement so that he can bring any conflicting scene to a resolution, beneficial to both parties.

A genius has the incredible ability to breathe life into conflicting things and bring it into harmony and order. His presence is a calming factor in any challenging scenario.

His granting powers of life to things and his high mental powers in creating new solutions to old problems give him a mystique and set him far apart from the average individual.

In short, a genius is a very highly trained being with several positive sets of skills, which enable him to deal with tough situations bordering on impasse. He is a truly live person with a keen sense of understanding of human nature, and how to bring about closures to conflicts and confrontations, without resorting to the use of force or expensive and stressful court proceedings.

Exercise 36: Imagine a situation in your life where you desire to obtain something from another and get a vivid picture of it in your mind with full color. Now devise a plan of action whereby you could approach this person to obtain the item in an amicable way. Implement it and see if you can obtain the item. Write down what your result was and what you learned.

Trait #37
Being a Great Futurist

By definition, *a futurist is a purpose-driven being whose view of life is wholly based upon the future, and his master plan of action is a rational use of the past to build a bright future.*

A genius is unglued and very detached from the past and actually lives in the far distant future and not in the immediacy of the present time at all. Even though he is actively involved in the present time projects and activities, but he has disengaged himself from the past fortunes and misfortunes and is seeking survival in a totally different plane of existence, the eternity of time which starts in present time and ends in an unbounded future. This is where his knowledge of own immortality of existence plays a big role in his futuristic view of life.

A genius is not resting on his laurels nor is he trying to get honorary recognitions from the "such-and-such society" or "so-and-so university" for his past accolades and achievements. He is just not content with his level of contributions and is constantly seeking to improve upon it.

A genius knows that he is not alone in this universe and is indeed surrounded by many other life forms and many grades of personalities in terms of ability and awareness, and that his own existence as an individual, let alone his potential survival is intimately connected to what happens to this timeless pool of life abounding all about him. Therefore, his approach to life and the solutions that he creates and puts forward to life's many enigmatic problems are not mechanically based or robotic, but are imbued by brilliant solutions that have a great root in the future and in the increase of potential survival as well as the preservation of the integrity of his fellow beings.

A genius puts an extremely great priority on the future goals and places a high level of premium on his future existence. He deeply recognizes that eternity is where he will be, and eventually it is where he will hang his boxing gloves at the end of the road of life, with the present time as just a small window of observation peering into that invisible realm called "the future."

A genius's current actions are motivated entirely by the future. He works and thinks quite contrary to the general belief that most older folks have, which is avoiding any future expansion or planning or new activities when they get to the ripe age of seventy or eighty years. They usually take up reminiscing about "the glory days," and "the good old times" and completely retire from work and activities at this age. Looking at the past, as a way of knowing who one is now is a backward look toward life and existence and a genius inherently knows it as a definite master trap and shuns it utterly!

He is a truly live being with a keen sense of understanding of future and knows how the neglect of it can bring wrong solutions and disaster to the world affairs. He knows how to bring about a closure to utterly impossible problems by injecting the future into the solution.

A genius knows that the tension, stress and wars in the world today are created by the short sightedness and vast ignorance of the leaders at large. He knows these unsavory conditions are primarily initiated by some unholy person in power who insists that the future will be very bleak, unpalatable and quite dangerous unless one does the unthinkable!

A genius knows that the mad men of the world are stricken with a serious malady, in fact a terminal illness called "futurelessness." He knows that the world powers who rule the earth's many nations are ignorant of the laws of life and are heavily manipulated by the powerful and heavily financed vested interest whose intentions are diametrically opposed to rational solutions that earth as a whole needs.

A genius makes it his mission in life to bring a great future to the people and projects in his vicinity and to those existing within his zone of influence. He actively works in this direction and is not deterred by small setbacks that life may throw at him.

In short, a genius lives in the future, views the portal of life through the present time lens, and does not focus his vision on the past in order to use it as a guide. He knows well that he can outcreate any obstacle so does not need to carry a great sack of past experiences (usually mistakes, accidents, mishaps, etc.) as a yardstick to measure the future or as an oracle to be guided by!

A genius knows to live in the future one must do a "past-ectomy" and shift his "present-time" thinking toward "future-driven" purposes and goals, while at the same time repelling and shunning all dark forces of life that may come his way!

Exercise 37: Imagine a situation in your life where there is a certain goal you have always wanted to achieve and see if you can get a vivid picture of it in your mind with full color. Now create a future reality in your mind where you have achieved the goal. In your mind devise a plan of action and give yourself plenty of time to execute each step of the plan. Write down your observations and what you learned.

Trait #38
Having Unlimited Space

By definition, **space (or more precisely, mechanical space or created space)** is *the delineated and designated region within a closed boundary line (2-dimensional space) or bounded surface (3-dimensional space) within which all things under consideration can be placed for observation or analysis.*

We loosely refer to "mechanical or created space" as "space" in all of physics and science textbooks. However, it has become evident that the source of space lies with the "viewpoint," since it is the viewpoint that delineates a "boundary line or bounded surface" and calls it space. Without this action of the viewpoint, we do not really have "a space" or more precisely a "created space" to work with.

Therefore, the concept of creating "space" is a mental phenomenon and is intimately related to a person's considerations and point of view, and is far different from the physical space of a room or a building, which is a byproduct of this mental action.

The physical universe space is "a created space" and is far different from "creating space" that a being can engage in through the power of consideration. The physical universe space is very deceptive to use as an exclusive form of space and can completely quagmire one's thinking if one recognizes it as the only "space" one can ever have. Because at that moment, one has fixated and equated one's own space with a finite commodity called "physical universe space." These two, "own space" and "physical space," are not synonymous at all and considering that they are, is a form of ignorance that should be cured rather quickly. The equivalence of these two distinctly different aspects of life is purely an apparency, and becomes more so as one descends to lower depths of awareness and understanding, but even there, they are not exactly the same, it just seems so.

A genius should be able to have a variable space, that is to say, he should be able to:

a) Create any space by consideration alone,

b) Be able to occupy and permeate any created space at will.

c) Withdraw or shrink from any space that he selects at will.

If one has a series of past spaces, which he is stuck in or are affixed to his mental consciousness, this will reduce his ability to have a variable space and he won't be able to expand or contract his space at will and he will as a result not be flexible in his space creation. He will be in a condition referred to as "fixed or frozen space" type existence. A genius has overcome this handicap to a very large extent and is totally free of the "fixed or frozen space" phenomena and its many limiting factors.

A genius's ability to perform many tasks by doing a "variable-space thinking" on them, makes him a breed of individual far above the average. This is a quality possessed by a few but one who has it is a genius sitting in the driver seat of a "bus called life" with many onboard passengers who really depend upon his driving skills. They will shower the driver with praise and admiration and be extremely delighted when they get to their final destination safely.

In summary, an ability to have a variable space and not confuse it with the fixed space of the physical universe space is indicative of a genius quality in a being. A genius must be able to create unlimited space at will and have a complete mastery of it. Through the application of this quality alone, one can achieve phenomenal solutions and results never before possible or imaginable.

Exercise 38: close your eyes and put a small cube of space (about one inch on each side) in your mind to view. Gradually increase the size of the cube by increments (of one inch at first and then one foot) until it is 20 feet on each side. Write down what you observed and describe your findings.

Trait #39

Being Able to Handle Any Incoming Force & Motion

We live in a world today that has enormous pressures, many hidden forces and large uncontrollable motions ready to pounce upon one in an unguarded moment. These factors are built into the fabric of our society unwittingly without one's consent.

Let us consider a few examples:

a) There are work deadlines that must be met.

b) There are many of one's enemies who spread black PR (public relations) in terms of a series of fabricated and horrid lies enough to ruin one's morale and productivity, for example through online blogs and sites on the internet, in newspapers, amongst friends, etc..

c) There are computer viruses and destructive emails aimed at one's inbox.

d) There are frivolous lawsuits filed against one for some totally bogus reasons aimed at one's wallet. Such loathsome characters are looking for a quick cash settlement, or else threaten one with a pending jury trial, a lengthy proceeding, high legal costs and long-term mental stress.

e) There are home burglars and car thieves scoping one's assets for an opportune moment.

f) There are drug dealers who are ready to get one's kid into addiction in a blink of an eye.

g) There are unscrupulous real estate brokers who will sell you a house by taking advantage of your naiveté. They will not put your best interest at heart but will milk you by selling a house at the wrong price just to get a good commission.

h) There are loan brokers who first befriend you and then will "help" you toward a home loan program that will enrich their pockets but will ruin your financial future and will eventually put you into foreclosure. They will not explain all of the pitfalls and traps in the loan program, just to collect a healthy commission premium. The list is almost endless.

Indeed, we live in a dangerous environment filled with many hidden threats that if not dealt with correctly will submerge one quickly in a downdraft motion of a quicksand.

A genius is well aware of these hidden threats and navigates himself away from these deleterious factors, and builds many guarding elements in his business by employing defensive moves that completely isolate him from these unseemly situations and characters. He employs proper insurance for every aspect of his business and never uses brokers as advisors. If he is in the stock markets, he insures all of his stocks by proper option strategies. If he is in real estate, he uses licensed and bonded contractors and property managers who are properly insured with workers comprehensive insurance as well as liability insurance.

A genius is well educated and understands the nature of human beings particularly the true nature of anti-social personality to such an extent that he knows their hidden evil intent and harmful toxic advices, which are dished out freely in his way. The moment he senses he has run into one of these characters, his next move would be a complete handling, coupled with filtering out their presence along with a total disconnection of all ties and affiliations.

Although he is wide open to helping anyone in trouble and considers it one of his greatest virtues, nevertheless he never tries to go near the dark side or understand the negative energy of the unholy. His actions are very clear-cut in nature: He promptly and effectively handles the incoming motion and force that these characters apply to him, and then permanently disconnects and unplugs the source of toxic power from his life. He will not bend down to their level or change his positive outlook toward life.

A genius is actually the positive and the bright side of life to such an extent that no present time negative event, or past misfortune could ever detract him or make him forego his positive future, which has a great base of optimism at its core. He does not hold grudges for his past tribulations knowing well that he caused it all even though the outcome was not what he intended.

In short, a genius is a very special being with extreme positive powers of understanding of life and its many forces whether positive or negative. This understanding enables him to love the positive people and shun the negative elements in life despite all invitations to get involved. He would rather build than destroy.

A genius's life-endowing powers to handle the incoming motions and force are based upon his high knowingness and superior understanding of life itself.

Exercise 39: Consider a negative incoming motion or force that you would like to handle in your life. Get a vivid picture of it in your mind with full color. Now handle it with proper measures and at the end disconnect the source. Write down what your result was and describe your findings.

Trait #40
Being a Great Scientist

The philosophical approach commonly employed by all exact physical sciences is referred to as the *"Scientific Methodology,"* which can be defined as:

"A systematic approach devoted to pure observation as a first step, followed by collection and classification of data (without observer's influence) and formulation of a hypothesis (based on the collected data), testing and experimentation to verify the validity of such a hypothesis and repeating this process for further refinement, until a workable principle is derived." The scientific methodology is shown below.

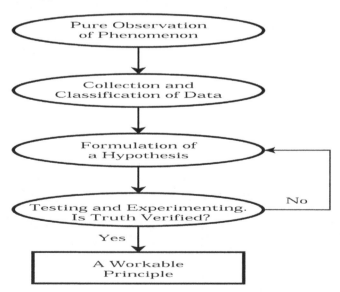

Use Of "Scientific Methodology" To Obtain A Workable Principle.

Sciences are organizing tools that, through a systematic process of observation of the chaos of the physical universe, try to uncover the governing principles, and in doing so, intend to bring about comprehension on a mental plane and a higher level of order on a physical level. Such a higher order on a physical plane is accomplished generally through the invention of intricate devices or systems, or the creation of new application mass.

A genius has a great ability to view life and livingness in a correct perspective, that is to say he knows that life is set up in a hierarchical fashion in the form of a pyramid where the viewpoint is at the top and tha produced product at the bottom.

A genius has a deep understanding of the scientific methodology and its ramifications in our lives. He knows that sciences as a pool of knowledge and a source of accurate information about our world are extremely vital in the decision making process and product development. Therefore, he incorporates pertinent sciences into all aspects of his endeavors and enterprises and solves problems not only philosophically correct or fundamentally error-free but also technically accurate and exact!

In short, a genius is a great scientist with extreme positive powers of analysis and understanding, which enable him to solve problems scientifically as well as philosophically! This is a far better method of solving than the mechanical band-aid unintelligent solutions sold to the public that only work for a short time before they backfire. Examples of mechanical solutions that are scientifically incorrect and unworkable include:

1. Psychiatric inhumane solutions of "curing" mental problems through: a) electric shocks, b) Lethal drugs, c) lobotomy, etc., to numb and paralyze the patient into a vegetable state at great cost to the patient.

2. Government's plan to drug children in order "to cure" lack of focus in students. This is done by first labeling and inventing a mental disease and then solving it by poison pills and powders (called medicine to really mask the intentions) at great cost and damage. This is done on a total mechanical basis and without ever solving the actual study problems that the student faces.

3. Government's "bright" and short-term solutions to improve the economy of our nation through the creation of unrest and conflict in two neighboring countries and then selling arms to both sides!

The list of incoherent and false solutions that betray man are really endless in our society. On the other hand, a genius can identify each and every one of these as falsehoods and steer his people clear of them toward more technical and accurate solutions, which have a deep foundation in philosophical truths and are based upon real sciences that actually help mankind!

Exercise 40: Consider the city or the country you live in. Look around to see one mechanical solution which is very short term and unintelligent. Get a vivid picture of it in your mind with full color. Now, think of a real solution that is technically correct and is based upon an actual science really helping mankind. Write down what you found and describe your results.

Trait #41
Being Able to Stay Exterior Stably

Staying **exterior** means *remaining on the outside of a situation, an event or a condition in life or business, and not being absorbed or drawn into it.*

This is a great quality that a genius possesses and because of it he is able to handle business problems and situations with great effectiveness.

A genius does not sympathize with someone's problems, instead he shows great empathy and by staying unemotional toward his client's problems, he would be able to come up with effective solutions leading to a swift resolution.

A genius's ability to stay exterior to a devastating and disastrous situation shows his great mental stability and inner power that can deal with a major crisis and still maintain good functionality.

He has a deep understanding and skilled knowledge in handling any form of bad news whether happening to own life or to friends and associates. He can take effective measures to handle the source of the negative enturbulence very quickly.

In short, a genius is a very special being with extreme positive powers of analysis and understanding, which enable him to handle "enemies posed as friends" who could cause mayhem in his vicinity. He always stays exterior to the most painful situations that most people cringe and usually avoid. He is like a doctor who stays calm and effective while attending a scene of carnage in an accident, dealing with mangled or dismembered bodies and broken bones in an unemotional and professional manner.

Of all of the abilities of a genius, the ability to stay exterior stably is one of the most precious traits because it allows him to stay in control of the scene and act to handle the problems with great focus and effectiveness!

Exercise 41: Consider a problem that you would like to see handled or make one up in your mind if there is none. Get a vivid picture of it in your mind with full color. First, move yourself to an exterior view of it and then from that angle handle it effectively to a resolution. Write down about your problem and describe how your exterior view helped you to solve it better.

Trait #42

Being Able to Select the Correct Game to Play

The English dictionary defines **game** *as any activity or undertaking that requires skill, knowledge, strategy, etc.*

As we look across the gamut of activities in life or business, every one of them could be likened to a game requiring one to know the rules, objectives and barriers well before he can become skillful in playing it.

A genius is no stranger to this concept and knows that any and all activities in life or business could be likened to a game. He knows to succeed in activities such as going to college, going to work, investing, handling a marriage, making money, consultation, negotiation, sales, learning a subject, etc., he needs to know the basic principles of games.

A genius grasps the fundamental concepts behind any game in life, which would then allow him to establish all aspects of operations such as goals, teamwork, inflow and outflow of particles as well as potential obstacles that could pose in his way.

A genius not only has a superior knowledge about the fundamentals of games, but also has a great ability to select games that enhance his main purpose and not get sidetracked or involved in games that detract from it. This is an essential difference between a genius and an ordinary person.

Whereas an ordinary person may get involved immediately in a fight with a belligerent personality that comes his way urging one to take him on as an opponent, a genius has a great amount of selectivity and sensitivity to what type of activities he would rather get involved that would further his envisioned goals on many fronts. If the intended activity would not be directly contributing to his goals, then he would intelligently divert his forces away from there and just like a commanding general would not deploy any soldiers or ammunition in that direction.

A genius is a very special being with a very high level of understanding and knowledge about games and the fundamental principles of operation. He knows that any activity can be likened to a game, and thus before he starts it he needs to know its purpose, rules of operation, the playing-field boundaries and the obstacles to deal with or avoid.

In short, a genius has a great vision to select the correct game that enhances his life and business income, as well as one that creates positive outcomes for the society and the world. He also has a high sensitivity to filter out the wrong games that will endanger his productivity and the quality of his life, or other people's abilities, possessions and morale.

Exercise 42: Consider a goal that you would like to achieve. Get a vivid picture of it in your mind with full color. Develop a game around this goal and see what obstacles are in your way. In your mind see if you can play the game properly and achieve the intended goal. Write down about your goal and the game and describe your findings.

Trait #43
Having Great Self-Cultivated Qualities

There are several qualities that one can cultivate in oneself, which would tremendously improve one's worth to himself and the society at large. These are:

a) High self-confidence,

b) High self-discipline,

c) High self-esteem,

d) High self-image,

e) High self-initiativeness, and

f) High self-reliance.

We discuss each one in more depth below.

a) Self-confidence by definition *is believing in one's own abilities, powers, judgments, decisions, etc.* In essence, it means having trust and confidence in self as a timeless being. It is allowing oneself to be the source of life and emanation point of all creations. Self-confidence means knowing without a shadow of doubt that one is capable of an infinite potentiality to be, to create, to radiate energy and endow matter with life and vitality.

A genius has a very high self-confidence and can transmit that feeling easily to anything he does or anyone that he meets. He fills others with an air of confidence and pumps them up with a lot of admiration and pride to a point that an ordinary individual feels joyous and very alive around a genius.

b) By definition, **"discipline"** refers *to training that develops control, character, orderliness and efficiency.* Therefore, **Self-discipline** is *the act or power of disciplining or controlling oneself, one's own character, one's own desires and actions through positive training of the mind.*

Because a genius has such a high level of self-discipline, he can achieve his goals rather easily once he decides to do it. His self-discipline allows him to engage in meaningful work and production far beyond average with total focus and dedication, and thus achieve extraordinary results. Others seeing these tremendous results in such short periods of time cannot help but get impressed and become encouraged to do the same in their own lives!

c) **Self-esteem** refers *to treating oneself with a high level of respect and considering self one's own greatest friend, never disparaging self out of rage or frustration.*

A genius has a very high self-esteem because he thinks extremely well of himself and his motives. He recognizes that in the final analysis, he is his own greatest resource and best friend and this fact alone allows him to overcome many unknown fears.

Therefore, a genius develops a steadfast friendship and creates a rock solid relationship, early in his life, with the best friend he will ever have: himself!

By having such a high self-esteem, a being has achieved a very high state of complete unity with self, a status referred to as indivisibility or unfragmented existence. He has achieved a high internal peace and enormous concentrated power. This high self-esteem state provides the most cohesive bond in a being and is the lone factor guaranteeing a high level of sincerity, honesty and integrity toward others.

d) **Self-image** means *an individual's conception of himself, his own identity, abilities and worth.*

A genius has a high self-image and invites others to achieve the same. Others perform to their fullest and achieve their highest efficiency working with a high self-image genius. This quality allows him to take on any desired project with complete confidence, knowing that he will carry through to its final completion, come hell or high water. This is a quality that our business world today needs plenty of and yet they have no clue where to find or how to develop it.

e) **Self-initiativeness** by definition *is the quality of an individual who originates new ideas or methods and is able to think and act without being ordered or urged forward.* Such an individual takes the first step or move and assumes full responsibility for beginning or origination of actions.

A genius has a very high self-initiativeness in that he takes an active role in initiating the first steps in any undertaking. This is the most cherished quality of a genius for leadership and one would bring much success to a group whose genius leader has this essential quality.

f) Self-reliance by definition *is depending confidently upon one's own judgments, abilities, powers, etc.* In essence, it means having total confidence upon oneself as the correct source of information and accurate judgment. It is allowing oneself a high level of importance, to be the sole source of abilities, power to decide and act in life or business.

Moreover, self-reliance means not allowing others to interfere with one's decisional and volitional powers in one's affairs, such that one would not get stopped toward his goals, or pointed in the wrong direction and sidetracked into a false goal.

A genius is very self reliant in own life and desires the same for others by encouraging others to rely on self as the true source as well as trusting their own instincts more often. He respects others as beings and their behavior. He recognizes that this ability alone can propel him to the top and help his group the most.

***

Concluding Remarks

A genius believes in himself and his ideals to such a degree that no one can take him off course or make him think less of others. He acknowledges the humanity as the force that has put him in power on this planet, thus he includes everyone in his plans of actions.

A genius he knows that his existence is truly dependent on many other beings that have gone before him and have contributed to the current scene on many levels whether technologically, culturally, or economically. Therefore, in all of his actions he includes everyone in the process as long as they are not part of another vested interest and serving other masters. He can detect the true group members. He respects those who associate with him and teaches them the self-cultivated qualities that he exemplifies.

A genius with his enormous belief in self as the source of life and a huge reservoir of élan vital (i.e., life force) makes it his top priority to help others and the existing scene of mankind in order to bring about toward a more ideal scene that even Greek gods would be very proud of. He stands for the greatest force of good that this world has ever seen!

Exercise 43: Think of an area where you need more self-confidence. This should be an area that could help you and everyone at home or work. Now try to improve that area by taking on more self-confidence, all done on a mental level in a quiet area. Write down the results.

Trait #44
Having Great Certainty

Certainty means *freedom from three conditions:*
a) *Doubt,*
b) *Indefiniteness (or vagueness) and*
c) *Confusion.*

Frankly, we live in a day and age that great efforts are constantly made to introduce and inject turmoil and tremendous amounts of confusions into our business world and daily lives.

One has to be well armed to handle this onslaught of uncertainties form many unsuspected sources just to keep his head above water, let alone soaring high to the mountain top.

It takes a great degree of certainty in one's mind and personality to combat these unhealthy sources of confusions and stay on course to achieve his intended goals. This is so because the injected uncertainties would absorb quite a bit of one's energy that could have been otherwise used for more productivity. Moreover, the economic challenges that these uncertainties introduce into one's thinking-ness could act as a roadblock to one's eventual prosperity.

A few examples of uncertainties that one could potentially run into at work or life are:

a) Economic depression,

b) High unemployment rate,

c) Price inflation,

d) High drug use (medical, psychiatric, street, etc.)

e) Rise of immorality,

f) Rise in crime rate,

g) Government bankruptcy,

h) Bank insolvency,

i) Rise in illiteracy rate,

j) Rise in divorce rate,

k) Rise in white-collar crimes,

l) Stock market crash,

m) Rise of commodity prices such as oil, gold, etc.

n) High drug addiction rate in school children and teen-agers,

o) Union strikes,

p) Interest rate manipulation, etc.

This list (a-p) is just a partial list of what could shake a person up one day out of his slumber party on earth without any warning and throw him into an enormous degree of confusion and a high state of degradation and uncertainty of future.

A genius has achieved a very high degree of certainty in many areas of his life and is thus unshakable as a being. He attains this state of high certainty by the following means:

a) Achieving a high certainty of himself as a timeless entity and a deep knowledge of self as a non-material source of life imbuing matter with abilities,

b) Achieving a high level of skill in being able to learn any new topic,

c) Achieving a high level of morality and purity of thought in himself,

d) Achieving a high degree of understanding about the motives of the confusion mongers and staying clear of their shooting range,

e) Achieving a high certainty in being able to produce a high income regardless of the economic conditions, thus achieving a bulletproof financial status,

f) Achieving a high certainty in making the right decisions,

g) Achieving a high understanding of what the economic traps are and steer self and his group into safety,

h) Achieving a high level of understanding about all poisonous substances (drugs, alcohol, pills, etc.) to such an extent that he educates others to abstain form the drug panacea syndrome currently promoted by the professional drug dealers (also known as psychiatrist, doctors, pharmacist, etc.) or other drug pushers acting as vampires in our society,

i) Achieving a high certainty in distinguishing between truth, facts and accurate technical data versus opinions, theories, untested hypothesis and hyped-up news data.

j) Becoming an independent thinker and achieving a high knowingness about life and business principles to a point that he has stopped worrying about what others think of him if he reasons differently than average, or if he does positive things that are helpful but unorthodox.

In short, a genius has a great certainty on self, others and the business world, and knows the correct actions and the right decisions in any situation based upon the truth and facts of the situation. This really means that he does not write scripts and assumes so and so without examining the facts and the actual data by using logic and pure observation of the situation.

Exercise 44: Think of something that you would like to gain more certainty about it right now. See if you can gather enough knowledge and understanding by: a) consulting with experts, or b) finding correct books, or c) search for the answer on the internet, or d) ask an experienced friend. Do it regardless of what others think, and thereby achieve a higher level of certainty. Write down the results.

Trait #45
Being a Great Visionary

By **visionary,** we mean *a person who has the ability to perceive something not actually visible, as through mental acuteness or keen foresight.*

This trait of a genius clearly depends upon several factors: a) First, one must have the ability to perceive the existing scene objectively and with a detached eye (***Perception stage***).

b) Second, one must have the power of imagination and the ability of contemplation of something that is not physically present through shutting off of all mental noises (***Imagination stage***).

c) Third, one must be able to get a vivid mental image or picture of it in the mind clearly and without interference from other thoughts or pictures (***Clarity of picture stage***),

d) Fourth, one must visualize a plan of action or a solution (or product) that could resolve and bring his mental image to a definite close (***Solution stage***).

e) Fifth, one must have a great degree of courage and certainty of his visualized solution to go ahead against all odds, and form a group and convince them to join him in bringing about the conceived plan of action (**Group formation stage**).

f) Finally, producing the solution (or product) in high quantity enough and implementing it widely enough to effectively improve the scene (*Implementation stage*).

A genius can easily overcome his fear of failure and take on a new enterprise or undertaking without much concern, knowing well that he can learn from his mistakes, overcome the obstacles and come out on top at the end.

A genius has such a high level of self-confidence that he is willing to experiment in new things, take on new challenges and make new waves in a new arena of activity.

A genius as a visionary has a great power of visualization of future goals and their attainment. He is not afraid of failure or rejection because he knows deep within that he is invincible as a being and thus does not allow small setbacks in life get in his way or discourage him from his main objectives or bright future ahead of him!

Exercise 45: Think of a new project that could take on or one that you have been thinking about for some time and see if you could get into the spirit of doing it mentally. Now, visualize the project as done and an achieved goal. Write what you learned.

Trait #46
Being a Great Adventurer

By definition, an **adventure** means *an exciting, unusual or bold undertaking usually involving some danger and risk.* An adventure has a certain degree of unknown risk that is quite different from a calculated risk in which one may engage for a certain transaction or business venture.

Many times in business or life, we encounter situations that require us to take the plunge, become adventurous and take a certain degree of unknown risk. In these instances, one needs to get into the spirit of a daring enterprise and disturb the monotony of life in order to open up new doors of opportunities.

Having a spirit of adventure is a great method to potentially gain valuable experience as well as a new territory to first conquer and then profit highly. A genius is no stranger to this concept and uses it to expand his own and his group's zone of operation and sphere of influence to a large extent.

A genius can easily overcome his fear of failure by realizing that if the gain is potentially high enough for self and others, then sacrificing his comfort zone and taking on the adventure is a worthwhile activity.

Moreover, a genius has an inherent knowingness and positive belief that:

a) He can enter an adventurous activity, persevere long enough to learn from his mistakes and identify the unknowns to such a degree that the obstacles encountered in the process will eventually surrender, and

b) No matter what events take place, he has enough personal stability and mental power to overturn the tide and come out on top at the end.

A genius is willing to experiment in new things, take on new challenges and make new waves in a new arena of activity. He welcomes new challenges and is not shying away from failure or rejection, because he knows deep within that he is invincible as a being. He knows that all negative obstacles can be learned from and in time be turned into positives!

He does not allow small setbacks in life or business get in his way or discourage him from his main objectives and will not rest until they are achieved. He figures that being adventurous is part and parcel of being alive!

Exercise 46: Think of a new adventure in life or business that you could take on for fun and see if you could take the risk without much concern. Now, get into the spirit of doing it in your mind by getting a vivid picture of going through all of the motions to the end of achieving the intended result. Write up your findings.

Trait #47
Being an Excellent Decision Maker

A decision by definition *is the act of making up one's mind and determining to carry on a definite course of action.*

The concept of "decision making" brings this observation to the forefront: Decisions derive from the priorities one has already set up in life or business! In other words, to make a correct decision one needs to take one step backwards and know *the order of priority* of actions before moving forward to the decision point.

The *order of priority* clearly depends upon *one's purposes and goals* that one has set up and solidified in his mind. The degree to which this is known and understood, establishes the sequence and pace of the decisions and actions that follow.

At this juncture, it becomes essential for us to clarify two basic terms:

a) **A purpose,** by definition, *is an intention for something desirable such as a condition, an idea, a result, etc. It is what one has in mind to achieve or is intending to do,*

b) *A goal suggests striving to attain something desirable through laborious efforts.*

A *purpose* implies achieving through an intention, whereas a goal brings forth the concept of attainment through effort.

The order of priority of things to do is directly established by the purposes one has setup in his life, which translate directly into a number of goals.

Considering a top-down view of life, we see that as one descends down from the ethereal realm of dreams and general purposes down to more concrete and well defined goals and sub-goals, one gradually enters the domain of projects and targets, which lead to sub-products and eventually the final product.

From the dreams, purposes, goals, we get the sub-goals, projects, targets with all leading to the sub-products and final products. This inevitably sets up a network of woven fabric, which altogether forms the vector of one's life and clearly indicates in whose direction one knowingly or unknowingly is moving forward.

The overall purposes, goals and sub-goals (leading to projects and targets) form a complicated network, which determines the order of priority of decisions that one makes. The clearer one can see his purposes and goals for life and livingness the easier and faster he makes decisions without regrets or loss of composure. The diagram on the next page illustrates this concept further.

Those who are in a confusion in some area of their lives take the longest and make the incorrect decisions, which are mostly regretted later on down the road.

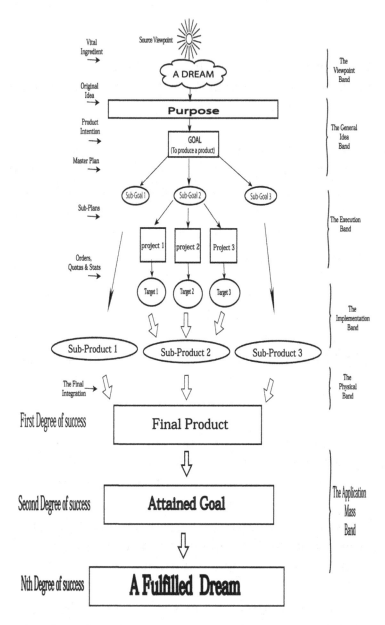

The Flow Chart for Attaining a Goal Based Upon A Dream.

A genius is a fast decision maker and is thus immune to regret and loss of composure due to several factors:

a) He is in intimate contact with his dreams,

b) He clearly knows what his main purposes in life and business are,

c) He knows the immediate goals and sub-goals that he needs to accomplish, well in alignment with his purposes,

d) He exactly knows the order of priority of projects and targets,

e) He can specifically name his final product and identify the sub-products that need to be produced.

Due to these five factors, a genius makes the most brilliant decisions in the shortest possible time with tremendous composure and certainty.

Exercise 47: Think of an area that you are in doubt and one that you have been thinking about for some time and have procrastinated it for a while. Now establish your purpose and goal in that area and see if you could get into the spirit of doing it and make a quick decision to do something about handling it in your mind. Write up your findings.

Trait #48
Having an Excellent Awareness Level

By definition, the concept of **awareness** *implies having knowledge of something through alertness of observation or by one's ability to interpret what one perceives through senses (such as sight, hearing, feeling, etc.), which is coming from different aspects of life and existence.*

The concept of awareness is not a constant factor for every being and is a variable depending upon one's state of mind. For example, at birth one is somewhat aware of his immediate people and surroundings. However, as one progresses in life and gains education and mental expansion in different subjects one's awareness could potentially increase to a very high level well beyond his immediate area and into many invisible realms of knowingness. On the opposite side of the coin, one needs to consider that one's awareness could also decrease equally by a simple drink, drug use, a mishap or a negative experience.

One's awareness of life is an all-important subject that has been really ignored and falsified into an upside-down definition to a point where to some people "going up in awareness" is painful and has actually come to mean "going down into the basement of perception." An example may elucidate this further: Let us consider a person who has become depressed over some failure or upset in life. The common solution advised by the most trusted authority today is to take pills (or even get drunk as advised by some friend) and one should instantly feel better by lowering one's awareness of the problem. So, instead of raising one's awareness to solve the problem one is led to believe that lowering it is the correct action.

Nothing could be further from the truth. Increasing one's awareness in life and business is at the core of a genius's life and he works on a constant basis to raise it for self and others and shuns those elements and people, with vested interest, who want to see it lowered.

A genius has many zones of awareness, which could be subdivided into levels, layers and sub-layers. These subdivisions of awareness make him one of the most indispensable forces of the good and positive side of life that the society has ever seen.

A true genius has an extremely high degree of awareness in many fields vital to man. He has a great awareness of:

a) Self as a power source,

b) Familial influence,

c) Power of groups and society,

d) Role of sciences,

e) Design of politics,

f) Role of art,

g) Correct education,

h) Goal of life,

i) Business principles,

j) Mental hygiene,

k) Spiritual aspects of life,

l) Attainment of high morale and happiness,

m) Protection of spaces and making them safe,

n) Anti-society individuals and philosophies,

o) Traps and their design,

p) Dark side of life, etc.

A genius, with his high awareness of many aspects of life as listed above in (a-p), is truly a gifted being far above average and in a league of his own. He is far beyond the humanoid level of operation commonly seen in our society.

In short, his high level of alertness and awareness of different aspects of life combined with his excellent powers of observation and communication as well as problem-vanishing ability, propels a genius to numerous discoveries in many essential and vital fields hitherto dead-ended and filled with enormous confusion and desperation.

The presence of an aware and alert genius in any field of activity is the most positive side of life in that arena, and the only hope any society would ever have in raising itself above the current level into a more peaceful and abundantly prosperous one!

Exercise 48: Think of an area that you would like to know more about and become more aware of it. This would be something that you could take on or one that you have been thinking about for some time. Now, in your mind see if you could get into the spirit of doing it and raise your awareness about it and thus learn something new about it. Write up your findings.

Trait #49
Being Able to Remain Always at Positive Cause

There are two basic terms that we need to address at the outset:

Cause: *Is anything producing an effect or result.* In modern times, cause is more precisely understood to be a live being (not an inanimate thing) who as the source point of life emanates thoughts and actions.

Responsibility: *Is a state wherein one is in charge of, answerable and accountable for something, which is within one's power or control.*

With these two definitions in mind, one can see that cause can be positive or negative. This really means that one can produce anything as a causative agent in life, and thus be the source of good or bad things. However, to be responsible for something one needs to exert positive control over it, which means that one must be at positive cause over it.

The moment one switches to negative cause (i.e., being and doing harmful things) one's responsibility instantly drops. This means that an insane genius is impossible to exist since he means harm, therefore, his intentions bad, his cause would be negative, his responsibility low, and his control very poor mostly done through blame and criticism.

A true genius, due to his high presence power and ability to create unlimited space at will, would be an excellent person to take charge of operations and exert positive control over them pushing them higher up toward survival and prosperity.

If a society is to move forward in a positive direction at all, if it is going to approach any positive degree of prosperity, it needs to have a lot of positive cause type individuals and responsible beings within it. This fact makes a genius the most qualified, the best-suited and tailor-made individual for this job, enthusiastically ready to take on the world, which desperately needs him and his high degree of responsibility along with his positive cause level and great life-endowing powers!

Exercise 49: Think of a task that you could take on or one that you have been putting off for some time and see if you could get into the spirit of doing it. Decide to become positive cause over it and by exerting positive control take a positive action in the direction of completing it. Write up your findings.

Trait #50
Being Able to Assume Any Identity at Will

Core identity, by definition, *refers to all the physical aspects and mental characteristics that make up a personality.* Creating all the physical aspects and mental characteristics for a particular profession forms an identity that enables one to perform a task in life or business.

An example of physical aspect could be a fireman's hat, which when worn along with a competent training and experience (mental characteristics) will create an identity called a fireman in an individual.

Due to innate abilities of a genius in creating unlimited space at will, his high understanding of life and his great leadership ability, a genius is able to assume identities that help him achieve his goals faster and more effectively.

Most often, when one encounters a failure or a serious obstacle, one tends to go into agreement with the failure and alter his original purpose or goal. This is surely a path to disaster and ultimate demise, because if every time one failed and decided to change his goals to something different, soon he will find himself in a jumble of unfulfilled goals and a shattered life. The solution is to improve the method of attaining the goal and assuming a more suitable identity rather than altering the goal.

A genius is well aware of the fact that life has many counter-flows to one's intentions and goals, so after having failed in an area, he just alters his identity and tries on a new method that would be more powerful. The new method would be more effective because of having gained the experience about the difficulties and the opposition or counter flows.

Therefore, invariably one never sees a failed purpose in a genius because he just assumes new identities on and on without altering the original purpose until final victory.

Therein lies the secret to a genius's unlimited prosperity, because the opposition usually has a fixed identity with a certain and yet limited number of methods in countering one's intentions. Therefore, if one could assume a different and yet more effective identity than the previous one, then one can cause a barrage of new flows from a different angle. The new identity would carry out a new plan of actions that are completely different but more effective than the previous. This shift of viewpoint or identity, which generates a higher morale and enthusiasm, will eventually influence the opposition into surrender.

Therefore, we can see that a genius cannot be contained in a box of limitations, unattained goals and failures, because his ability to assume new identities at will gives him an unlimited weapon to conquer any counter-intention or opposite force. *Amongst all the fifty, this is the absolute zenith (highest in rank) trait worthy of mastering.*

In short, this last is the ultimate key trait, essential in a genius, that makes him the most precious being in the society. His positive view of life, great perseverance and his relentless pursuit of his goals without allowing compromise or failures to creep in, is the most invaluable quality that a genius exemplifies when it comes to life and livingness and achieving one's goals, purposes and dreams as shown on the next page.

Exercise 50: Think of a failed project that you have been thinking about for some time, and see if you could rekindle that failure by assuming a new identity, tackle it now and get a mental victory. Write up your findings.

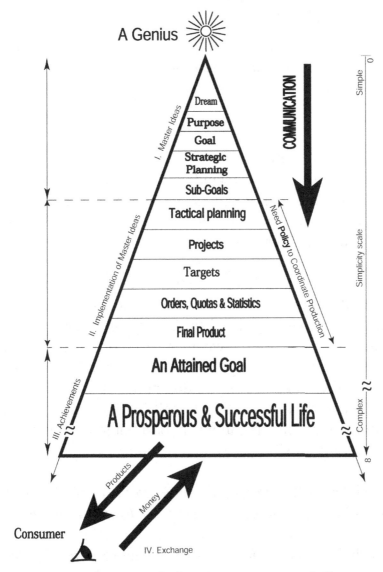

The Pyramid of Prosperity in a Nutshell.

The Gradient Scale of Genius

"When every physical and mental resource is focused, one's power to solve a problem multiplies tremendously."

—Norman V. Peale (1898-1993)
American Writer

The concept of genius, especially in sciences, has gained quite a bit of misunderstanding and many think that scientists are the most qualified individuals for the status of a genius, primarily because of their technical or scientific contributions.

However, even more liberal thinkers have this erroneous concept of calling someone a genius because he can do something in a spectacular fashion and can rise above all in some particular arena whether, in sports, in arts, in science, etc., even though he may be horrible in his personal life and have a disastrous financial life. Nevertheless, everyone seems to call him a genius, which according to our classifications, at best could be a called a "single-trait genius".

However, truth be told, one is genius to the degree that he can acquire all or most of the genius traits discussed in this book. In other words, there is a gradient scale of genius and as one gradually masters more and more of these traits, then one is ascending in the direction of a complete or "absolute genius."

With the panoramic view of all of the possible traits of a genius and what each mean and encompass, we come toward a crossroad of redefining the word genius more accurately in this work. Several classifying terms could be coined at this juncture to consolidate this work and align it more effectively with the vocabulary of our existing society.

We coin the following new terms:

I. The Single-Trait Genius
The Basic Genius: Is an individual who is brilliant in an area and solidly possesses just one of these fifty traits (a 2% genius).

II. The Multi-Trait Genius
The Grand Genius: Is an individual who is extremely brilliant in an area and solidly possesses up to five of these fifty traits (a 10% genius), not necessarily in the order given in this book.

The Advanced Genius: Is an individual who is extremely brilliant in having up to ten of these fifty traits (a 20% Genius).

The Pre-eminent Genius: Is an individual who is extremely brilliant up and solidly possesses twenty of these fifty traits (a 40% genius).

The Ultra Genius: Is an individual who is extremely brilliant and solidly possesses thirty of these fifty traits (a 60% Genius).

The Superior Genius: Is an individual who is extremely brilliant and solidly possesses forty of these fifty traits (an 80% genius).

The Supreme Genius: Is an individual who is extremely brilliant and solidly possesses forty five of these fifty traits (a 90% genius).

The Absolute Genius: Is an individual who is extremely brilliant and solidly possesses all fifty of these fifty traits (a 100% genius).

We have had partial geniuses in many fields who could only master a few of these traits, but certainly a full genius is a very rare bird.

Since the recorded history, no one except a very select few have ever achieved the title of full genius and those who have, rank amongst the highest and finest quality of beings, close to the level of saints just below the level of angels and gods. The table on the next page summarizes all of the traits one needs to master to achieve the title of an absolute genius:

Table 1- All Of The Traits To Achieve Absolute Genius Status

Trait#	Genius Traits
1	Having a Great Drive
2	Having Great Courage
3	Being Highly Devoted to Goals
4	Being Immensely Knowledgeable
5	Having a High Honesty and Integrity Level
6	Having Great Optimism
7	Having a High Ability to Judge
8	Being Highly Enthusiastic
9	Being Highly Willing to Take Calculated Risks
10	Having a Dynamic Energy flow
11	Being Highly Willing to Undertake an Enterprise
12	Being Highly Able to Motivate and Close People
13	Having an Outgoing Personality
14	Having a Great Ability to Communicate Well
15	Being Extremely Patient
16	Having Great Perception Powers
17	Being a Great Perfectionist
18	Having a Great Sense of Humor
19	Being Highly Versatile
20	Being Highly Adaptable
21	Being Highly Curious
22	Being an Excellent Individualist
23	Being a Great Idealist
24	Being Immensely Imaginative
25	Having a High Ability to Grant Beingness
26	Having a Great Balanced Life
27	Being a Great Leader
28	Being an Intelligent Investor

Trait#	Genius Traits (continued)
29	Being an Expert Salesman
30	Being a Great Humanitarian
31	Being a Great Environmentalist
32	Having a Great Spiritual Understanding
33	Being Highly Divine
34	Being a Clever Innovator & Problem Vanisher
35	Being a Superb False Data Detector
36	Being a Master Negotiator
37	Being a Great Futurist
38	Having Unlimited Space
39	Being able to Handle Any Incoming Force or Motion
40	Being a Great Scientist
41	Being able to Stay Exterior Stably
42	Being Able to Select the Correct Game to Play
43	Having a High Self Confidence
44	Having Great Certainty
45	Being a Great Visionary
46	Being a Great Adventurer
47	Being an Excellent Decision Maker
48	Having an Excellent Awareness Level
49	Being Able to Remain Always at Positive Cause
50	Being Able to Assume Any Identity at Will

Examples of Geniuses in History

"Fantasy, if it's really convincing, can't become dated, for the simple reason that it represents a flight into a dimension that lies beyond the reach of time."

— Walt Disney (1901-1966)
American Animator, Entrepreneur and Entertainer.

Since the recorded history on earth, there have been many genius individuals who have graced this planet with their magical presence and incredible powers of thought and innovation. They have truly brightened up our lives in many ways and have made our daily existence truly a pleasant experience far more than we can ever realize or imagine. In other words, we are forever indebted to these extremely bright forces of positivity and owe a great debt of gratitude.

We have inherited their work and their ingenious legacy of help and assistance toward mankind in the direction of better survival in this forlorn corner of Milky Way galaxy. Our only and ultimate salvation from the yoke of such a huge debt to such genius minds of the past is to return the flow, no matter how small. We should strive strongly and pledge a solemn promise to make this world a better and a happier place than how we found it at birth! "To repay our debt by meaning well and doing noble deeds" is our final redemption to unburden the heavy obligation passed onto us from our genius ancestors.

We are indebted to them forever for their work and creative ability in bringing us their gift of ingenuity of thought and wisdom, thereby blazing the path for many generations to come and benefit from their work.

Examples of geniuses of different calibers and quality are many but some have had extremely far-reaching effects, which extend into modern times and thus tremendously affect our current lives in many ways. These geniuses have built the foundation of our modern life, our society and the whole culture on earth with their ingeniousness and brilliance.

There are stellar names in history, which are worth noting here, such as: Galileo (developed scientific methodology), Sir Isaac Newton (discovered the laws of motion), Johann Gutenberg (Invented printing press), Nicola Tesla (invented electric power distribution systems), William Gilbert (discovered static electricity), Charles Coulomb (Discovered laws of charge interaction), Alessandro Volta (invention of battery), Hans C. Oersted (discovered laws of interaction of magnetism with electricity), Ampere (laws of interaction of electricity with matter), Michael Faraday (developed the force field theory), James Clerk Maxwell (developed the wave theory and unified light with electricity), and Hertz (provided experimental proof of wave theory).

In more modern times the list of geniuses includes such names as: Thomas Edison (invention of light bulb, etc.), Graham Bell (invention of telephone), Albert Einstein (developed the theory of relativity and unified energy with matter), Shockley (invention of PN junction Diode and transistor), Walt Disney (invention of Imagineering), Bill Gates (invention of Windows computer operating system and Graphic User Interface), Steve Jobs (Computer/Internet innovator), etc.

Quizzes #1

Quiz 1.1

What are "**The Misconceptions of being a Genius?**" Give an example.

How does one "**Develop Genius Traits?**" Give an example.

What are "**The Character Traits of a Genius?**" Give an example.

What are a few examples of "**The Fifty Genius Traits**" that you have personally observed?

What is meant by "**Having a Great Drive?**" Give an example.

What is meant by "**Having Great Courage?**" Give an example.

Quiz 1.2

What is meant by "**Being Highly Devoted to Goals?**" Give an example.

What is meant by "**Being Immensely Knowledgeable?**" Give an example.

What is meant by "**Being Extremely Honest?**" Give an example.

What is meant by "**Having Great Optimism?**" Give an example.

What is meant by "**Having a High Ability to Judge?**" Give an example.

Quiz 1.3

What is meant by **"Being Highly Enthusiastic?"** Give an example.

What is meant by **"Being Highly Willing to Take Calculated Risks?"** Give an example.

What is meant by **"Having a Dynamic Energy flow?"** Give an example.

What is meant by **"Being Highly Willing to Undertake an enterprise?"** Give an example.

What is meant by **"Being Highly Able to Motivate and Close People?"** Give an example.

Quiz 1.4

What is meant by **"Having an Outgoing Personality?"** Give an example.

What is meant by **"Having a Great Ability to Communicate Well?"** Give an example.

What is meant by **"Being Extremely Patient?"** Give an example.

What is meant by **"Having Great Perception Powers?"** Give an example.

What is meant by **"Being a Great Perfectionist?"** Give an example.

Quiz 1.5

What is meant by **"Having a Great Sense of Humor?"** Give an example.

What is meant by **"Being Highly Versatile?"** Give an example.

What is meant by "**Being Highly Adaptable?**" Give an example.

What is meant by "**Being Highly Curious?**" Give an example.

What is meant by "**Being an Excellent Individualist?**" Give an example.

Quiz 1.6

What is meant by "**Being a Great Idealist?**" Give an example.

What is meant by "**Being Immensely Imaginative?**" Give an example.

What is meant by "**Being Highly able to Grant Beingness?**" Give an example.

What is meant by "**Having a Great Balanced Life?**" Give an example.

What is meant by "**Being a Great Leader?**" Give an example.

Quiz 1.7

What is meant by "**Being an Intelligent Investor?**" Give an example.

What is meant by "**Being an Expert Salesman?**" Give an example.

What is meant by "**Being a Great Humanitarian?**" Give an example.

What is meant by "**Being a Great Environmentalist?**" Give an example.

What is meant by **"Having a Great Spiritual Understanding?"** Give an example.

Quiz 1.8

What is meant by **"Being Highly Divine?"** Give an example.

What is meant by **"Being a clever innovator and Problem Vanisher?"** Give an example.

What is meant by **"Being a Superb False Data Detector?"** Give an example.

What is meant by **"Being a Master Negotiator"** Give an example.

Quiz 1.9

What is meant by **"Being a Great Futurist?"** Give an example.

What is meant by **"Having Unlimited Space?"** Give an example.

What is meant by **"Being Able to Handle Incoming Force or Motion?"** Give an example.

What is meant by **"Being a Great Scientist?"** Give an example.

What is meant by **"Being Able to Stay Exterior Stably?"** Give an example.

Quiz 1.10

What is meant by **"Being Able to Select the Correct Game to Play?"** Give an example.

What is meant by "**Having Great Self-Cultivated Qualities**?" Give an example.

What is meant by "**Having Great Certainty**?" Give an example.

What is meant by "**Being a Great Visionary**?" Give an example.

Quiz 1.11

What is meant by "**Being a Great Adventurer**?" Give an example.

What is meant by "**Being an Excellent Decision Maker**?" Give an example.

What is meant by "**Having an Excellent Awareness Level**?" Give an example.

What is meant by "**Being Able to Remain Always at Positive Cause**?" Give an example.

What is meant by "**Being Able to Assume Any Identity at Will**?" Give an example.

PART 2

The Slant of Life
Is
Toward Selling

To Succeed, Think Unlimited!

"The best things are never arrived at in haste. God is in no hurry; His plans are never rushed."

— Michael Phillips(1946-), writer and novelist.

By **infinite** we mean *something without bounds or limit; unlimited.*

Most people including business professionals do not seem to grasp the essence of unlimitedness when approached or directly questioned, and still seem to be immeresed in a twisted philosophy called "short term profits at any cost." This is the philosophy that most businesses are grappling with everyday and never seem to carve out a deep riverbed of longevity wherein the river of life can flow and embed itself in an incessant and forever manner.

Instead, they deal with short term survival goals, underhanded techniques to take down the competitor, backstab joe-the-inventor or badmouth bill-the-innovator in order to keep their own survival raft one more day afloat in the ocean of life. This is where we find the average professional lives: from the medico, to the lawyer and down to the drug dealer; from the educator, to the priest and down to the lowly psychiatrist with his poison pills and shock machines.

Each one seems to have no respect for life and its infinite potential to survive and heal. Each is trying to enforce his own erroneous theory on life and force it to obey the artificial system set up in doing business and make profits.

Example #1: Let's take the doctor. He believes in the disease theory of life one hundred percent (100%) to the point of eliminating all other methods of healing such as nutritional healing, chiropractic methods of healing, stress-relief healing (through counseling), mental therapy through debug and confusion resolution, lightwave therapy, vitamin and mineral therapy, etc. He is trying to shut down all other forms of healing (through American Medical Association, AMA) and exclusively devote his entire practice to chemical healing or surgical operations and cutting off body parts. He works avidly to outlaw all other forms of therapy to maintain his exclusive rights to a healthy income flow!

Example #2: Another example is the legal system and the lawyers. These groups of individuals are hired guns who go after anybody with deep pockets and create such enormous amounts of confusion, illogic, causes of actions, conspiracy theories, etc. that one's head spins after getting one of their paperworks (called a lawsuit), especially if one is a defendant in a case. Their stock in trade is lies, untruth, omitted data, allegations, accusations, distorted facts, creation of doubt, threat of punishmnet and financial penalty.

Lawyers are not interested in finding truths except to use it against the opposite party, because they are not trained in basic principle and laws of how to debug life and remove conflicts. They know the artificial and man-made laws and channels of operation and communication in the legal system, and as such they are not even vaguely interested in aiding and abetting people by solving people's problems or resolving impasses. They do not emphasize conflict resolution methods and actually prevent communication between parties in order to extend the conflict so that they could get paid more handsomely. They do not bring about solutions to confusions of life and as such they are a pretty ineffective group.

Therefore, from examples #1 and 2 we can see that to think unlimited and in an ever widening sphere of influence, one must:

a) Have no vested interest to promote any single idealogy but only truth,

b) Have a sound knowledge in principles and laws of life,

c) Have an honest desire to help others with no hidden motives to betray or destroy,

d) Have an expert training level in conflict resolution and problem solving.

Given these four requirements one can engage in problem solving successfully and bring about calm and order in the society and actual prosperity for self and others.

To solve a problem, one needs to solve it in such a way that it encompasses all aspects of life and integrates all factors into a long-term positive solution with truthfulness and honesty toward people who are directly involved.

To have an unlimited income, one needs to engage in those activities that actually help mankind on a broad scale and those that do not betray, by pretending to help only on the surface, but deep down meaning harm.

The key to unlimited prosperity is three-folds:

a) A willingness to help as many groups of people as possible and really mean it by being honest, respectful and helpful in one's endeavors in life or business.

b) A genuine desire to treat people well and help them to grow stronger, to make them more powerful, and to free them of falsities that surrounds them in education, healthcare, selfcare, finances, investment, etc.

c) A great motivation to create an exchangeable product that truly benefits people, and at the same time stand behind it one hundred percent by means of forming a dedicated group that provides a great customer service. This third criteria is directly derives from and is totally a result of one's intentions to help as delineated in (a) and (b) above.

The Five Echelons to Climb

"You may delay, but time will not."
— Benjamin Franklin

As one rises through the ranks of professional to the top of his field, especially if it is a very technical area, one cannot help but to note certain powerful principles at work.

These principles in the order of seniority can be subdivided into three large divisions of principles and facts as follows:

Echelon I— "The Dream Echelon," which forms the backbone of all that a person will ever achieve or attain in life or business:

a. **Dreams**—Create big dreams for yourself and do not let anyone or anything take them away or trample on them.

b. **Purposes**—Have self-fulfilling purposes for your existence; intentions that are positive and aligns with your personality.

c. **Goals**—Translate your dreams and purposes into well-defined and exact goals. Shoot at a fixed target, which is written down and is specific in nature.

d. **Plans**—Create a strategic plan, a tactical plan and a mental system to accomplish what you have enevisioned as goals.

Echelon II- THE FIFTY GENIUS TRAITS, which should be mastered one by one at an early stage (see Part 1 for complete details) to enable the individual achieve the enormous success that is waiting for him in the wings!

Echelon III — THE TEN ULTIMATE KEYS TO SUCCESS, which in the order of importance are:

1. *Identity or role*—who do you have to be to succeed?

2. *Knowledge*—how workable is your knowledge?

3. *Leadership*—what are your execution capabilities?

4. *Idea*—what is your winning edge in the market?

5. *Communication* —how connected are you?

6. *Niche market*—do you know how to succeed in your niche market?

7. *Organization*—who is on your team?

8. *Exchange*—how many streams of income do you have?

9. *Trends*—are you aware of trends and fashions in your business or society?

10. *Legal and Ethics*— do you know the laws of the land and how ethical are your business decisions?

Beyond these ten ultimate keys and principles of life, one can employ other tools. These tools are summarized in the next two echelons:

Echelon IV —THE FIVE LAWS OF SUCCESS, which deal with the hidden principles at work as follows:

1. The Law of Leverage (LOL): Leverage is defined to be *"increased means of accomplishing some purpose."* The law of leverage states *that to accomplish much with little effort one needs to use leverge to his advantage.* This is done through the use of all of life's available resources to get what one wants. There are seven levers to this law which will be discussed in a later section. This law will increase one's effectiveness in life or business enormously.

2. The Law of Operating Space (LOS): This law concerns with *giving yourself vast space to operate in, whether mentally or physically, in order to see far ahead and well beyond the curve, on the road of life.* This law will decrease the stress level in one's life dramatically.

3. The Law of Operating Time (LOT)— This law concerns with *giving yourself unlimited time to operate and succeed without making hasty decisions.* This really means that one is allowing enough operating time for doing actions to a point that time (as a vriable in the equations of life) is rendered powerless and one's decisions become less time-dependent and more logical and correct. By giving self a vast operating time, one expands his decision power enormously and comes up with long-term solutions to problems.

This law allows one to develop an uncanny ability to plan ahead and foresee the future and become the master of time and actually stretch it mentally to see what the scene is evolving into without the need for resorting to rushed decisions and hasty actions. This law will reduce one's stress and anxiety in life dramatically.

4.   The Law of Money (LOM): This law is based upon the fact that money is actually a particle that requires a high level of understanding if one is going to have an abundance of it.

The **"Law of Money"** states that *money is an inflow particle and to create it one must first outflow an exchangeable product or service in a positive and constructive direction.* Without this initial positive outflow, there will never be an inflow or any incoming money particle.

This law will decrease one's dependency upon the exterior environment as a source of money and puts the burden of money generation upon one's own shoulder. By applying this law properly, one will increase one's incoming flow of cash greatly.

5.   The Law of Prosperity (LOP): Using the law of money sets up the stage for the law of prosperity to come into its own and into view. As it turns out, money is actually one component of prosperity but there are several others that will help to create a prosperous scene.

Therefore, *"the law of prosperity"* is actually a generalization of *"the law of money."* Whereas the law of money applies only to money particles, the law of prosperity expands this concept further into any and all particles.

The **Law of Prosperity states** that *one must start to create outflows of positive things in many helpful and constructive directions in order to generate an inflow of many positive and desirable things, which would lead to one's eventual well-being and prosperity.* This law will increase one's degree of prosperity greatly and will hasten one's entrance into the realm of propserity.

Caveat: Lack of an ample survival wherewithal on many fronts signifies that one has exited or is gradually departing from the realm of prosperity. This is a definite indication of one's failure to create an outflow of positive and constructive particles and furthermore, acts as a red flag of warning that one needs to heed and handle with great urgency!

Echelon V—THE FIFTEEN RULES OF OPERATION, which deal with the less essential and yet very important facts of life and business that one needs to know well. These are as follows:

a. **Increasing Decision Power Rule**: Allow self a high level of respect and believe in self as a an enormous source of poewer. This will create a high degree of self-confidence and self-certainty such that one can decide more correctly and with more accuracy.

b. **Building a Cash Cushion Rule**: Have an abundance of cash to operate in your life and business. This will prevent one from excessive borrowing in order to survive.

c. **Creating a Stress-Free Work Environment Rule**: Identify and remove stress producing elements from your work and enjoy your time while producing. This could include certain people or things such as newspapers, TV news, etc.

d. Setting up a Reward System Rule: Reward people to operate and act in your favor with a positive reward system.

e. Having a Postive Mental Attitude (PMA) Rule: Have a mental attitude that approaches life with a smile and a warm personality.

f. Removing Negativity Rule: Filter out negative people, negative news, negative attitude, and intend to make a conscious effort to eliminate negative and hostile elements from your envirnment. This is done by first identifying the negative sources and their harmful acts and then disengaging their power and eventually purging them from your system altogether.

g. Removing Broker-Tips Rule: Use broker's mechanical knowledge of the rules and the set-up of systems, but never use their tips or knowledge as the main cornerstone for decision making step in your life, investment or business. This concept equally applies to cold callers and all people of this nature.

h. Never Arguing Rule: Never engage in arguments with the boss, market's up and down motions, with associates, clients or business prospects, etc.

i. Constantly Improving Rule: Develop the habit of making constant improvements in self and business by reading, listening and taking classes or courses on a lifelong manner.

j. Noise Filtering Rule: Make a serious effort to rise above and filter out the noise of life, and understand the emerging pattern in any situation by zooming out and seeing beyond the daily clutter, stress and the obstacles that life and livingness constantly presents to one.

k. Outflowing More Than Inflowing Rule: To get an outflow, one should know that life is set up in the form of a machine that requires an input first before the output leaps out! Therefore, always use a technique that first puts something positive in before expecting to get something positive out. This is the foundation of a principle we call *"Prime The Pump,"* which will be discussed later.

l. Long-term Thinking Rule: Every one of us are dealing with problems of different magnitudes and qualities on many levels everyday of our lives, which cry out for our proper solutions constantly. We need to know that when faced with a problem in business or life, we should a) search for a long-term handling, b) not be happy with band-aid level type of solutions, and c) not try to resolve it purely to our own benefit while leaving others out of the equation. Instead, we should attempt to solve it in such a way as to include and benefit all parties involved, thus bringing forth a solution that all can agree upon as a long-term cure.

m. Winning the War Despite of the Battles Rule: This is one of the most fascinating concepts that one can get entangled in life. Most of us are so involved in the battles of life that we seldom see the bigger picture and confuse the war arena with the battle zone that is at hand. The war arena is clearly maked by the dreams, the purposes and the major goals one has to achieve. On the other hand, one is usually opposed and prevented to reach by the major barriers that block the road. One's awareness should be high enough to realize that as one travels along the road to one's dreams, there may lay many battles for survival which need proper handling. These battles include such things as doing daily house chores, paying bills, buying groceries, handling minor body sicknesses, etc., but one should never take his eyes off of the dreams and jeopardize losing the war to save the battle.

n.   **Never Giving Up Rule:** In the process of one's pursuit of his dreams, one would inevitably run into situations that seem hopeless and beyond one's worst expectations. In such instances, one should never give up on his dreams and realize that he has found one method that did not work. He should now reorganize his efforts and plot a new path to attain his goals no matter what the universe throws at him.

o. **Reinvesting the Profits Rule**: This is a powerful concept that enables one to start with just one asset (one stock, one real estate building, a sum of money in the form of cash, etc.) and then through the process of proper maintenance and good management produce a profit. Reinvesting the profits back ino the syatem, places one in an affluence state and causes one to accumulate wealth at a much faster rate than normal. This concept leads to the *"compounding principle"* which will be revisited and treated in more depth in a later section.

There are other rules and concepts that will be explored and discussed in future sections. These rules and concepts lay the groundwork for all future development of the advanced principles as well as the evolution of the highly practical investment strategies. These will become more transparent as this work unfolds in the ensuing pages of this book.

⊷℘✶✿✺✿✶℺⊶

The Law of Leverage

Leverage is defined to be *the multiplication of the applied force or power through the use of a lever toward accomplishing a purpose.*

A lever is an instrument that moves around a fixed pivot point (called a fulcrum, which is a stable datum-- a static) to magnify the input force or energy by several folds so that a heavier weight could be lifted. Such an instrument could be mechanical (such as a crowbar, a pulley, etc.) or nonphysical as discussed further below.

The whole essence of a lever is a stable pivot point (a static) around which a larger force (outcome or purpose) can be controlled or managed (a kinetic), all through the application of a smaller input force, energy or effort. The central datum in all of this is based upon a static (fixed pivot point) and a kinetic (motion of forces around it). Therefore, every lever must have a fixed pivot point to operate.

The Law of Leverage on a mental level, is based upon the concept of "a lever" and can be stated as *"accomplishing much with little effort by using all of life's available resources to get what one wants."*

In the business world there are many non-physical levers one could employ to multiply one's power greatly as described next.

The Seven Levers in Leverage

There are seven levers in life and business that one could utilize effectively in order to attain his dreams and goals much faster and with more certainty. These non-physical levers of life could be summarized as follows:

Lever #1- Own Resource Leverage: *Using One's own valuable resources,* which can be subdivided into:

a) *One's Own Knowledge (OOK):* By developing an expert knowledge in one's chosen field of study, one begins to create a sphere of influence and put the world in motion in a positive direction toward his intended goal.

b) *One's Own Time (OOT):* By cutting out all of the time wasters and thus creating distraction-free and high quality time periods, where much production can be achieved.

c) *One's Own Work (OOW):* By applying one's technical knowledge in his chosen profession, one can create a high quality and exchangeable product, which if mass produced will bring him solvency and much prosperity.

d) *One's Own Money (OOM):* By being frugal and saving one's money efficiently as well as staying away high interest personal loans, one would create his intial capital nest egg. This initial saving has no string attached to it by anyone, therefore can be used worry-free as a down payment to build one's financial empire.

Lever #2- The Network Leverage: *Having a good network of people and contacts, which is a result of positive relationships with a network of professionals, will form a great pool of skill and knowledge ready to assist one in any project.* This is a great leverage one can utilize in business and life. It is one of the greatest resources one can have available at his finger tips to quickly find the most qualified person to do the task with the highest quality and least expense. This could also be called *"Other People's Resources"* Leverage, which *is essentially teaming up with other people and utilizing their valuable resources.* There are four types of resources that can be summarized as:

a) *Other People's Knowledge (OPK):* One can tap into another person's expertise and professional knowledge and benefit tremendously. This person should not be one's rival or competitor but one who is free of bias and vested interested, and has one's best interest at heart. Such a person would become one's personal coach, mentor, advisor or counselor and could leverage one's thought into a brainstorm session wherein one could multiply his potentiality many times.

b) *Other People's Time (OPT):* One can multiply his time many folds if one had a group of professionals who could spend their time toward furthering one's goal and push it further along the road. This could be such people as office workers, information organizers, administrators, technicians, and accountants.

c) *Other People's Work (OPW):* One can multiply his production and work many folds if one could tap into the existing workforce in the society and have them create products aligned with one's goals. These could such professionals as laborers, subcontractors, licensed and bonded vendors.

d) *Other People's Money (OPM):* One can multiply his money many folds if one could tap into the low-interest pool of money available so that one could indeed take control of larger assets. These could include such things as loans through banks, credit cards, and lines of credits through financial institutions.

Lever #3- The Option Leverage: *Using option instruments in Assets (such as Stocks, Futures or Real Estate,* etc.) *will enable one to control large quantities of assets with small sums of money.*

Lever #4- The Insurance Leverage: *Having An "All-Encompassing" Insurance Policy will effectively manage and minimize the risk of loss in any type of asset class.*

Lever #5- The Ten Keys Leverage: *Having a Misconception-Free and Solid Knowledge of the Ten Keys will turn one into a skilled business entreprenure as well as an info-prenure (one who deals in information and knowledge at a professional level such as counselors, consultants, lecturers, professors, philosophers, teachers, salesmen, etc.).*

Lever #6- The Genius Traits Leverage: *Having genius abilities, which are achieved as one establishes self as a positive force in life by helping self and others, gives one a huge lever to successfully lift many heavy undertakings.* This becomes an inevitable fact as one gains more alertness through positive cultivation of the genius traits, and thus awakens from his own long slumber party. Through the genius traits leverage and by increase of one's own mental powers of perception of truth, one truly rises above the clouds of life and the constant noise of existence.

Lever #7- The Automation Leverage: *Creating certain positive habits in self as well as helpful mechanisms in business or life to help the customers will help one to speed up his success rate.* This lever will create a higher level of efficiency wherein decisions and actions are executed faster and more accurately. For example, there are internet devices called "Remote Capture Deposit (RCD) Machines," which will save one's time in standing in line at the bank by depositing all of one's checks at home. There are many such devices one could employ in personal life or business to free up one's time from tedious and mundane work and thus increase one's effectiveness and productivity. One could also polish up his personality and develop many positive traits and habits such as greeting others and acknowledging them automatically when they talk, in order to increase the acceptance and influence of one's ideas over his desired public.

Living a life without any form of leverage is living at a disadvantaged, handicapped and unhappy level of existence full of hard toil and heavy efforts.

On the other hand, constantly employing these powerful and yet magical levers in one's life and business could create such an enormous level of propserity that one would often wonder "how in the world he ever lived" before his discovery of the law of leverge.

As one ascends to higher levels of awareness, it dawns upon one that life becomes truly a joy for one who knows and can use leverage. One's dreams become a reality, one by one, as one gradually utilizes more leverage in every aspect of his existence.

Note: *The dark side of leverage is actually a form of blackmail, which is the crime of threatening to tell something harmful about someone unless certain actions are done or certain amount of money is paid. This form of leverage, commonly employed by the unsavory and criminal element in our society,   is equivalent to getting someone to do something by the threat or force of exposure of his hidden secrets and has no place in the normal and healthy business environment.*

Understanding The Ten Ultimate Keys

"The future starts today, not tomorrow."

— Pope John Paul II

It seems that nature has handed us ten keys to create life and existence, without which we crumble and perish in a short order of time. These are the keys to success in any business activity, however, the magic to unlock these ten keys and create unlimited income lies in selling or more precisely closing!

The theme of this book is set around the concept of the ultimate form of leverage of all times: employing the ten keys along with the genius traits (as the input) to achieve infinite prosperity (as the final outcome)! This concept can be understood more concisely as "putting in ten to get out an infinity," or "ten in - infinity out (10 to ∞)."

The ten keys essentially give us a roadmap to a plethora of actions and infinite income potentials! In this work we will look at some fundamental reasons why we even need to have these ten keys to life and why everything else becomes a subset and subordinate to these ten golden principles.

The Two Stages in the Selling Process

"The whole history of science has been the gradual realization that events do not happen in an arbitrary manner, but that they reflect a certain underlying order, which may or may not be divinely inspired."

— Stephen Hawking (1942-)
English Physicist

To begin, we need to define precisely what we mean by selling. **"Selling"** means *a) exchange for money or other form of payments, and b) cause to be accepted widely or convince someone to do something.*

Furthermore, let's define **closing** *as "to conclude something successfully by properly arranging the final details.* This is the end point of what began as a sales pitch!

One can say that selling is the beginning of journey on a road to prosperity, whereas closing is the end point or the destination of this journey. Even buying by some could be considered to be a precursor to sell or a pre-sell step.

So what we normally call **"Selling Process"** could be subdivided into two stages:

a) Pre-close, and

b) Close.

In this book we call "pre-close" as the "sell or the enlightenment" stage, which is anything that takes place before we close. The end stage or the "close" action is the commitment or the signature stage of the selling process.

To sum, the "selling process" to be successful by definition, must have a close! The close is the "product" one is looking to achieve in the sales process. In other words anything can be considered a selling process, but without an actual close or commitment it is purely a sales pitch!

For example, the process of going to school and getting educated at first glance appears to be a process of acquiring knowledge, but upon close examination we see that it is the preclose step in the selling process. Education and gathering knowledge by itself, without an exchange with the society, is not a meaningful action. A wise man who cannot do anything or help anyone is really worthless to the society. Therefore, by getting educated one intends to sell himself to the job market upon graduation and thus close the employer on himself as a bona fide employee and a valuable work force.

There could be many steps or cycles of action in the pre-close process, but there is only one close which ends all of the prior steps and acts as a concluding and culminating point in the selling process.

To be closed on a product or activity one could take his first step in the sales process in many possible ways. In other words, the selling process could potentially have many starting points, such as:

a) One is given a sales talk by a salesman,

b) One inqures about it through one's own curiosity,

c) One gets introduced into it as a result of taking a high school or college course,

d) One finds out about it through experimentation,

e) One gets a job interview, etc.

The closing part, however, is a different story altogether. It has a definite and precise end point and no variation in it is allowed. It is a signature on an agreement or a contract. For example, a car sold and delivered to a customer, a goal scored in hockey or soccer, a trophy won in a championship series, a loan commitment from a bank, a job offer, a marriage engagement leading to a wedding ceremony, etc.

The list of closes are too many to catalog here, but the concept still remains as a point of accomplishment after a series of sales presentations and successfully meeting the customer's requirements! It is considered to be a product, a stat on a graph and a "done".

The close of every selling process generates power and propels the person one step closer to his goals and dreams. With each close, one builds up his self confidence and increases his zone of influence and success in a company, in the society or in a nation.

Closing as an activity, all by itself, ranks extremely high on the list of skills that one needs to acquire to attain unlimited prosperity. In fact, without one's great ability to effectively close self, people and the whole world around oneself on his ideas, dreams, goals and ambitions, one will be considered an average, a mediocrity at best and one who will be travelling toward a state of poverty, quite in the opposite direction of the road to prosperity.

Therefore, closing as a concept, if mastered well, will orient one vectorially toward the entrance gate of the realm of unlimited prosperity!

"Human history becomes more and more a race between education and catastrophe."

—H. G. Wells (1866 - 1946)
English Novelist and Historian

⊶ ᘓ ✶ ❀ �֎ ❀ ✶ ᘐ ⊷

What Is the Backbone of Selling?

"Reason, Observation, and Experience — the Holy Trinity of Science."

—Robert G. Ingersoll (1833-1899)
American Statesman and Orator

If we consider selling and closing as a process, which bridges point A to point B, then the girders on the bridge are the ten keys that will delineate the steps one should master to begin selling and closing on many levels. If done right, selling and closing will empower one into a high level of expansion and prosperity, which would make one practically the envy of his peers and associates in the community or at work!

If one considered his life as a series of steps toward ultimate success, then mastering each of these keys will become a tremendous mental asset that will carry one far along the path of life.

If for instance, one considered going to school as one-step in the selling process, then one would probably pay more attention to his knowledge base rather than focusing just to pass the exams to get his sheepskin!

If one bought his first house as one of the steps in the selling price, then one will focus on essential things such as price per square foot, or land size or whether it has copper plumbing or not, rather than buying it just because he fell in love with it.

If one always keeps the end point of any process in mind then many wasteful or harmful actions could easily be avoided. For example, if one realized the havoc and confusion that can be created in a friend's life and his children as result of a divorce (the end point) then one would never even think of, much less do any flirting advances toward his friend's wife!

This means that the endpoint should drive all of our actions and activities in life or business. However, our mental vision of life and existence as well as our ability to predict the future to see the outcomes may have to be worked upon before any meaningful change in our conduct can be obtained.

When one thinks or considers selling as an action, he is very consequence oriented and actually lives in the future. Therefore, the selling process starting with buying an asset and then managing it (as two pre-sell stages with closing as the endpoint) as a general concept puts one at once into the future and one no longer is focused on the present time. Of course, one must consider the present time parameters to make the decision to buy but the buying process is done with an eye on the future sale of the item or activity.

For example, if one bought a fancy and expensive car on credit and drove it off the dealer lot with the hope of making payments every month for the next 5 years, then this could be a very costly mistake. He did not put the sale of the car as his first priority! This is because usually buying it on credit and making a monthly payment for the next 5 years (for example at a rate of 10% interest per annum) would make him pay an amount 50% more than the actual price of the car. As a result, if the car's purchase price is $60,000, then by the time he has paid for it in full it would be close to $90,000. However, the car itself after five years is now worth 1/2 of its original price due to depreciation, wear and tear and many other hidden factors. Therefore, in this simple example we can see that the car buying decision can make one lose about $45,000 to $100,000 ($90k-$45k). This is because one was more concerned with the present time luxury status and having fun with the car itself rather than its future value.

However, there are cases when our car buyer is actually a multi-millionaire and buying an expensive car barely puts a dent in his finances. However, here is the catch: he had made a lot of selling with his eyes peeled totally on the future to make him a multi-millionaire before he could do such a thing. So even in this case, selling had taken place years before the purchase date and even then, he still had to sell himself on the concept of the expensive car.

The concept of "selling and closing" is so predominant and interwoven in our lives and existence that we cannot help but to notice that even a baby is selling his parents to take care of him by giving them occasional smiles or kisses. Later on when older, he would bring a bunch of flowers from the garden with a scribbled note attached to it saying, "I love you mommy!"

"Science does not know its debt to imagination."

—Ralph Waldo Emerson (1803-1882)
American Essayist

Therefore, selling and closing is the cornerstone upon which everything in life is founded and every successful person is doing plenty of it. Those who are unaware of selling or are uneducated about its consequences usually end up in the ditch of unhappiness, dungeon of insolvency, and more often than not in the bankruptcy court!

In the final analysis, the backbone of selling is based upon a solid understanding of the ten keys and one's ability to apply them successfully in life or work.

"There are in fact two things, science and opinion; the former begets knowledge, the latter ignorance."

—Hippocrates (460 – 377 BC)
Greek Physician, known as the Father of Medicine

᭸ ℘ ✶ ✿ ✖ ✿ ✶ ℧ ᭸

Selling as a Way of Life

"Never waste a minute thinking about people you don't like."
—Dwight D. Eisenhower

Succesful people sell in many creative ways that ordinary people do not even dream of or care to investigate. However, having said that there are wrong ways of selling that needs to be delved into at this stage.

One of the wrong ways commonly touted by nonprofessionals, especially stock or commodity brokers, is selling short something with the hope of buying it later at a lower price. This opens up the door to unlimited losses, which if not dealt with early on, could be devastating. So this type of selling is purely wrong and an easy way to the poor house.

This opens up the concept of reward to risk ratio (RRR) which is paramount in any form of transaction or trading.

The "**Reward to Risk Ratio—RRR, Triple R, or R^3, R-Cubed**" is defined *to be the "amount of reward or profits" divided by the "amount of risk" in the transaction.* This can be written as:

$$\text{RRR or R}^3 =$$

(Amount of Reward or Profits)/(Amount of Risk).

If one is risking X as an amount of money (the risk capital) that one is willing to spend or lose at worst, then at the close of the transaction he should expect to get out at least a minimum of 3X as a reward, with a high probability of success. That is to say, we want RRR=3 with 90% or higher probabilty of success.

Sometimes one may want to consider $1 \leq RRR \leq 3$ if probability of succuss is high somewher close to 95-99%.

So the key to correct selling is RRR. If one is doing a lot of buying with no eye on RRR then his future survival and prosperity is at risk and he is potshooting at best as an investor.

For example, one may buy a 16-unit apartment complex at a price of $1.150 million in a down market with $12,000 gross income, generating a net income of $2000. This transaction corresponds to to $75,000 per unit. Let us say, he invests $230k (20%). His expectancy of price per unit in "a normal market" is $100,000 corresponding to a $1.6 million price tag. This is a good example of buying it right in the first place because a) it has a built-in equity, and b) it has a good positive cash flow. So by buying the asset and managing it correctly, while waiting for the market to improve, he is in an excellent presell position. After 20 months, the market picks up and the realistic price in the new market conditions improves and he sells the asset for $1,450k for a tidy profit.

Therefore, we have:

RRR=(1,450k-1,150k)/(230k)=300k/230k=1.30

This is a good investment because we have a keen eye on selling when we buy. This is what most professionals in real estate refer to as buying wholesale and sellig retail!

So the investor invests 20% or $230,000 and within 20 months finds a buyer for $1.450 millon. He sells and pockets a gross profit of $300,000. The actual RRR=1.3, but given the fact that market was not quite healthy and chance of a quick and immediate sale was slim, the investor had to wait for 20 months to cash out. However, he still made the correct decision by buying it right in teh first place!

The Make-Break Point

Considering the fact that the make-break point of any profitable investment is RRR=0, we can see that there are instances when the investor buys the asset wrong; so he can never sell it right because he bought it at too low a "triple R" value.

For example, if one is buying at 0≤RRR≤1, which corresponds to an RRR more than zero but less than one, then one is barely above the make-break point of any successful investment (i.e., RRR=0), and usually ends up selling the asset with a negative RRR (i.e., RRR<0).

For example, if one buys a $250,000 investment house with 20% down payment ($50,000) in a down market and has no clue what the future price of the house will be within a few years, then he is entering into a negative RRR territory. Even if he wants to keep it as an investment rental property, he will soon be forced to liquidate the asset or face foreclosure.

The empirical rule in rental housing is to have an incoming rent equal to 1% of the purchase price. So in this case, if he cannot rent it out for $2,500 per month then he should not even consider buying it at all! Even if he sells it at the same price that he bought it in two years, he still has a negative RRR because of the carrying costs, cost of maintenance, and other negative cash flow expenses.

This is how investors lose in the market. They take their eyes off of selling and the RRR (triple R) value and fall in love with the asset, be it a house, an apartment building, a car, gold bullions or coins, big-name stocks, commodities, etc. and never realize that the game of investing is all about selling and not buying. The buying itself is actually a pre-sell step, which needs to be handled well if one expects at least a positive RRR, to say the least let alone the expected minimum of 3 as a value!

A hyped up example of negative RRR value is commonly advertised by the front-line brokers in the stocks and futures markets and is done by telling the investor to sell short options in order to collect its time decaying premium, or sell short a certain stock to benefit from its down-slide. These brokers are just the sounding board for their bosses who are very keen on collecting a healthy commision without any hint of understanding of the selling concept or the RRR value.

They dupe the green investor into the trade by promising him green pastures of prosperity and encouraging him to start selling far out of the money option premiums with no eye on RRR value, which in this case is negative and far below a zero number (since it has an infinite risk built into it):

Reward=limited premium (a limited positive number),

Risk=Infinite loss potential (potentially an unlimited negative number),

RRR= (limited premium) / (Infinite loss potential) < 0.

Even if one does not experience a finacial loss, his loss would be in the mental realm. He will experience heavy mental anguish, coupled with relentless and worrisome feeling. His self-confidence will be at risk and his free attention units will be occupied by a pending threat looming around, ready to pounce at him at any moment! One is subjected to such an enormous amount of stress in volatile markets as stock moves unfavorably toward the short leg that one's sleep and peace of mind is greatly disrupted. This is not investing by any stretch of imagination, but gambling at best!

"Science can purify religion from error and superstition. Religion can purify science from idolatry and false absolutes."

—Pope John Paul II (1920-2005)
The Polish Pope

Economics as a Subset of Life

"To read means to borrow; to create out of one's readings is paying off one's debts."

—George Christopher Lichtenberg (1742 - 1799)
German Physics Professor and Scientist

Sciences in general, and econmics in particular, are organizing tools that, through a systematic process of observation of the chaos of the physical universe, try to uncover the governing principles, and in doing so, intend to bring about comprehension on a mental plane and a higher level of order on a physical level. Such a higher order on a physical plane is accomplished generally through the invention of intricate devices or systems, or the creation of new application mass.

Since life and livingness, as imbued by the life force, is set up in a hierarchical fashion at the top of the pyramid of knowledge affecting the entire pyramid, therefore we realize that sciences as a pool of knowledge and a source of accurate information about our world, created by and for the viewpoint, are merely a subset of life.

"Science is simply common sense at its best that is, rigidly accurate in observation, and merciless to fallacy in logic."

— Thomas Henry Huxley (1825-95)
English Biologist

◦⌐ ℘ ✶ ❀ ✕ ❀ ✶ ℃ ◦⌐

The Gradient Scales to Prosperity

"Facts are stubborn things."

— John Adams (1797-1801)
Second US President

The idea of using a graduated or gradient scale is not a new concept in mathematics but using it to plot relative data is! It is a common practice to plot for example real positive numbers on a scale that extends from zero to infinity.

However, what we are doing here is actually generalizing the concept of scale of gradients in mathematics, which up to now has only been applied to numbers. Using it to plot out any and all data (numerical, conceptual, physical, etc.) concerning the physical universe materials (e.g. voltage, current, power, etc.), is a way to plot out their order of importance, validity, etc. as shown below.

The Graduated Scale Of Abstract Concepts Or Physical Quantities From The Lowest To The Highest Absolutes.

Since this graduated scale is based on the data derived from the finiteness of the physical universe, it would not permit any of the absolutes at either end (0 or ∞), to be achieved but only approached.

The *Fifty Genius Traits, the Five Laws of Success, the Fifteen Rules of Operation* as well as *the Ten Ultimate Keys* provide examples of gradient scales that one needs to use in order to gradually climb up the ladder toward the realm of prosperity.

In other words, one cannot suddenly jump to prosperity overnight or become prosperous on a one-shot basis. A high mental understanding of wealth principles, genius traits, and the ten ultimate keys should precede any physical level of prosperity.

This principle is quite evident in events such as lottery ticket winners, who become millionaire overnight. The track record of success of such people is quite dismal as their lack of mental fortitude and high misunderstandings of wealth principles lead them to the poor house in a short order of time, and causes them to declare bankruptcy as a way to protect themselves from the creditors.

Prosperity & the Ten Ultimate Keys

"The man who doesn't read good books has no advantage over the man who can't read them"

—Mark Twain
American Humorist, Writer and Lecturer, 1835-1910

To **prosper**, *by definition, is to thrive, flourish and grow vigorously into health, wealth and success in life.* Since time immemorial, Man has been on a long road to a higher level of survival and with each turn of the century, his level of survival has dramatically increased. This can only be stated now that we have a better understanding of our past as a race.

Our relentless search for the answers to the riddles and puzzles of this universe has cracked the atom on a microscopic level and has mapped our solar system, our galaxy and many of the neighboring stars or galaxies on a macroscopic level.

It has been a long search, and many great scientists and philosophers have been at work to bring about a higher level of understanding for the general public. We have inherited a mountain of know-how and expertise and are in possession of a tremendous amount of information concerning many aspects of our existence such as farming, bridge building, home construction, electronic devices, highly advanced computing machines, so on and so forth.

Armed with this knowledge, we have vastly improved our own lives and paved the way for many future generations to come.

There have been bits and pieces to this puzzle discovered through the millennia; however, the formulation of these ten "Ultimate Keys" has occurred over the last one hundred years. These keys will open the doors to many hidden treasures.

What we are attempting to undertake in this work is what has embroiled many generations in the past ages through the strikes, revolutions and other social upheavals and still beckons to many as unreachable and impossible to achieve even today.

Mastering these keys depends upon several main factors, especially the identity of the individual, which plays a major role, as will be seen shortly. Understanding these keys will undoubtedly bring about a clarification of the spiritual or mental aspect compared with the material side of life, clearly pointing out its true origin.

The ten ultimate keys are essential in one's business of survival toward prosperity and form a coherent and solid bedrock to spring into action in a world that desperately is asking for brighter solutions to new or existing problems.

A Prosperous Business

"All business depends upon men fulfilling their responsibilities."
—Mahatma Gandhi (1869-1948)
Indian Philosopher,
internationally esteemed for his doctrine of nonviolent protest.

The English dictionary defines "**business**" as "*buying and selling of a) ideas (as in education, consulting, etc.), b) commodities and application mass (as cars, TVs, buildings), and c) services (as accounting, car repair, medical treatment, etc.).*" With this definition, we see immediately that anyone living on a physical plane in association with other people needs to be able to buy and sell effectively, and also know how to overcome problems related to these activities through correct solutions.

To prosper and excel in life, one needs to have an abundance of survival goods and services, which he needs to purchase. On the other hand, to create this scene of abundance, which is an inflow in essence, he now needs to create many things whether in the form of goods or services and then sell it effectively to others to generate the cash flow needed for his prosperous life.

Since buying is a pre-sell step, therefore to buy anything really means that one knows about the selling process as a first step, because if one does not know how to sell as an initial action, then he has no money to buy anything either and the whole scene falls apart! With this one sentence, we have cracked open the whole puzzle of how to enter the realm of prosperity: **to be prosperous one needs to sell in abundance!**

Any adulteration and degradation on the sequence and purity of these two basic actions will cause an imbalance and produce major repercussions in a person's life.

There are certain laws and key concepts about these two basic actions that one needs to be aware of and heed carefully before one can gain prosperity in the physical or mental universe.

The knowledge about the methods of implementation of the ten keys is essential for those brave-hearted individuals who desire to soar like an eagle into a higher plateau of abundant existence. This book is your road map and the bullet train to the realm of prosperity.

Production Vs. Selling

There happens to be a misconception in our world about production and selling. To produce means to create something whether ideas, goods or services. There is no concept of exchange when one is producing something, so one can produce quite a bit and still be poor. The laborer at the construction site works hard and puts out a lot of energy for little pay. Therefore, increase in production is not quite the answer and acts as the wrong why and will not make one prosperous necessarily.

On the other hand, there is an entirely different concept when we put forth the concept of "selling." Selling has a much higher significance and goes far beyond mere production. It brings into focus the concept of "exchange" and places it in the limelight and the forefront of activities. It is such a powerful concept in the world that nothing seems to come even close to it in the business world.

Everything we see around us from personal items such as the car, the TV, the house we live in to more impersonal and national things such as welfare programs, taxation systems, healthcare systems, wars, etc. in practice at the governmental level, had to be sold by the politician to the public and the legislation body before they could be approved.

Even a little baby sells the concept of "take care of me" to his parents by his beautiful smile and cute behavior. In fact, if you look around carefully you will notice that every living creature is selling something!

Selling is one of the most powerful concepts one can ever employ in his business because its essence is based upon the concept of outflow and causation of an effect!

At the core of every healthy and rational being is a pure source of energy and vitality. This source manifests itself in the form of a constant and never-ending outflow of mental and conscious energy in every being. This is so even when it appears that one is inflowing such as reading a book or listening, because one cannot help but to notice that the reader or listener is still outflowing causative energy to see the words and hear the sounds! If one can somehow tap into this eternal source of energy and turn it into an exchange machine, which can produce things that are sell-able, then his prosperity is quite assured.

The key concept is not to produce, but "produce things that sell." Obviously to produce to sell requires communication to find out about the buyer and knowing what he needs. One also needs to have a team and a system to produce buyers and keep them happy after being sold to and closed. Furthermore, one needs to keep track of buyer's name, inventory and the receipts as well as having a system to bank the money and pay the bills.

Therefore, to sell one must communicate, and develop a whole team around this one main function. Every project or effort must be geared toward selling and contribute to this one main action. If not, it will eventually create an extra expense and drain the potential income of the organization parasitically!

In the final analysis, selling is a specific type of outflow and production and one that is the holiest in the business world because it puts one's business on the map and guarantees his prosperity. In other words, if one makes the selling action as the centerpiece of his operation and considers everything else subordinate to the main function, then the operation is being run with the correct emphasis and priority.

The moral of the story is that one must develop selling skills as his number one skill in the battle for survival and eventual prosperity!

One must transform himself into a genius selling-machine and an expert salesman to stamp a commanding presence in life or the business world around him.

Why Do We Need Keys to Prosperity?

"Education is the key to unlock the golden door of freedom"
—George Washington Carver (1864-1943)
American Chemist,
who started his life as a slave and ended it as an educator.

The word **"Key"** means *the answer to a puzzle or a problem.* Since life and the business world alike are filled with seemingly unsolvable problems and difficult puzzles of one kind or another, therefore we need to have a series of keys to guide us and to open doors to practical solutions, which would reward us in return and take us one-step closer to our final destination of prosperity.

Having the ten keys that can bring about a high level of positive control to life's perplexing scene is a saving grace and an essential factor that will distinguish success from failure. These keys when applied correctly will be an asset in any business and will keep the doors of that business successfully open to the outside world.

Each of the ten keys opens a different door so when we apply all of these keys simultaneously in a systematic manner to any business, we will create an avalanche of positive solutions and an ample of prosperity coupled with a large cash flow on a regular basis, which will guarantee long term survival.

These keys could also be called the "code combination" to the vault of any business that when properly combined in a methodical fashion will open up the vault of that business activity to the individual successfully and expose the hidden treasures hitherto invisible to the uninitiated!

The proper employment of the ultimate keys ensures ultimate success of the business and will establish it as a going concern (i.e., a successful activity).

On the other hand, if the business starts shrinking it will be due to one or several of these keys not being known or applied properly. The business shrinkage will cause disruption of the positive cash flow, which is accompanied by a threatened survival potential and a clouded future.

Therefore, to have a business that can withstand the test of time and market forces, one needs to build it with an understanding and implementation of the powerful keys described in this book.

Implementing the Ten Keys

"Three keys to more abundant living: caring about others, daring for others, sharing with others."

—William Arthur Ward
American dedicated scholar, author, editor, pastor and teacher.

To obtain the ultimate keys for any business activity we need to crack the codes of different aspects of that business enterprise systematically. Once these codes have been cracked successively, we obtain a series of exact keys, which become the guiding principles, the road map if you will, guiding us through any turmoil in that business activity and point out what to do in order to expand.

The most essential code to be cracked, which forms the fundamental of any business is the **"viewpoint key."** The viewpoint's vision and understanding of the business world lights up the entire business activity and brings to life all of the remaining keys!

The next key is **"the knowledge key,"** which more precisely we mean "workable knowledge." This workable knowledge, first and foremost, must be acquired early on in one's road to prosperity and is the essential launching platform to catapult one into a higher degree of affluence. Special attention must be paid here to the concept of "workable knowledge" to mean a knowledge free of misconceptions, opinions and false data, but one that is totally based upon solid truths, time-tested principles, practical laws and pertinent facts.

The next key in the lineup is "**the leadership key.**" This key emanates directly from one's capability to round up a competent personnel to do a job and oversee them until it is done to a full completion. This is purely an ability, which one as an executive needs to possess and master in order to manage people, projects and things. Such an ability is usually attained through precise executive and management training under the supervision of a professional.

The next code that needs to be cracked in a sequential series of codes is the "**the idea key.**" As we will see this is the most important aspect of any business. This key contains what we normally refer to as the "edge" in the business. Without this code cracked very early on in any business, one should not even think about going into business. It would prove to be fatal!

Having gotten the right idea for the business, we can aptly call it the "idea key."

At this point one then needs to get into communication with the environment and find out what communication medium is best for a certain public and in this process establish a powerful communication system. Solving this problem and obtaining the exact answer to the communication problem would hand us "**the communication key.**" As we will see the lack of a powerful communication system is the sole reason for the downfall of many a would-have-been successful business enterprise!

There are five other keys that one needs to acquire before one can have a successful business. However, the process of obtaining these keys are the same, that is to say, one needs to crack the code of a particular aspect of the business and then use the obtained results as the guiding principle to formulate the exact "key" and apply it throughout the business without any alteration in the key except perhaps improving it as more experience is gained!

The Keys Form a Pyramid of Seniority

"I am a general. My soldiers are the keys and I have to command them."
Vladimir Horowitz (1903-1989)
American Virtuoso Pianist.

The ten ultimate keys forms a hierarchy of essential elements in a business, which can be arranged in the form of a pyramid (see next page) with the most important at the top and the least at the bottom as shown below:

1. **"Viewpoint Key"**
2. **"Knowledge Key"**
3. **"Leadership Key"**
4. **"Idea Key"**
5. **"Communication Key,"**
6. **"Niche Key"**
7. **"Establishment Key,"**
8. **"Exchange key,"**
9. **"Trends Key"**
10. **"Legal & Ethics Key"**

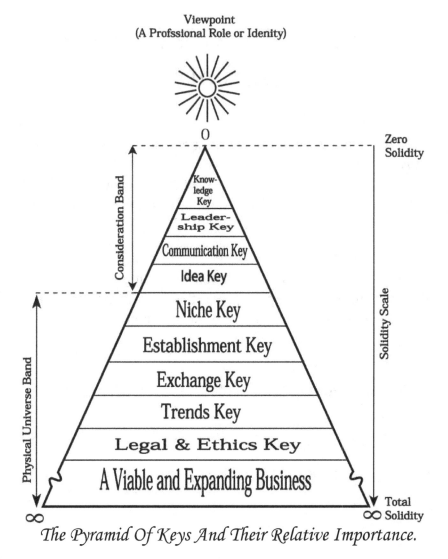

The Pyramid Of Keys And Their Relative Importance.

As can be seen from this pyramid, the most important factor is the **"Viewpoint Key,"** the visionary or the founder of the business, without whom there is no real driving force behind that activity.

Having established the viewpoint as our first factor (this could be called "Key one"), the next essential key is the **"Knowledge Key,"** where we actually mean "workable knowledge," which is essential to put one on the correct path of thinking and the right technical thoughts. It also prevents one from diverging into the byroads of inferior and mediocre concepts and methodologies, usually touted, marketed and sold to the public as pseudo-technical knowledge.

The next key is the **"Leadership Key,"** which gives one enough boldness and mental stability to proceed down the pyramid of keys successfully by bringing forth the remaining keys into existence so as to produce the desired product.

The fourth key is the **"Idea Key"** from which an innumerable number of business forms and practices can be developed.

The next key is the **"Communication Key,"** which requires one to get into communication with the environment and find out what communication medium is best for a certain public and in this process establish a powerful communication system. Solving this problem and obtaining the exact answer to the communication problem would hand us the "communication key."

Proceeding down the pyramid, we need to obtain the **"Niche Key,"** which is any particular zone of activity one needs to specialize in, and around which one will build a business enterprise.

The next key is the **"Establishment Key,"** which can only take place only after obtaining the **"Niche Key"** by cracking the niche code. This is where one needs to establish a company fully staffed with trained personnel and knowledgeable in different aspects of the business. Part of this key also requires one to establish a physical location, which would mean the proper facilities being fully equipped with the state of the art machines, office equipment, and gadgets at a suitable geographic location.

The next key in this process is the **"Exchange key,"** which is the delivery of goods and services to the consumers in exchange for money, which is needed to procure the services of the employees and materials, and pay for the bills incurred by the operation of the business.

The next step in the pyramid deals with numerical data and digitizing the critical aspects of operation into a series of plots or charts. To improve one's business, one needs to plot or chart its operation on a regular basis such as daily, weekly, monthly, or annual and by monitoring the plot one can then improve the quantity of production while maintaining the quality. By identifying the pattern of the chart in terms of health and stability of its trend, one can examine and interpret this numerical data and develop a plan of action to correct (if trend is down) or strengthen (if trend is up). This analysis capability of a numerical-data chart becomes an essential aspect of developing and utilizing the **"Trends Key"** in one's business.

Mastering the final key called the "Ethics Key" adds the final touch to one's business activities and equips him properly for long-term survival. Cracking the ethics code and obtaining the **"Legal & Ethics Key"** adds another important weapon in one's arsenal in the fight against the onslaught of physical universe requirements.

The "physical universe requirements" would include such things as government agencies' codes and laws pertaining to business operation and conduct (both at the Federal and the State level) as well as work or insurance related mandates and demands, which are imposed on the business almost on a constant basis by the city and the public at large.

Moreover, these requirements also include the legal aspects of operation such as proper licenses and permits for the business activities and for the creation of the company's different products. The establishment of legal entities for asset protection, reducing exposure to risk and limiting liability also comes under this heading.

Observation: *As one descends the pyramid from the apex, the activity becomes narrower and more specific in concept but wider in terms of mass of things and activities. Conversely, as one ascends from the bottom toward the apex one gets more and more nonspecific and gets more of an ethereal concept—more conceptual and less massy.*

In conclusion, we can see that once one discovers and masters these ten keys, he will be ensured that he will have a successful business, defined *as one that is stable, viable and expanding on a regular and constant basis.*

As these ten keys will be treated amply and explored in more depth in the ensuing pages, one cannot help but to see that in the final analysis, knowing and applying these ten keys will put the goal of prosperity well within one's reach.

Quizzes #2

Quiz 2.1

What is meant by **"Don't Think Big, Think Infinite?"** Give an example.

What is meant by **"The Five Echelons to Climb?"** Give an example.

What are **"The five laws of Success?"** Give an example for each.

What is meant by **"The Law of Leverage?"** Give an example.

What are **"The Seven Levers in Leverage?"** Give an example for each.

What is meant by **"Understanding the Ten Ultimate Keys?"** Why is this so important in life? Give an example.

What are **"The Fifteen Rules of Operation?"** Give an example for each.

Quiz 2.2

What is meant by **"Two Stages in the Selling Process?"** Give an example.

What is **"The Backbone of Selling?"** Give an example.

What is meant by **"Selling as a Way of Life?"** Why is this so important in life? Give an example.

What is meant by **"Economics as a Subset of Life?"** Give an example.

What is meant by **"The Gradient Scales to Prosperity?"** Give an example.

What is the relationship of **"Prosperity & the Ten Ultimate Keys?"** Give an example.

What is meant by **"A Prosperous Business?"** Give an example.

Quiz 2.3

What is the difference in **"Production Vs. Selling?"** Give an example.

Can you describe **"Why Do We Need Keys to Prosperity?"** Give an example.

How can we **"Implement the Ten Ultimate Keys in our business?"** Give an example.

What is meant by **"The Technical Side of Any Business?"** Give an example.

What is the meaning of **"The Keys Form a Pyramid of Seniority?"** Give an example.

PART 3

Key 1
Who Do You Have to Be to Succeed?

Who Do You Have to Be to Succeed?

"Those who are free of resentful thoughts surely find peace."
— Buddha, *'The Enlightened One'* (563-483 BC)
The Title of Indian Prince Gautama Siddhartha,
Founder of Buddhism

To be successful in any business one must be able to endow "life and ability" in things he sees around him and make them more powerful than they initially are. The keynote of all these actions is "to create" in various forms and actions.

In other words, one must take charge of life and be willing to assume command of operations before anything significant happens.

Following this line of logic, one's identity and role in any business activity boils down to just a few things:
1. one must create a **safe and stable space** to operate in,

2. One must be able to create **mental and physical energy**,

3. One must be able to create an **exchangeable product or service**, and

4. One must be able to create **long-term solutions** in any intended activity.

If one can create in these four arenas as specified above, then one's initial effort in the business world has a strong footing, and his ultimate success is assured to a large degree, and one is on the right path toward prosperity.

"Whatever you cannot understand, you cannot possess."
—Johann W. von Goethe (1749-1832)
German Poet and Novelist

A Safe and Stable Space

"What is my life if I am no longer useful to others."
—Johann W. von Goethe (1749-1832)
German Poet and Novelist

If one wants to succeed in any line of work, he must assume a position of leadership within his zone of activity. Any zone of activity in an organization has posts within it acting as the building blocks of operation, much like bricks to a building.

By a "post," we mean a position from which a person operates in an organization. These people holding the posts are the fixed points in space amongst which the communication particles flow. The flow of particles as well as their speed of travel generates power, very much like an electrical motor connected to the mains and fixed on a platform, creating electrical power when current flows through it.

This is very much like electricity, where we need to have both voltage (potential energy) and current (kinetic energy) to generate power. The presence of one without the other will never generate power!

As we will see this ability to create a safe and stable space is one of the most essential factors of a business owner.

Mind's Energy Can Create Power

"The energy of the mind is the essence of life."

—Aristotle (384 - 322 BC)
Greek Philosopher and Scientist

One has to envision the flow of particles between posts in the company fully in his mind's eye, before one can command his area and emerge as a leader.

After one has established a stable and safe space, vital to any operation, the flow of particles and services that are passing through the fixed posts brings about power.

The number of particles of any establishment depends to a large degree upon how trained the personnel are in handling and managing the particles!

The leader must make it feasible for people to get trained and become more responsible for their own zone of operation, thus reduce the amount of dependence of his juniors to act solely on his orders and initiatives.

This ability to take more responsibility by getting trained will generate more power and will lead to a more expanding operation, which can have a bigger effect on the society and world at large.

⊢৪০ ✷ ❀✹❀ ✷ ৫৪⊣

An Exchangeable Product or Service

"When the product is right, you don't have to be a great marketer."

—Lee Iacocca
Former Chrysler President

An exchangeable product by definition is one that has value in the consumer's eye and performs the intended function as advertised. Anything short of this leads to returns, repairs, recalls and overall non-viability for the group as a whole.

The ability to create a product or service should be well mastered by all related personnel before a company gets into the production, promotion and distribution stages.

This is an area where promotion and advertisement for the goods and services need to be financed sufficiently so that the company goes into proper exchange. The flow of particles, particularly money particles, for the transportation and promotion is an important step.

Longevity

"The quality, not the longevity, of one's life is what is important."
—Martin Luther King, Jr. (1929-1968)
American Baptist Minister and Civil-Rights Leader

One needs to think long-term solutions to stay in business. Thus creating a product or service for long-term exchange as well as customer care, if perfected and refined over a period of time, will lead to a viable and expanding business that will begin to take a life of its own. This will create a time stream for the business activity and eventual longevity.

When one starts to employ long-term solutions in his business activity by not short-cutting the production process, handling customers with care and solving problems methodically and rationally, then one places himself in a totally different modality of operation in business and life.

One will soon garner public's highest level of respect for his work and quality of product and the few catcalls (from the competition or ill-intentioned individuals) that may come his way will quickly die out in the huge din of his howling success!

The Core Principles

"A business absolutely devoted to service will have only one worry about profits. They will be embarrassingly large."

—Henry Ford (1863-1947)
American Industrialist and Pioneer
of the Assembly-Line Production Method

A leader has core values with a distinct role in a business, which is different from any other post. While the business exists and operates in the physical universe, a leader's viewpoint exists exterior to the business for its guidance, protection and smooth operation on a team basis.

A fundamental study of any business requires us to analyze and outline the basic qualities of a leader. These qualities are based upon a series of fundamental principles, which underlie all of life and existence, and form a hierarchy as follows

1. The Cause Principle: Being cause in any activity,

2. The Identity Principle: Assumption of a professional identity or role with ease, and one that is suitable for the activity.

3. The Awareness Principle: Having a keen awareness of the flow of particles and activities.

4. The Consideration Principle: Being able to form pertinent thoughts and considerations that help the activity.

5. **The Communication Principle**: *Being in good communication with others and environment.*

6. **The Solution Perception Principle**: Being able to think on one's feet, perceive solutions and execute them rapidly.

There are other facets of life that could be analyzed in terms of these basic principles, such as:

a) *Observation* of facts in any situation: which is a combination of the *Awareness and Communication Principles*,

b) *Correct reasoning or analysis* of a given problem: which is a combination of the *Identity, Communication and Solution Perception Principles*,

c) *Positive control* of an object, a conversation or a life situation: which is a combination of the *Cause, Awareness and Communication Principles*,

d) *Learning* a new subject: which is a combination of the *Awareness, Consideration and Communication Principles*,

e) *Working* on a project: which is a combination of the *Cause, Identity, Awareness, Communication and Solution Perception Principles*,

f) *Playing* a game, which is a combination of the *Cause, Identity, Awareness, Communication and Solution Perception Principles* (same principles as working on a project, but perhaps less seriously!).

The point to emphasize here is that many of the factors and concepts of life become a subset of these basics, and can be derived or analyzed in terms of any single one or a combination of these six core principles.

☙ ✶ ❀ ✂ ❀ ✶ ❧

Quizzes #3

Quiz 3.1

Why is it important to know "**Who do you have to be to succeed?**" Give an example.

What is meant by "**Safe and Stable Space?**" Give an example.

What is meant by "**Mind's Energy Can Create Power?**" Give an example.

Quiz 3.2

What is meant by "**An Exchangeable Product or Service?**" Give an example.

What is meant by "**Longevity?**" Give an example.

What are the six fundamental principles in the "**Core Principles?**" Give an example for each.

PART 4

Key 2
What Is Your Knowledge Base?

The Precious Knowledge

"Science and art belong to the whole world, and before them vanish the barriers of nationality."

—Johann W. von Goethe (1749-1832), German Poet and Novelist

Since the beginning of recorded time, we seem to have been in a contest with the physical universe. When it comes to sciences, we seem to be totally inclined in the direction of trying to understand the physical universe with the idea of using the obtained knowledge for improving our own conditions of existence. This is done sometimes to a point of obsession. However, this obsession may be justifiable because our very survival on the physical plane depends on this point alone and no other.

In our daily existence, we are faced with enormous factors. We are faced with this unthinking and imposing thing called the physical universe, which cannot be dealt with or reasoned with on any level other than force. It only knows force. It is a universe of unintelligent force, which has submerged all living beings within it.

Being confined to a fragile and physical entity (called a body), which cannot tolerate much force, however, our main tool against the onslaught of the physical universe's demands and mandates is our organized bodies of knowledge called the physical sciences. This knowledge has been obtained through millennia of postulation and observation of the cause-effect of the observed phenomena in nature using the scientific methodology.

The knowledge about the physical universe has been handed down like a precious lore, improved and polished from generation to generation and has been preserved dearly. It is rightly so, because knowing this precious knowledge well and applying it effectively to ourselves and our surroundings has meant a higher level of survival for us, our progeny (children) and symbionts (codependents, pets, etc.).

"Human history becomes more and more a race between education and catastrophe."

—H. G. Wells (1866 - 1946)
English Novelist and Historian

☙ ❀ ✳ ❀ ✳ ❀ ❧

The Relativity of Knowledge Principle

"Mathematics would certainly have not come into existence if one had known from the beginning that there was in nature no exactly straight line, no actual circle, no absolute magnitude."

— Friedrich Nietzsche (1844-1900)
German classical Scholar, and Philosopher.

We can extrapolate and expand Einstein's theory of relativity and obtain a highly generalized principle: *The Principle of Relativity of Knowledge.* This generalized version of the theory of relativity is vastly workable, since it clearly demonstrates to one the highly viewpoint-dependent nature of the world in which we live. This principle goes far beyond the perimeter of scientific arena and actually applies to any and all parts of our existence particularly our business world.

Utilizing the concept of "absolutes" in the physical universe, we are now ready to define an important principle, which has ramifications throughout the entire field of science and technology. That principle, of course, is *The Relativity of Knowledge Principle*, which is defined as:

"Any datum, such as a natural law, a principle, a fact, a measured value, etc., (which is derivable from the scientific postulates and axioms), can never have an absolute value, but only a relative value whose relationship to other data is based on the point of view of the observer."

This principle actually broadens the concept of relativity and brings out a much bigger arena for examination than has ever been envisioned.

Applying this principle to any field of study such as "a small business," at once demonstrates to us that the concepts therein are only relatively true and lie somewhere on a gradient scale and therefore, should never be considered to be absolutes!

For example, let us consider the field of economics (the science of production, distribution and consumption of goods and services) and ask ourselves this question, "Can economics contain an absolute law, which would be true under all conditions?"

Using the concept of "absolutes," we can see that such a condition of absoluteness is impossible since all laws are derived from scientific, business or life postulates. We know that these postulates are the only absolutes and anything derived from a postulate is perforce conditional or relative and therefore not absolute. This applies to all of our beloved economic laws, such as exchange, supply and demand, etc. Simple or complex, the laws of economy, as presented in the modern textbooks, are only realtively true! They all have definite limitations and peculiarities that must be understood well before applying them.

This is a direct consequence of working within a finite physical universe. Even if one achieves a workable law, which is expressed and cast into absolute terms of an exact mathematical equation, however, when that equation is put into practice, it immediately falls into the category of a relative law and can never be held true unconditionally in all locations and under all conditions without any further qualifications. This applies to all laws even those of hard core sciences such as physics: Newton's laws, Maxwell's equations, etc.

From the above discussion and example, one can conclude that, "The only absolutes in a business activity or a scientific arena are the postulates. All of the physical laws are relatively true and can never achieve absolutes in actual practice, unconditionally and for all times. Absolutes can only be approached."

Moreover, we can observe that all of the laws of the business world do not have a monotone order of importance. Each law has a different weight, which should be evaluated properly relative to other laws before it is applied to a practical situation; therein lies their inherent relative value.

"What wisdom can you find that is greater than kindness?"

Jean-Jacques Rousseau (1712-1778)
French Philosopher and Writer,
Whose Novels Inspired the Leaders of the French Revolution

The Pyramid of Knowledge

"I have just three things to teach: simplicity, patience, compassion. These three are your greatest treasures."

—Lao Tzu (600 -531 BC)
A Chinese Philosopher

Workable knowledge is like a pyramid, where from a handful of common denominators efficiently expressed by a series of basic postulates, axioms and natural laws, which form the foundation of a science, an almost innumerable number of devices, circuits, and systems can be thought up and developed. The plethora of the mass of devices, circuits, and systems generated is known as the "application mass," which practically approaches infinity in sheer number.

By "**Application Mass**" we mean, *"A very specific type of mass consisting of all of the related masses that are connected and/or obtained as a result of the application of a science."* This includes all physical devices, machines, experimental setups, and other physical materials that are directly or indirectly derived from and are a result of the application.

The inter-relation between the postulates and the application mass of a science is an important point to grasp, since the foundation portion never changes (a static) while the base area of the pyramid is an ever-changing and ever-evolving arena (a kinetic), where this evolution is in terms of novel implementation techniques and new technologies.

It can be observed that the fundamental postulates of a science, as a whole, form the bedrock upon which all natural laws rest. Furthermore, we can see that the postulates and the discovered natural laws, altogether, form the foundation of a science. It is an important concept, which is omitted in the majority of scientific texts.

All the remaining considerations such as scientific conclusions, technical data, design methods, rules, etc., as well as their byproducts (space, energy, matter, and time) and the entire application mass of the subject is derived from the foundation.

The business leaders, through years of trial and error, have learned that to create a viable product and have the lion's share of the market and thus dominate their niche, they need to employ sciences to provide unique technical solutions to their production problems.

Any business today starts with the viewpoint of the founder and puts forth certain and definite goals to attain. Using laws and axioms of the business world, they use sciences and technical knowledge to set up an operating space for the company. Then with correct positive mental attitude and enthusiastic energy, they bring in the raw materials and by proper scheduling and coordination of actions they engage into action and produce an exchangeable product. The Figure below shows the pyramid of knowledge in any business enterprise.

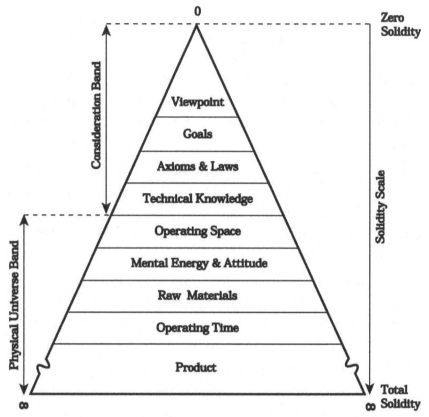

The Pyramid Of Knowledge In A Business Enterprise.

"Kindness in words creates confidence. Kindness in thinking creates profoundness. Kindness in giving creates love."
—Lao Tzu (600 -531 BC)
A Chinese Philosopher

The Circle of Knowledge

"It is the mark of an educated mind to be able to entertain a thought without accepting it."

—Aristotle (384 – 322 BC)
Greek Philosopher, Scientist and Physician

By observation we can generalize the pyramid of knowledge for a business enterprise to include all of the extant activities and sciences of mankind in a nutshell. This generalization would take the shape of a circle or a pie as shown below.

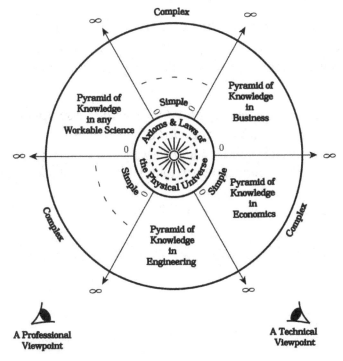

The Circle Of Knowledge And Its Relation To The Pyramid Of Knowledge.

From this Figure, we can see that the entire field of knowledge of mankind about the business world, as well as the physical universe, takes on the form of a circle (or a pie) where each workable subject or science is a slice of the pie.

At the center of the circle lies the viewpoint (or a collective viewpoint), which puts forth a series of the fundamental purposes as the guiding factor for the development of the product or application mass at the perimeter of the circle. This factor is held in common by all of man's activities, whether done in a business enterprise or a scientific activity.

This common area, at the center of the circle, forms an inter-relatedness of concepts and thought patterns amongst all activities of man across many subjects and activities.

"It is not enough to have knowledge, one must also apply it. It is not enough to have wishes, one must also accomplish."
Johann Wolfgang von Goethe (1749-1832)
German Playwright, Poet, Novelist and Dramatist

Unique Vs. Arbitrary Principle

Any unique and exact solution in the business world is surrounded by an almost infinite number of "arbitrary solutions" which are all deviations from the central datum. These deviations are all based on an introduction of an "arbitrary factor" at some point along the way in the solution process. Thus, we can conclude that:
Use of arbitrary factors produces arbitrary solutions, which are all deviations from the exact and unique solution of any given problem (see the Figure shown below).

The Unique Solution In A Sea Of Arbitrary Solutions.

The English dictionary defines "**arbitrary**" as "pertaining to something, which is based upon one's own wishes, whims and personal preferences without regard to specific laws or rules." Generalizing this concept, we now obtain a definition more appropriate to our work, as follows:
An arbitrary factor is any datum or assumption, which is unnecessary and irrelevant to the resolution of a problem

and thus does not fit into the framework of the problem. It is derived from mere opinion, misunderstanding, or preference and usually violates known natural laws.

It can be further observed that the introduction of an arbitrary factor generated by authoritative sources or based on one's misunderstandings will invite the introduction of more arbitrary factors. This is where the old maxim "Deviations from truth of a situation beget more deviations," meaning, "Lies beget more lies," comes to mind and illuminates this concept even further. Moreover, because the concept of "arbitrary factors" applies to a much wider sphere of existence on a physical plane; therefore, it is applicable to the field of science and engineering as well as the business world.

We can have a reverse look at the "number of arbitrary factors in a subject" and by observation conclude that those fields of study (e.g., arts, politics, humanities, etc.), which mostly depend on authoritative opinions for their source of data, contain the lowest number of natural laws.

It is important to note that the uniqueness axiom only applies to "analysis" type problems and excludes all "design" type problems. This is a rather obvious observation, since for example, while there is only one unique answer to a broken TV set (an exact part number!), a skilled designer could easily design several electronic circuits, leading to different TV models, all functioning satisfactorily.

An example could illustrate this point further. Let us see how the concept of "unique and arbitrary solutions" apply to a field of study such as "politics" and what conclusion can we make about this subject.

To answer such a question, we need to observe that the field of politics has been pockmarked with arbitrary ideas of politicians, opinion leaders, political educators, senators, newspaper editorials, etc. to a point that a completely unworkable subject has been created.

This is a field of study, where lives of human beings, their happiness and future survival on a national or a global level hang in the balance and yet nothing is known about it on an inexorable and axiomatic level.

Nevertheless, the field of politics has been aggrandized and is now called "political science," which is an oxymoron of terms to the nth degree. It is a field of study where many strange and arbitrary solutions to global or societal problems are constantly offered to the populace and passed as workable solutions. The public instinctively senses this arbitrariness but cannot identify it as such in terms of axioms and natural laws, thus, the political charade goes on.

There is not one single axiom or natural law that has been discovered or stated in any textbook published on politics and yet it is one of the most vital fields of study to mankind, far more important than physical sciences.

It has not achieved the status of "unique solution type of science" as all physical sciences have. Thus, it has stagnated for centuries, if not millennia, as a field of study.

Furthermore, we can conclude that the solutions to the problems of mankind as proposed by politician "X" are totally arbitrary and not unique, mostly unworkable on a larger scale, even if somewhat workable on a micro-scale and "band-aid" level of operation.

Generalizing the concepts discussed in the example above, we can make a general conclusion: Any field of study (such as politics, economy, arts, etc.), being filled with many arbitrary factors and authoritative opinions, which form the foundation material of that subject, shall perforce become unworkable.

One can conclude this article by understanding that: "There exists many wrongnesses (arbitraries) but only one or a few rightnesses (unique-nesses)"

"The whole history of science has been the gradual realization that events do not happen in an arbitrary manner, but that they reflect a certain underlying order, which may or may not be divinely inspired."

— Stephen Hawking (1942-)
English Physicist

☛ ఎం ✶ ❀✖❀ ✶ ♋ ☚

Utilizing Sciences to Create any Business

The business world is really a general field of study and has many divisions and sections in it that one needs to understand well before becoming a powerhouse of success. A few examples of the different businesses one may encounter today are shown below:

The Business World And Its Many Subsidiary Realms Of Activities.

We now examine the essential factors that enable us to construct any desired hub of activity or business enterprise such as stocks and options trading or real estate leasing and management.

By observation and the presented material in this book so far, we can conclude that to construct any business enterprise we need to have the following series of elements in place:

a) **THE FOUNDER'S VIEWPOINT**—The first step is having a founder and his unique viewpoint. This is the first and foremost step in the creation of any business.

b) **Operating SPACE**— The founder needs to set up a region, which is delineated by a boundary surface. This region effectively creates a workable space in which all future creations can take place.

c) **PRIMARY PURPOSES**— The founder needs to put forth a series of primary purposes, unconditionally true at all times, which are capable of creating different mass and forms, each with its own distinctive characteristics and peculiarities.

For example in the field of apartment business, one can set up a primary purpose of owning 100 units in ten years, which is an essential step to be established well before the start of the business activity itself.

d) **PRIMARY GOALS AND TARGETS**— The founder needs to put forth a series of workable goals and targets, which create a workable gradient scale or ladder steps to make achievement of the primary purposes possible.

For example, in the field of apartment business, one can set up a series of attainable goals of:

1) Acquiring knowledge and the business skills to manage apartments,

2) Accumulating a sufficient initial capital for down payment,

3) Approaching banks to borrow,

4) Identifying potential apartment candidates to purchase,

5) Putting an offer that can be accepted by the seller, and

6) Successfully closing escrow on the subject property.

e) **LAWS AND RULES** — The founder needs to learn the subject well and identify a series of laws and rules based upon these primary purposes, goals, and targets which will uniquely define the interactions and inter-relations amongst the ideas and the created objects or entities.

For example, in the field of housing rentals there is a hidden "rents law" which states that the rent from a rental house should be about 1% of the purchase price in order to have the operation stay solvent.

These laws and rules can all be obtained purely by observation. For example, purchase price=$100k, rent=$1000, result=solvency.

Therefore, steps (a-e) define all the considerations built into the field of any business.

f) APPLICATION MASS—The final aspect of any business universe is the creation of its application mass, which could approach to a high quantity in sheer number.

By application mass, we mean any mass derived from the application of the business principles. For example, in the field of apartment leasing business, it includes such things as rental offices, the mass of the buildings and accessories, a thriving organization, the apartment appliances, storage units, expense bills, rent money, bank accounts, equipment, materiel, etc.

The mechanics of creation of a business as delineated in steps (a-f) is shown on teh next page.

Viewpoint

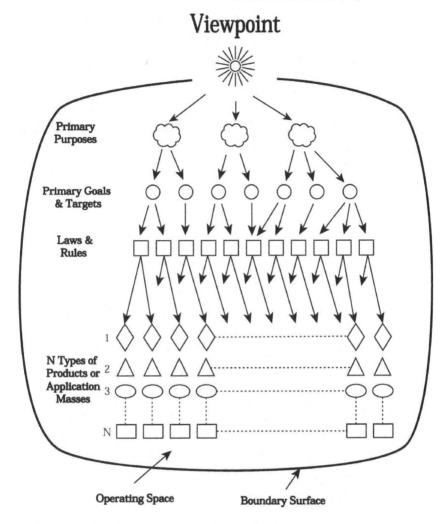

The Mechanics Of Creation Of Any Business.

In summary, the first action after assuming a founding viewpoint and setting up an operating space, is to put forth a set of primary purposes to hold true at all times followed by a series of workable goals and targets. One then by learn the subject establishes a series of laws and rules to operate the business by. The laws and rules bring about and define an exact relationship between the ideas and masses and assist one in eventually arriving at the final destination of intended application mass.

"In creating, the only hard thing is to begin: a grass blade's no easier to make than an oak."

—James Russell Lowell (1819-1891)
American Poet, Critic, Editor and Diplomat

Business Knowledge

"Opinion is the medium between knowledge and ignorance."
—Plato (428 BC-348 BC)
Ancient Greek Philosopher.
He was the world's most influential philosopher.

An expert knowledge of the business in which one is engaged, is an essential part of one's stock in trade if one is to be popularly considered as a leader in a field. Having this essential factor one can control business activity and be truly successful.

One may ask at this point, "How does one get such an expert knowledge?" The first and foremost prerequisite for gathering knowledge in the business world is "an intense desire to learn the subject at hand." He should be self-motivated and should really desire to learn the fundamentals of the business. Mastery of the fundamentals of any field of business and final success as an end product, follow from this factor!

Given such a desire on one's part, then and only then the teacher may appear and even then one will encounter numerous obstacles on the road to knowledge. Such obstacles could be financial, emotion-related, schedule-related, etc., but one's intentions and desires will override them and in time one will achieve his intended goal, provided one stays the course and does not get sidetracked by unrelated byroads and wasteful activities!

๏-ฏ ✳ ❀ ❇ ❀ ✳ ฆ-๏

The Technical Side of any Business

"I have seen men incapable of the sciences, but never any incapable of virtue"

— Voltaire (1694-1778)
French Philosopher and Writer,
One of the greatest of all French Authors.

Before one can be called a businessman in the truest sense of the word, one must have a familiarity with state of the art in technology and acquire a good knowledge about the scientific laws and a good technical vocabulary of his profession. This set of data would be called the fundamentals of that business, and should be based upon sound scientific principles, which are but irrefutable.

For example, if one is planning to get into "car business," one needs to understand the basic purpose of cars, and how as an application mass, they have exchange values based upon the science that created it. Gasoline powered cars, electric cars, hybrid cars, solar cars, and hydrogen cars all have different engines, different operating parts, and thus different technologies and supporting infrastructures.

This is the technical aspect of the business, which must be understood and properly cared for through trained team of technicians and scientists who can produce or repair these different types of cars.

Moreover, one needs to get trained in the management and marketing aspects of cars and get trained in the sound business principles, such as exchange, cycles of business, trend recognition, so on and so forth, in order to create a thriving and self-sustaining operation. One that will not go out of business after 5 years, as is the current norm for 90% of small businesses! It should be designed to have a longer life span than hopefully one's own lifetime so that his progenies and future generations can also benefit.

Conversely, one needs to be a businessman (or more precisely a salesman) before one can be called a scientist. He must learn how to find where the demand for his skills lie or create a demand for his knowledge and then market himself properly to the potential employer in order to get employed in the firm.

Furthermore, once he gets the job he needs to apply the proper trends formula to improve his lot, move up the ladder and thus achieve a greater degree of influence in his job and the company as a whole. This is in addition to his technical knowledge that he has painstakingly acquired through years of education at the college level. This is essential or else he will soon find himself in the employment line asking for a handout.

Thus, the business of life requires us to not only be trained technically, but also have a deeper understanding of higher principles of life and existence, of which the business fundamentals, especially sales and marketing, is but a subset!

Quizzes #4

Quiz 4.1

Why is it important to know "**The Precious Knowledge?**" Give an example.

What is meant by "**The Relativity of Knowledge Principle?**" Give an example.

What is meant by "**The Pyramid of Knowledge?**" Draw a sketch of it.

What is meant by "**The Circle of Knowledge?**" Give an example.

Quiz 4.2

What is meant by the "**Unique Vs. Arbitrary Principle?**" Give an example.

What is meant by "**Utilizing Sciences to Create any Business?**" Give an example.

What is meant by the "**Business Knowledge?**" Give an example.

What is meant by the "**The Technical Side of any Business?**" Give an example.

PART 5

Key 3
What Are Your Leadership Qualities?

What is Leadership?

The English dictionary defines **"Leader"** as *a person who can direct, conduct and guide the operations of a group or an activity and enable it to achieve its intended goals.*

Utilizing this definition, we see at once that the leader must be able to communicate well and possess a high degree of responsibility, understanding, intensity and courage to motivate the group in carrying out the intended actions, oversee the operations and enforce the orders until the goals and targets are met.

The leader is very product oriented, which means that he guides the group to obtain certain outcomes and products, and does not rest until targets are attained and quotas are met.

The founders of business enterprises are the leaders of the society who have brought forth, through centuries of development and observation, a positive atmosphere of commerce where goods and services can be exchanged among different individuals, groups or nations and thus a higher level of survival for the earth inhabitants has become possible.

"The greatest book is not the one whose message engraves itself on the brain, but the one whose vital impact opens up other viewpoints, and from writer to reader spreads the fire that is fed by various essences, until it becomes a great conflagration (big fire)."

—Romain Rolland (1866-1944), French Writer.

The Importance of Leadership

People have long since recognized the importance of leadership in any business activity and when an operation is awry and needs mending, the first action usually taken on in the business world is changing the leader.

The concept of a leader is extremely important because without it the business is really blind and has no mental vantage point to view things from and no space to create or look at and then it has no energies or objects to place them in for future exchange. So the leader or the founder forms the rock bottom foundation of the business activity. It is far more important than the project goals, business rules and targets, since the leader can infuse all of these things into his group and make them into a powerhouse of production and a hub of prosperity.

Therefore, we can see that an implicit concept is built into all of our extant businesses, and that is "the leader" which is taken totally for granted in all of business operations.

This is something far beyond the scope of operation of most educators in business colleges and most professors do not have a clue as to what makes an effective leader, let alone train one into existence and turn loose into the society which desparately is in need of such people. Most educator's stock in trade is turning business graduates who can work for somebody else (usually a leader) and make a living by trading time for money!

This is an observable fact that our business schools are not turning out business founders, but rather people who are trained to take on jobs or occupy different posts in a company. The business schools across the land have no clue how to train or create founders, who can create a new company or take on the leadership role of a company and take it to the next level. There is a major dearth of leaders in our society!

The concept of "leadership" is often introduced rather late in the study of a subject and the student feels like "Why do I need to know this?" It seems kind of out of place since the business authors do not often recognize the importance of the subject.   Conversely, even if the subject is introduced at an early stage, not enough emphasis or importance is placed upon it to make it worth studying or delving into.   Therein lies the problem of our current commerce world!

"One of the true tests of leadership is the ability to recognize a problem before it becomes an emergency."
—Arnold H. Glasgow

Good Leadership

"I can live for two months on a good compliment."
—Mark Twain (1835-1910), American Humorist, Writer and Lecturer.

A Good Leader works on high survival goals and approved projects, issues positive orders, and oversees their execution and completion in a timely manner. These facts are as true of a leading governing body such as a business council, as they are of an individual leader.

Moreover, a *good Leader* should be an able and competent person who can do many things impeccably well. He must be able to:

1. Provide Good Service: The public expects good service, which translates into positive scheduling, accurate billing, accurate addressing of letters, good delivery of services, etc.

2. Provide Good Control: The public expects good control, which translates into swift and prompt delivery and actions once the customer has ordered the product.

3. Provide Good Communication: The public expects good communication, which translates into rapid message handling and an effective response from the right person within the company. The establishment of a good communication line is a must for proper leadership to occur.

4. Provide Good Execution: The public expects courteous and prompt execution of orders, fast shipment of goods and proper delivery in a reasonable length of time.

5. Provide Good Management: The public expects good management at the helm, people who care about what happens to the customer, the quality of the product and the work, how the place looks, and how trained are the staff to produce and deliver exchangeable products. A good manager is dedicated to getting the show on the road and taking out of the line-up obstacles to the business's or staff's progress. The basic concept here is "Caring what goes on," and the opposite motto "not caring and just worried about own profits" is heavily shunned.

6. Create an Ideal Scene: The public expects to see an ideal scene, which is: a well-run and harmoniously organized company producing high quality products. This is a simple concept in the business world and a leader should work hard to exceed it in the public's eye, in order to make them more than a customer, but a repeat customer, a client!

7. Train Employees to Become Good Workmen: The public expects to see professionals in the work environment who can produce high quality products. Professionals are people who can positively control their equipment or tools of trade and control the communication lines in order to create a decent product that can be exchanged for money.

8. Develop an Eye for Positive Indicators: The public expects the leader to be aware of positive indicators as well as red flags in the workplace, for proper steering of the business ship so that it arrives at the destination. For example, fast progress, high quality products, higher efficiency, more presence on the job, better health, less pain in life, etc., are all positive indicators and should be acknowledged and re-enforced often.

A good leader knows the above inside out and applies them on a constant basis in the work environment. This will assure a high degree of success, and eventual prosperity on many levels, for himself and the group!

Quizzes #5

Quiz 5.1

Why is it important to know "**what leadership is**?" Give an example.

What is meant by "**The Importance of Leadership**?" Give an example.

Quiz 5.2

What is meant by "**Good Leadership**?" Give an example.

What are the eight areas a good leader should concentrate? Give an example for each.

PART 6

Key 4
What Is Your Winning Edge in the Market?

Having the Winning Edge in Business

"The liberty of the individual is a necessary postulate of human progress."

—Ernest Renan (1823-1892)
French Philosopher and Historian

Before one gets into business, one must be aware of four *Primary building blocks*:

a) **Establishment,**
b) **Production,**
c) **Exchange, and**
d) **Longevity.**

One's leadership in any business gets asserted to the degree that one can:

I. **Exhibit a proper identity for the job at hand.**
II. **Exhibit a good set of communication skills at the post.**
III. **Implement practical ideas in the work environ.**

A leader with the proper identity on the job inevitably comes up with correct goals and plans (correct considerations and ideas) and then with proper communication can execute them well, and as a result his business will survive over a long span of time and he gets longevity as depicted on the next page.

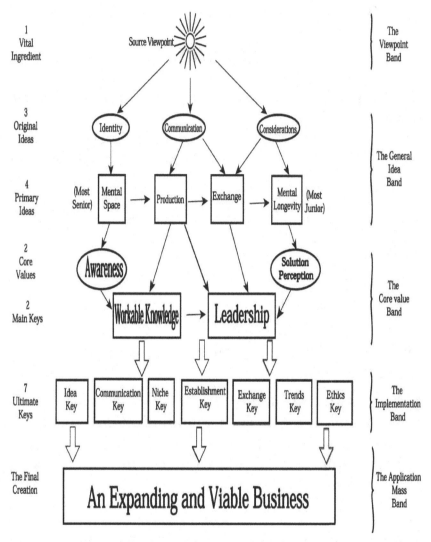

The Main Components Of Any Business Activity.

Therefore, we can see that from a one-man-band small business to a national government and beyond we can become an enormous success and bring a considerable degree of simplification to any business activity. We can display a higher level of truth than one can ever obtain from a detailed examination of the components of the business activity as done endlessly in business schools all across the land.

"The ability to convert ideas to things is the secret of outward success."

— Henry W. Beecher (1813-1887)
American Liberal Congregational Minister

Setting Goals

"A goal is a dream with a deadline."

—Napoleon Hill (1883-1970)
American author

The English dictionary defines "goal" as "an objective that one strives to attain." In simple terms a goal is a result toward which an effort is directed.

A business leader is goal driven and understands how essential it is to have definite and established goals, and the important role they play in one's business.

In fact most business educators' first step in guiding someone along a path to financial prosperity is through the establishment of his goals. Usually, such goals should be written down and kept in a secure and yet readily accessible place for constant feedback to one's progress, and immediate correction if one is deviating from these goals.

"A man is not idle because he is absorbed in thought. There is a visible labor and an invisible labor."

—Victor Hugo (1802-1885)
French Poet, Novelist and Dramatist

☞ ೞ ✳ ❁ ✺ ❁ ✳ ೞ ☞

What Gives You the Winning Edge?

"Simulated disorder postulates perfect discipline; simulated fear postulates courage; simulated weakness postulates strength."

Lao Tzu (600 BC-531 BC)
Chinese Taoist Philosopher, founder of Taoism,
wrote "Tao Te Ching" (or "The Book of the Way").

One's edge in any business boils down to several factors and can be roughly summed up as:

Edge #1: An Expert Knowledge of the Product

This edge deals with the creation of a professional role or job identity, who knows the job functions, and has an expert knowledge of the products and understands the niche market he is in.

Edge #2: A Good Ability to Communicate

This edge deals with the first action of a professional identity, which is putting out communication lines to the world around him. He does not argue, make hostile remarks or make people wrong for making a comment. He is a very likeable person because he respects people, wants to work things out, and deisres to solve problems through mutual understanding and two-way communication alone.

Edge #3: A Good Ability to Assume Leadership

This leadership edge requires that one can effectively "Decide, Execute and Oversee," which means that when facing a problem, one should make a quick decision on a certain course of action and get the cooperation of others to excute a plan of action and see that it is done. This edge encompasses a) quick thinking on one's feet, b) ability to see solutions to problems, c) taking fast action within the company policy, and d) seeing that it does get done by actual reports and customer satisfaction.

Edge #4: A High Ability to Take Responsibility for Self and Group Actions

This sub-idea is the production of a product or service, which produces viability for the business. This concept deals with turning or condensing ideas into products or services, which leads to the concept of atoms and molecules on a microscopic level and products/services on a macroscopic scale; and,

Edge #5: A High Understanding of the Exchange Principle

The main consideration in business is to have a going concern, that is to say that it is expanding on a regular basis and is in exchange with the environ around it. This means never accepting money unless one can deliver the product as promised. This priciple encompasses a) Great degree of honesty, b) A deep regard for one's word once given, c) Great focus on the product itself and its quality, and d) Being survival oriented and wanting to help others with a useful product, which brings in the money only as a byproduct!

Edge #6: A Caring Attitude

The main consideration in business is to have a going concern, that is to say that it is expanding on a regular basis and has a stable operation guaranteeing long term survival (i.e. has longevity).

This edge of a caring attitude for self and others encompasses a) One's watchful attention on the customer's satisfaction, b) One's concern for own group's well being, c) One's ensuring that all money is collected and d) One's establishment of a high enough monetary exchange value for the product so that longevity of one's own group is amply guaranteed.

From this discussion, we can easily see that *"exchange and longevity"* are two direct sub-products of utilization and relentless pursuit of employing these six edges in actual practice; one's group eventual soaring to the top of any profession and business activity will be inevitable, as the sunshine follows the dawn!

"I want to know God's thoughts. The rest is just details."

—Albert Einstein (1879-1955)
German Born American Physicist, Nobel Prize in 1921

Quizzes #6

Quiz 6.1

What is the concept of **"Winning Edge?"** Give an example.

How do you get **"The Winning Edge in Business?"** Give an example.

What is meant by **"Setting Goals?"** Give an example.

Quiz 6.2

How can a business prosper by knowing **"The Elements That Give One the Winning Edge?"** Give an example.

How can a business fail by ignoring **"The Concept of Winning Edge?"** Give an example.

PART 7

Key 5
How Connected Are You?

The Positive Communication Principle

"Never, never rest contented with any circle of ideas, but always be certain that a wider one is still possible."

—Pearl Bailey (1918-1990)
American Entertainer

The "Positive Communication Principle" is a fundamental concept, which is at the heart of a wide sphere of existence called "life and livingness," Therefore it behooves us well to define it at this juncture:

THE POSITIVE COMMUNICATION PRINCIPLE: This principle states that positive communication is the process of giving and receiving correct information, which is free of false data. It is essential to anyone who intends to carry out a healthy and expansive life style, whether personal, business, social or otherwise. In its absence there is no life, no business, and no income, only shrinkage and death.

Communication in Business

"Start with good people, lay out the rules, communicate with your employees, motivate them and reward them. If you do all those things effectively, you can't miss."

—Lee Iacocca
Former Chrysler President

Communication is a basic principle in life. This basic principle, as precisely defined by the positive communication principle, states that communication is the process whereby information is transferred.

In life, the most important thing is communication. A business is no exception to this rule. In absence of communication any business activity, however well intentioned, will break down and would not function properly.

In any business activity, there must be a producer (source point) and a consumer (receipt point) and to exchange the product a certain amount of positive communication should take place.

Therefore, the first key to success in any business is communication since with it we can open up a whole new vista of activities and operations.

Most of the communication jams are found to be at the top where the executives are. Upon a thorough study of the way the communication between the executives and managers are handled, we can form a plan to improve the flow lines of the business and achieve a faster particle flow in that business activity.

Thus, our biggest and the most profitable area of investigation and improvement lies in the area of communication and with it, we have our biggest and most important tool to achieve our goals in any business activity.

Thus, we can conclude that *"Communication Is the Most Fundamental Key in any Business or Science."*

Specialized Particles in Business

"The most important thing in communication is to hear what isn't being said."

—Peter F. Drucker (1909-)
American Educator and Writer

Communication is defined as the act of giving or exchanging of information, signals or messages by words, symbols, sound, video, electrical, optical signals or physical motions and gestures.

Communication generally encompasses the concept of **"information exchange"** as a wide sphere of activity, which is essential to life and livingness.

Communication is a simple concept; however, implementing it can be quite complicated, especially when it involves inexpert and untrained personnel. Misunderstandings, alteration of content and distortion of data can lead to disastrous results in any business activity.

However, it is an observable and noticeable phenomenon, which is successfully followed in all efficiently run companies and business enterprises. The prosperity of these organizations is directly proportional to the implementation of the communication and its component parts.

Thus in a prospering business we need to have a communication system set up. A properly set up communication system provides the infrastructure, through which communication particles can flow. Communication is the lifeblood of any company and its neglect could mean death for that business activity just like a body perishing soon without a healthy blood flow!

To have a prospering business we need to have a *specialized type of particle* as input. *This particle is a suitable and qualified consumer of a product or service.* For example, for a grocery store, it would be paying customers who need the grocery items and do not argue or shoplift the items; for a school it would be bright students who can study and be trained to apply the materials without cheating, difficulty, upsets or complaints. Obviously, every business has its own particular specialized particles and needs to develop a system to weed out the unqualified or the trouble-makers. Therefore, we can conclude an inexorable fact:

Every business needs primarily one thing to survive: **the specialized particle.** This concept is very similar to a car engine that runs on nothing else but only one type of fuel: gasoline, which is the specialized particle!

Acquiring the specialized particle is actually a filter action or a selection process based upon an understanding of what is needed best to engage in for the proper exchange process to take place, and thus create an income flow.

The filter action for the proper selection of the specialized particle (i.e., an actual consumer or a customer who has the potential to become a client) is a selective process. It allows only a series of select particles to flow in from a pool of many available particles of different forms and shapes (i.e., many applicants who desire the product). Depending on the type of the produced product, one engages the marketing department for the initial filter and then later on (if needed), the legal department for further selection, as shown below.

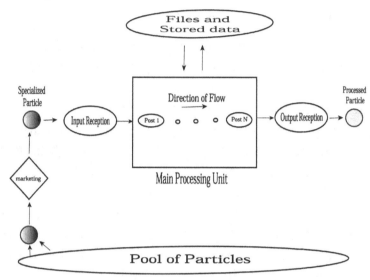

The "Specialized Particle" is the desired particle in any business.

An example of a specialized particle would be a car buyer who comes in, from an advertisement in the newspaper, to a car dealership and buys a car. Another example of a specialized particle would be a qualified tenant coming (from an outside advertising banner) into a property management office with good credit history and great income and rents an apartment at market value.

The specialized particle is created by a strong marketing campaign and its abundance can boom any company to its highest level of success. On the other hand, the absence of the specialized particles, no matter how well organized the main processing unit is, will lead to disaster and eventual nonexistence as a business entity.

☙ ❀ ✳ ❀ ❀ ❀ ✳ ❀ ❧

The Importance of Communication

"Electric communication will never be a substitute for the face of someone who with their soul encourages another person to be brave and true."

—Charles Dickens (1812-1870)
English novelist, generally considered the greatest of the Victorian era

The first point of contact of public with any company or business activity is through a company employee and by means of the communication system already in place. The form of the communication may be by audio (phone conversation, CD, etc.), mail, email, in person, or visual (TV, DVD, video tape, etc.). Whatever the form, all of the communication principles apply and one's efficiency in handling that communication is essential.

A business enterprise encompasses the production of a product or service, the distribution of the product, advertisement, marketing, client mining, customer service and many other aspects of the business, which goes into the make-up of that particular business enterprise. The interesting part is that the common denominator of any of the above-mentioned aspects of a business is communication and its associated communication systems. A communication system can also be referred to as a communication network in engineering.

It is an essential aspect of any business to have a superb communication system set up so that the particles can flow on it with maximal speed and minimal delay. Therein lies the success and the efficiency of that business. Take the communication aspect out of any business enterprise and we get a totally unprofitable and declining business that is doomed to failure.

To the degree that we employ high-speed communication devices to facilitate and implement the positive communication principle into our business, to that degree we succeed, advance and expand our business activity.

The most successful business activities have the communication concept implemented down to a "T." Their communication system is expertly setup, operated by responsible and high-morale individuals, and is well maintained by technical experts with minimal down time.

"To listen well is as powerful a means of communication and influence as to talk well"
—John Marshall (1755-1835)
American Founder of constitutional law
and the Supreme Court of the United States.

Therefore, the importance of the communication concept and its implementation in terms of an efficient communication system should never be underestimated. It is the lifeblood of any worthwhile activity.

From the above discussion, we can make the following powerful conclusion about the business world:

A business activity is as prosperous and profitable as it has mastered communication and can use it effectively to handle the outside world.

⊷ ఴ ✳ ❀ ✄ ❀ ✳ ఴ ⊶

Your Connections to the World Count

"Society cannot share a common communication system so long as it is split into warring factions."

—Bertolt Brecht (1898-1956)
German poet and playwright

Due to the importance of communication, we need to set up an efficient communication system. This communication system establishes the infrastructure in which we can create all future plans for prosperity in life or business.

A **communication system** is a system consisting of fixed communication devices (such as telephones, FAX machines, video/data devices, computers, etc.), connected by communication channels or links, in which communication particles (e.g. voice, video, data, etc.) can flow to and from.

The money is invaluable in any business activity, but actually is an inflow and the result of the exchange process. Money is the inflow value received in response to the product or service rendered. The mistake most businesses make is purely focusing on the cash flow and never realizing that it is of secondary importance to having a great product to exchange. Then and only then, the cash flow will be there as well as the specialized particle (i.e., the customer) who bought once, will be satisfied enough to buy again and again, soon becoming a client!

The establishment of the communication system along with its constant maintenance and constant vigilance to safeguard it from subversion and sabotage, is the foremost key in one's arsenal in the business battle for survival. A good example of such an attack on the communication system is the computer viruses sent through the internet that could potentially paralyze a company and bring it down to its knees and cost millions if this point is not kept in!

A Modern communication system for a small business must at least have a minimum of the following devices:

1. One dedicated phone line for incoming calls with an answering machine if line is busy; also preferably an answering service outside operating hours to handle calls.

2. One dedicated phone line for outgoing calls.

3. One dedicated Fax line.

4. An e-mail account.

5. A fully-manned cell phone functional with unlimited minutes.

6. A highly trained receptionist who can greet the customers with a smile and with politeness and respect.

7. A physical location for the business, where it provides proper accessibility via roads, travel paths, mail, etc.

8. A high-speed internet link for fast audio/video communication.

9. A sophisticated communication center or better yet a trained receptionist who can route the incoming signals properly to proper posts, who then can handle and answer the public's needs and questions effectively. This will ensure that there will never be a dropped call.

10. A closed feedback loop where the public is contacted again 7-10 days after their initial inquiry, so that the communication loop is closed and a potential consumer can be generated. This would be a specialized particle!

11. Above all, one needs to be well trained to receive, originate and handle communication with great confidence and alertness. In other words, one may have access to information on a mechanical level and yet be completely out of communication!

To the degree that one can implement and put these points of communication into practice and operation, one has answered the question "how connected are you?" and to that degree one survives and becomes prosperous.

"We shall never be able to remove suspicion and fear as potential causes of war until communication is permitted to flow, free and open, across international boundaries."

—Harry S. Truman (1884-1972)
American 33rd President of the United States

⋇ ৪৩ ✶ ✿ ✾ ✿ ✶ ৪৩ ⋇

Quizzes #7

Quiz 7.1

What is meant by "**The Positive Communication Principle?**" Give an example.

Explain why those business, which have mastered "**The Positive Communication Principle**" succeed the most?

Why is it that we need "**Communication in Business?**" Give an example.

What is meant by "**Specialized Particles in Business?**" Give an example.

Quiz 7.2

Can you explain "**The Importance of Communication?**" Give an example.

Why is it crucial to have "**Connections to the Immediate Environment and the World at Large?**" Give an example.

PART 8

Key 6
What Is Your Niche Market?

What is a Niche?

"Good business leaders create a vision, articulate the vision, passionately own the vision, and relentlessly drive it to completion."
— Jack Welch

The English dictionary defines **"Niche"** as *a recess, a nook or hollow in a wall (or a vast space) suitable for something, such as a vase, a statue, etc.*

The concept of **"niche"** can be generalized and applied beneficially to any business activity and thus redefined as:

"A specialized business activity, which is a cut down of a larger sphere of activity."

Having a niche business is specializing in a particular activity or arena, such as having a practice as an eye specialist or as a heart surgeon, rather than a practice in general medicine.

For example, we know that the world of real estate is comprised of any and all entities that pertain to land, building and construction. It has many business components and subcomponents, around which many business enterprises could be created. Each one of these could be considered to be a niche business.

Homes, apartments, retail centers, shopping centers, real estate management (renting and leasing, etc.), land development, condominiums, industrial buildings and commercial high rises are just a few "niche businesses" in this vast arena of activity.

☞ ❊ ✳ ❊ ☜

How Niched Are You?

It is often said but seldom followed the famous maxim: "Niche Thyself," which simply translates into *find a niche for yourself in the business world and your success is practically assured*! Its lack of adherence could be associated with a lack of understanding of its meaning and importance.

What we mean by this phrase is that one should find an area of specialty and specialize in that area to a point of its mastery. In other words, specialization pays off handsomely when it comes to a business activity and people are willing to pay a higher premium if you are expert in a particular business niche by knowing it inside out!

In other words, if one has niched himself, then his chance of success has already increased dramatically. This is one of the keys to success of most, if not all, business founders. For example, if you have an eye problem you would not go to a doctor practicing general medicine, rather only to an eye specialist. Therein lies the truth in niching one's business and attaining great prosperity!

For example, if one is entering the real estate market, one should niche himself into a small niche such as buying and renting or selling only houses in good neighborhoods and establish himself as the best and most reliable owner in the area. One's chances of success could go up greatly by doing just this one thing.

On the other hand, trying to get into buying raw land, apartments, shopping centers, strip malls, triple net properties, commercial and office buildings, trailer parks, etc., all at the same time can prove to be disastrous because each one has its own rules, profit zone and city and state regulations and requires a huge team of professionals to manage each sector efficiently! If one is not prepared to handle and master each effectively, one could potentially lose his shirt in a hurry.

In the niche business arena several great examples come to mind: Aamco Mufflers, GoodYear Tires, Mayo Heart Clinic, Rolex watches, Souplantation restaurants, McDonald's, Subway, Dell Computers, Milgard Windows, OptionsXpress trading firm, so on and so forth.

So the moral of the story is **niche yourself** and succeed, just like the old maxim, "divide and conquer," which means by dividing an area into smaller pieces and handling each part, one can eventually conquer any large task. There is great wisdom in this saying!

One can put this to work in any business with great success. The only remaining issues are:
a) Where is a high-growth business sector?
b) Where is a good niche in that sector, which has a high demand and a low competition?
c) How niched one should get so that his products offer an irresistible edge?
d) Who are the players and competitors in that niche?

e) How one should market and position his edge in the market so that it would attract more attention than others?

Quizzes #8

Quiz 8.1

What is meant by **"a Niche?"** Give an example.

Explain why one needs to **"niche"** himself?

Why is it so important to know **"the Niche one is in?"** Give an example.

Quiz 8.2

Explain how one can fail by not being in **"a Niche?"** Give an example.

Explain why those who **"niche"** their business succeed?

What are the consequences of not using **"The Niche Concept in Business?"** Give an example.

PART 9

Key 7
What Team Are You Working
With?

Team

"Individual commitment to a group effort -- that is what makes a team work, a company work, a society work, a civilization work."
—Vince Lombardi (American Football Coach, national symbol of single-minded determination to win, 1913-1970)

We are living in a very interdependent world, which means no one lives alone. The loners are mostly thinkers, introverted into themselves and are usually non-doers. Therefore, if one is planning to achieve a worthwhile goal, he needs to assemble a team of competent personnel who will aid and assist one in his progress toward the intended goal.

A competent team is a necessary element in the goal equation and without it not much can be accomplished even if one has many far-flung goals and ideas. There simply is not enough man-hour in one day for one person to achieve his dreams in a timely manner.

So lesson one in goal accomplishment on a large scale is a lesson in humility and that is one needs to recognize one's own insufficiency and that others are needed to hold up the corners of one's existence in many ways, so that one can go about planning and accomplishing what he intends!

When the team members bond and coordinate well with one another and all agree on the worthwhileness of the intended goal, then and only then should one expect some level of production far beyond the ordinary!

A team is composed of team members and each should be respected by the head of the business as well as other team mates. Each team member should have an inherent trust in the other and know that he will make the right decision and do the right thing when the proper time comes.

The mutual respect between team members goes far beyond ordinary greetings and daily platitudes normally exchanged amongst one another. It should be instilled deeply within one's belief system that his teammates will come through and can be counted upon to contribute to the common goals and purposes of the company to the best of their abilities.

In other words, the team is a coherent and committed group to the cause. A true group is one who handles the outside world as a unit in unison, with high confidence and composure. Only in this fashion, one will have a successful business operation, which will prosper and flourish for a long time to come.

Group

"Just as the individual is not alone in the group, nor any one in society alone among the others, so man is not alone in the universe."

— Claude Levi-Strauss (French Philosopher, 1908-)

As we discussed earlier, a team is a necessary and required element in the equation required for accomplishing one's goals.

To create a team one needs to create a group of people who believe in the goal. Then and only then the group turns into a team.

The individual does not submerge into the group but remains as an individual who is freely thinking within the scope of the team and the guidelines set by the management. His production is not an unrelated and random thing but is directly correlated with the ideals of the team. In other words, his actions and activities coordinate and contribute to other products and activities of the team.

Once we have achieved this factor alone, then and only then, we have created a unit entity whose power has multiplied by many folds. This power is not a direct mathematical summation of each individual's power but has an added factor of comradery and brotherhood. It is a far greater force to reckon with, a force that can literally move mountains!

There are two more factors that truly bond the group into a more cohesive unit:

1. To have an efficient group we need to have a good level of *communication* amongst the members. We discussed the concept of communication as the second key and here we see that it comes in again as an indispensable factor in cohering the group from within.

2. There must be a series of sensible *policies* that the team members can and will agree upon and abide by. This factor will further enhance the power of the group and make it into a force in the business world. These policies should be based upon and built around the goals and ideals of the group and not a series of separate and stand-alone rules and guidelines.

A Business Enterprise

"An enterprise, when fairly once begun, should not be left till all that ought is won."

—William Shakespeare (1564-1616)
English Dramatist, Playwright and Poet

To survive well one needs to hold a post in a company and from that point put many particles into motion to achieve the aims of the group. The motion of the particles and their speed of travel determine the quantity of production, which directly determine the power produced by the business activity.

A company's production has a great analogue in the field of electrical engineering. In other words, it is very similar to electricity, where the voltage in the wire sets up the force to move the electrons, resulting in an electric current to flow.

The multiplication of the voltage by the current is power; very similar to an organization where the power of the post (similar to the voltage on the wire) multiplied by the size of the particle he handles (similar to the current in the wire) determines the productivity of that activity.

For example, a business that has 10 cashiers (the number of posts) who can handle 5 transactions of $10,000 per hour (the size of the particle), has $500k production (10x5x$10,000=$500,000 per hour) and thus generates

1000 times more power than one with one cashier handling 5 transactions of $100 per hour (5x$100=$500 per hour)!

However, given the same exact two companies and the same number of posts (i.e., fixing the voltage), then it is the rapidity of the particle flow (i.e., the amount of current flow) that determines the power of each business.

The English dictionary defines "power" as *A source of physical and mechanical force or energy. It is also the capacity to exert physical force or energy and is expressed in terms of the rate at which it is exerted (Joules per second or Watt).*

We can generalize this concept in business to define **power** as *"money, influence or authority, which can be used to create or procure a desirable effect."*

In simple terms, **power is the capacity to exert energy or influence and the rate at which it can be delivered**.

In our modern business world, the power of a business is usually measured in terms of its cash flow, cash reserves, net worth, its solvency, and its political affiliation and clout. The most important factor, however, seems to be the hard and cold cash in abundance and its continuance of flow, which plays a major role in the overall power of a company.

"The magic formula that successful businesses have discovered is to treat customers like guests and employees like people."
—Thomas J. Peters (b.1942)
American Author and Consultant

⊷ ℘ ✳ ❀ ✄ ❀ ✳ ℃ ⊷

The Fundamentals of Teamwork

"The golden rule for every business man is this: "Put yourself in your customer's place."

—Orison Swett Marden

Any team activity is based upon very simple and very basic concepts that are easily understandable and observable. The basic factors in establishing a team, an enterprise, or a company in the order of importance are:

a. First, we need a system at the thought level that can produce an exchangeable product and get money for it.
b. Next, we need to put this mental system into a physical format to produce a product. This step requires the production team to come into existence.
c. Then, we need to create a quality-check team to make sure the product that is produced by the production team functions correctly before shipment.
d. Finally, we need to create several other teams that will support the production team as well as the quality-check (or quality assurance) team as follows:
   - A *marketing and promotion team* that can create a demand for the product by constantly tapping into new territories, and can bring in new public.
   - A *treasury team* to collect the money, bank it and pay bills.

308 Advanced Principles of Success & Prosperity

- A *repair team* to handle the damaged or faulty products.

- A *customer satisfaction team* to handle production problems and repair issues, and to keep existing customers happy.

- A *planning team* to implement broad goals and to create future expansion possible.

- An *administration and records team* to keep accurate records of production, scheduling, etc.

- A *legal team* to protect one against claims and litigation.

- An *acquisition team* to acquire new facilities, buildings and equipment for the creation of new or future products.

- A *registration team* to introduce and route new public to the company products and to register new people as they enter the system. There could be other teams, such as personnel, cleaning, maintenance, etc., that one would need to survive the business world effectively.

We need to have all of these teams to support the production team as the main function of any company. However, the quality check team plays a highly important role in correcting the product and its equipment of production. So one needs to take an extra step of seeing that any produced product is also exchangeable before it is shipped to the customer.

For example, in the case of car production, one needs to see the car functions properly after production. This is done by the quality check or quality assurance team. This team also recalls all faulty models and repairs them at no cost to the consumer—thus the car's performance is enhanced and the consumer's confidence in the producer is restored.

Thus, the moral of the story is that when personnel are poorly trained and equipment is also faulty, a correction of both becomes mandatory, otherwise the production will definitely suffer! This is a job all by itself and should not be thrown back into the lap of the production people or be expected of them to do. It has its own training and expertise and is therefore assigned to the quality check or quality assurance division of a company.

Proper Correction

> "The heart of every man lies open to the shafts of correction if the
> archer can take proper aim."
>
> —Oliver Goldsmith (1730-1774)
> Irish born British Essayist, Poet, Novelist and Dramatist

At first glance, by spending time and energy to do a quality check, it seems that we are adding extra costs and manpower and thus reducing our bottom line profits. However, if one looks carefully, the opposite is found to be true.

If one only focused on producing the product as the main function and took no further responsibility for the produced product then he will eventually run into a high rate of returns and customer dissatisfaction, a lower demand for the product and thus a lower bottom line profit.

It is a scientific fact that a machine or an electronic amplifier with an open loop system has a high production level, a high output gain but has a short longevity in the longer timeframe, which corresponds to a smaller bandwidth of operation. If we now lower the output through a feedback loop, we effectively drop the gain but increase the life of the machine and increase the bandwidth of operation. Taking this piece of wisdom from the engineering world to the business arena, we find out that if there are no corrections of any kind soon the word gets out about this irresponsible type of production activity. It would quickly get labeled as a bad brand name, and then no one would be buying the product, which would cause an eventual cut in production. In other words, the drop of sales signifies a lowered demand and leads to a drop in production and a lowered longevity level.

Therefore, "quality assurance" is the most important factor after putting the wheels of operation and production in motion. This factor puts **responsibility** for the product as well as **control** of the future of the company back into the hands of the executives.

Thus, we can conclude that *Lack of awareness and a deep understanding of the role of proper correction is where a person or a businesses can go off the rails and fall into a state of shrinkage, eventual demise and a state void of prosperity.*

"Drive thy business, let not that drive thee."
—Benjamin Franklin (1706-1790)
American Statesman, Scientist, Philosopher, Printer,
Writer and Inventor.

Role of a Team in Goals

"Opinion is the medium between knowledge and ignorance."
—Plato (428 BC-348 BC)
Ancient Greek Philosopher He was the world's most influential philosopher

To understand prosperity at its core, one needs to understand well his role in his own team, how he fits within it as well as the broader picture of the company and its products and how he can assume a leadership role in it.

Any team that one is engaged in and gets support and assistance in the direction of one's goals, could make or break one! In other words, one should know the team and its goals of operation thoroughly before one joins or participates in it!

If one is the leader of a team, then an expert knowledge of the job function, the products of his team and the people in the team is an essential part of one's stock in trade. This is a must, if one is to be popularly considered the leader in that zone of activity.

The first and foremost prerequisite for gathering knowledge in the business world is a desire to learn. One should be self-motivated and should intensely desire to learn the fundamentals of the business despite all obstacles. Such obstacles could be financial, schedule-problems, lack of preparation, etc., but one's intentions and desires could override all of them.

As long as one stays the course and does not get sidetracked by unrelated byroads and wasteful activities, one could rise to the top as a leader in his team or his company and set new standards of excellence in any desired field of activity, and in the process use the team's power to achieve one's own goals.

"I am not bound to win, but I am bound to be true. I am not bound to succeed, but I am bound to live by the light that I have. I must stand with anybody that stands right, and stand with him while he is right, and part with him when he goes wrong."

—Abraham Lincoln (1809-1865)
American 16th US President (1861-65), who brought about the emancipation of the slaves.

Who is on Your Team ?

"Executive ability is deciding quickly and getting somebody else to do the work."

—Earl Nightingale (1921-1989)
US motivational writer and author

One as an executive in life or at work gets things done and completes projects through the power of a team. His function in the team is coordination, administration and management of the affairs of the team.

Just like a captain navigating a ship, an executive assumes the navigation function of his team and company through the chaotic business world.

The executive must be an able individual who can formulate positive solutions in emergency situations, within the confines of the company policy, and take full responsibility for his actions.

He must be a very confident person and have a good ability to make realistic goals and correct decisions, and then with the help of his team implement them through the use of practical plans, projects and orders, and finally oversee their execution.

An executive needs to be an alert individual, well aware of distracting factors that would enter the work environment and take immediate actions to remove them with efficiency.

For example, one should isolate and stamp out lazy workers, rumor mongers, agitators, and certain individuals generating false reports.

In the final analysis, whether at home or work one must surround himself by a team of professionals as follows:

Home Team
1. A good household (spouse and children).
2. A good gardener.
3. A good pool man.
4. A good insurance agent.
5. A good utility provider (phone, internet, TV network, etc.).

Work Team (as an office worker)
1. An excellent and reliable assistant
2. A good office staff
3. A pool of good clientele (specialized particles)
4. A great company with great benefits such as healthcare, retirement program, etc.

Work Team (as a stock investor)
1. An excellent computer system with reliable internet access.
2. An excellent brokerage firm open on a 24/7 basis (i.e., 24 hours/7 days a week) allowing portfolio margining.
3. An excellent trading platform without fees and no broker interference or solicitations.
4. A pool of highly liquid stocks (specialized particles).
5. Access to up-to-the-minute and accurate charts.

6. A library of books, CDs, videos and courses dealing with the best investing ideas, all available at one's fingertips.

7. Above all, one needs to have sufficient funds (at least $50k to $100k) in the account to act as one's army of employees ready to be deployed at one's command.

Work Team (as a real estate owner/investor)

1. An excellent and reliable superintendent who can manage and deal with vendors and managers.
2. A good and friendly office staff.
3. A well-intentioned and professional real estate broker who has one's best interest at heart, can filter out the existing portfolio and bring one the best deals available in the market and market the ones ready to be sold.
4. A good loan broker who is honest and has great loan knowledge and connections.
5. A good insurance broker who can help you get the best coverage and protection against unforeseen events and litigation.
6. A great library of the best books written by the experts on real estate.
7. Access to cash either from one's own account or from readily available lines of credit with high limits.
8. A good cookie cutter formula for identifying proper buildings to purchase at wholesale prices, and likewise a proper formula for unloading real estate properties at retail values to generate cash and profits.

Therefore, one must recognize that no matter what one does in life or at work, first and foremost one is an executive within his own sphere of influence, and only then in his business enterprise, and thus needs to have an honest and reliable team to back one up and turn one's planning into a reality.

Quizzes #9

Quiz 9.1

What is meant by "**Team**?" Explain why one needs a team to attain his goals? Give an example.

What is meant by "**Group**?" Give an example.

What is meant by "**A Business Enterprise**?" Give an example.

Quiz 9.2

Why does one need to know "**The Fundamentals of Teamwork**?" Give an example.

What is meant by "**Proper Correction**?" Give an example.

What is meant by "**Role of a Team in One's Goals**?" How does a team help one to achieve one's own goals? Give two examples.

Why is it so essential to know "**Who is on Your Team**?" Give an example.

PART 10

Key 8
How Many Streams of Income Do You Have?

Exchange

"If you have an apple and I have an apple and we exchange these apples then you and I will still each have one apple. But if you have an idea and I have an idea and we exchange these ideas, then each of us will have two ideas."
—George Bernard Shaw (Irish literary Critic, Playwright and Essayist. 1925 Nobel Prize for Literature, 1856-1950)

The English Dictionary defines "exchange" as *"Giving one thing for another thing."* It is also further defined *as an act or process of interchanging of goods and services in return for money.*

Exchange is an inexorable principle in nature that seems never to be violated on a long term, even if slightly ever so on a short-term basis.

From this simple definition, we can see that in order to exchange, we need to have a product in sight and have the means to produce it, but more importantly we need a customer or more precisely from the earlier discussions, a specialized particle to sell the product to and complete the exchange process.

From this observation, the **"Law of Supply and Demand"** evolves. This is a subject much discussed in classical economics textbooks, but poorly understood by most economists.

Using the concept of supply and demand, we see that exchange happens to be one of the most fundamental laws of existence without which we seem to be in a complete chaos. It is exchange that creates an inflow and an outflow on a large scale and thus gives one a degree of survival potential. That degree clearly depends on the rate of exchange of the individual with the society per unit time.

For example, if a person or (a group) creates a product (such as a car, a TV, etc.) and exchanges it once a month with the society, the survival potential could increase if the product could be produced and exchanged once a week! This is where the marketing department comes into play and becomes crucial in order to constantly tap into new territories for customers and create the needed demand to balance the flow of increased supply for the exchange process and keep prices the same or higher to guarantee an increased survival potential. If this is not done, then the increased production will not be offset by a higher demand and prices will sag, leading to a lowered production quota — back to square one!

It is rather obvious that one has to produce something to exchange for money. If this give-take process is altered or interrupted then we get a flow that is one-way flow like a DC battery, and will eventually run down and stop.

How Supply and Demand Determine Prices

"Time is the most valuable thing that a man can spend."
— Diogenes

If we examine the supply of a quantity and compare it with its demand versus time, we will see that some neat patterns develop from pure observations.

Case I – Increasing prices

If supply decreases while demand keeps increasing, then prices will increase as shown below.

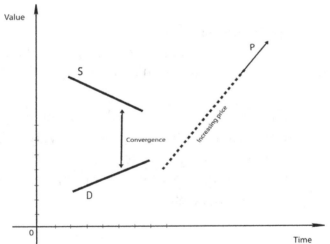

Price increases due to an increase in demand and shrinkage of supply.

Case II – Decreasing Prices

If supply increases while demand keeps decreasing, then prices will decrease as shown below.

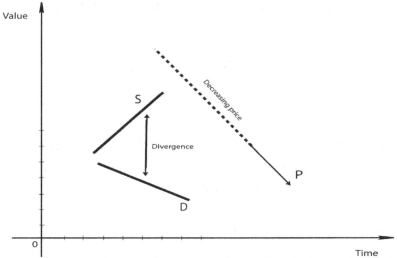

Price decreases due to a decrease in demand and plenty of supply.

Case III– Stable Prices

If supply keeps pace with demand at all times, then prices will remain stable as shown on the next page.

This is a situation where every earth government on the public relations front wishes for, but actively fights it through improper handling of exchange factors (such as printing money, heavy taxation of producers, creating unexchangeable products, etc.).

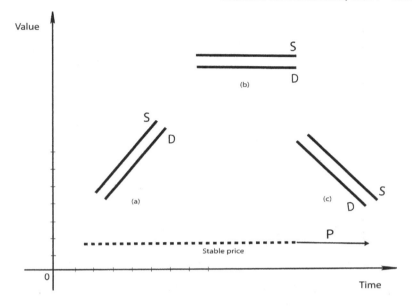

Price stabilizes due to both supply and demand both a) increasing at the same rate, b) remaining constant in time, or c) decreasing at the same rate.

Case IV–Increasing Prices Become Stable

If supply decreases while demand keeps increasing, then prices will increase at first until both rates keep pace with each other, at which time the price will remain stable as shown on the next page.

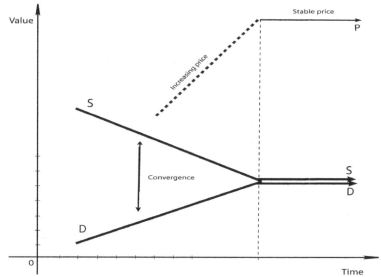

Price increases due to an increase in demand and shrinkage of supply. Price stabilizes due to both supply and demand remaining constant in time.

Case V–Fluctuating Prices Become Stable

If supply and demand lines diverge, prices will decrease; if they converge, then prices will increase until both rates keep pace with each other, at which time the price will remain stable as shown on the next page.

This is what happens in good economic times and periods where planning in advance by the company leaders and their adjustments of production of a commodity (the supply side) to meet the actual demand results in stability and prosperity.

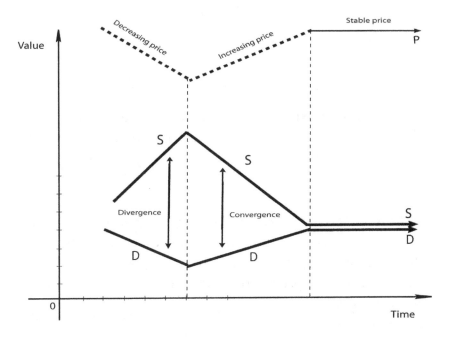

First, Price decreases due to an increase in supply and shrinkage of demand (divergence). Then, Price increases due to an increase in demand and shrinkage of supply. Finally, Price stabilizes due to both supply and demand remaining constant in time.

Building a Business Upon Exchange

From a study of exchange so far, we may have noticed that it is an extremely important subject in the society and the whole civilization, whether locally or globally depends upon it.

There are three primary and yet very basic methods one can get into exchange with the society and create the many pillars or streams of income that can support the huge weight of one's prosperous life. These can be briefly summarized as:

Basic method #1: know information on the *supply or demand* side - Have a good information network to get access to a readily and available pool of goods and services owned by people who want to be willing sellers or buyers. In this case, one is a **catalyst** for the exchange process, and is commonly called a broker. This category includes access to all communication media, all of the data bases available, and all names and addresses of interested parties. This requires a great public relations (PR) presence to contact people and close the transaction, etc.

Basic Method #2: Enable people to assume the role of *demand*- Have a good marketing and promotion network to generate the desire in people and thus create a readily and available pool of interested people, which translates into willing and eager buyers. This category could include helping the buyers through financial assistance, loans, grants, consulting, education, and proper guidance to enable people to assume the role of a proper demand.

Basic Method #3: Become the *supply*- This is done by producing a Product, which means that one has the means and capability of producing an exchangeable product, which can enhance life and the survival potential of others.

These three methods cover all of the fundamentals of exchange, wherein one can build many flourishing businesses around each of these with a huge degree of success.

There could be other secondary factors but the above is the main points that must be present to increase the ways one can get into exchange and begin traveling on a road that leads to the realm of prosperity.

Failures in Exchange

"Lost time is never found again"
— Benjamin Franklin

When a person fails to take on the role of the supply side of life primarily, or the demand side secondarily, then to that degree his life falls apart and he starts a parasitic existence.

A parasitic need and desire on the part of people who want to have the products or services but not willing to become the supply for something else is the major point of disintegration of the society. This means that they are not going to have the money to pay for things, making it impossible to assume the role of an actual demand. This means that *demand* by definition is really not there and no one can assume the role of a willing and eager buyer. At this juncture, the exchange formula completely falls apart.

An example clarifies this situation in the world of investment. Let us say one owned an asset such as a stock, a commercial building, silver or gold coins, etc. If one does his research work well and investigates the trend in that particular market, then investment would be an easy task and he would be prosperous. Because if the market was in an uptrend he would buy (become the demand), and if in a downtrend he would sell (become the supply). However, if stagnant and stable he would hold onto the asset for trend clarification.

Now imagine an investor who would rely on TV news, and listen to the neighbor's or friend's advice or worse yet his broker's recommendations to trade. He would live a chaotic investment life and would soon find himself in the poor house or the bankruptcy court.

Some people waste their time on *unexchangeable products*, such as playing video games, watching TV listening to gossips, spreading lies and destroying lives, studying outmoded subjects for which there no jobs, etc. This translates into a nonexistent personal economy based upon non-production.

Another way one can fail in exchange is not planning and not setting up a real system for the production process. Any system set up by the business owner if not protected by a set of exact policy and an actual knowledge of the applicable laws could open up major litigations against him and his company, which could not only cost him his sanity but also his bank account.

Another way one can fail in exchange is operating through dishonest means. This means having a team of executives, and staff who cannot operate the system competently but cover up the truth and present many unethical solutions to exchange problems. Their company would experience many upheavals coupled with up and down cycles of lost production and unforeseen losses.

We can see that all ills of the society can be obtained through a manipulation of the exchange equation by one's inability

a) To be the *supply*.

b) To become an actual *demand*.

c) Not producing a product or producing a false product or service (such as bombs, drugs, prostitution, etc.).

d) Not setting up a system of exchange thus putting everyone at risk through a total ignorance of the laws of life!

There are many laws to life and livingness but exchange happens to be a fundamental one and lies dead center at the heart of a prosperous life!

☜﹏℘＊❀✳❀＊℃﹏☞

Exchange and Prosperity

So far, we have examined the exchange principle purely as an economic principle concerning supply and demand for the transfer of goods and services.

Examples of exchange abound all around us. Plants, animals, human bodies and all businesses, governments and companies are all dependent on this principle. It is fascinating how the modern economic theory and PhDs in economics and most economists who work for the government have missed this vital principle and have come to believe in things such as interest rates, taxation, etc. as the primary ways to handle and remedy the ills of the society when things go wrong.

Applying this concept to a business enterprise, we can see that building a company is no different from a biological organism. That is to say, it has to be built on the principle of exchange and without it being fully incorporated in all aspects of any business activity, it will eventually die, perhaps gradually but certainly!

In conclusion, to operate a company we need to feed it (as an inflow) the personnel, information, policy, money, guidance and technical expertise. It is only when these are available, and in the correct proportion, that the organization will produce (as its outflow) the superior and exchangeable products or services that can then be exchanged to procure future survival wherewithal.

From this discussion, we can extract the inexorable fundamental rule pervading the entirety of the exchange principle to be:

Exchange should be present at the core of all of one's activities, before one can even consider himself a) a success or b) one who is traveling toward abundance and prosperity!

The Generalized Exchange Principle (GEP)

Upon careful observation, we can see that the exchange principle does not just apply to the business world, but is interwoven into any and all aspects of existence on any imaginable level of existence, large or small. This leads us to the generalization of the concept of exchange called the "Generalized Exchange Principle (GEP)," which encompasses all of life and its many varied levels of livingness. All of life seems to be based on the GEP!

The generalized Exchange Principle (GEP): *This principle states that every part of life is in constant exchange with every other part of life and nothing can exist without exchange principle being constantly at work on a macroscopic or microscopic level.*

In essence, we can observe that life on a physical level exists as a result of exchange from many sources, material and immaterial. The solid matter exists because of the exchange of electrons between atoms in the form of bonding (whether covalent, ionic or metallic bonding). The car moves because of the exchange between the fuel and oxygen as the intake, and the exhaust and fumes as the outgo.

Everything has exchange built into it, which really means that nothing can exist on its own as a far-isolated entity! A single atom is an anomaly and cannot be found in nature. One must work hard to achieve such an isolated atom and even then, it is not stable and will soon combine with other elements to form new compounds.

GEP is visibly at work for all life organisms on a cellular or organic level and any larger aspect of life such as investment, prosperity and survival. By not understanding GEP or following it, one will jeopardize the operation of his business and future survival of any aspect of his life.

Let us consider a human body. Let us say we starve it constantly by inputting junk food and highly processed products, have it drink soda and chemically treated water and have it breathe smog and polluted air, we will soon discover that the body cannot produce much energy and has much problem in the survival process. It gets sick easily and cannot withstand any level of force or action. It gets tired very quickly and lacks vitality and health.

Our observation tells us that "The generalized exchange principle" was violated. The cells have no building parts to build the body organs from inside on a cellular level. These cells cannot go into exchange with their immediate environment, thus the body on a functional level (macroscopic level) cannot exchange either, and thus has no vitality or health worthy of mention.

Similarly, we need to use GEP in building a company, an investment account or any other activity.

To have a company exist in such a way that it cannot produce any product, or when it does it is not up to par, we have to feed it wrong information, set up incorrect policy, and not fund its many operations with adequate money, give it incorrect and inexperienced guidance and provide no technical expertise! Even worse, we would have to man it with either inadequate personnel or a set of green employees who are unaware of the business itself or the exchange principle as a governing factor. With the above as the inflow into the company, one will expect nothing but bad news and poor products or services generated as the outflow. The outflow will be an inferior and non-exchangeable product or service which cannot be sold and exchanged for further survival wherewithal.

In conclusion, we can see that without a full implementation of the GEP in all aspects of a business operation, we should not expect a thriving company with any noticeable longevity to come about, and its doom will be in the offing, as certain as nightfall after sunset!

The Two Major Categories of Exchange

Exchange by its very definition concerns a product that will enhance the lives of both the supply (i.e., the seller) and the demand (i.e., the buyer). This is what we normally refer to as **"Constructive Exchange"** such as selling a car to someone who does not have it and has a need for its use and having it will enhance his life. The money given to the car dealer will enable it to pay its bills and procure other cars for other customers. Therefore, the car dealership also benefits from this transaction

However, there are situations where exchange does take place but the product or service exchanged destroys both the seller and the buyer alike. This is called **"Destructive Exchange."** A good example would be a bomb factory, where the buyer obtains a bomb that will destroy many people, whereas the seller will also destroy itself eventually, having destroyed so many lives—by pure karma! Therefore, both sides will eventually experience demise. The list of such destructive exchanges throughout human history has been a long one, but notable amongst them are illegal drug transactions, prostitution, human smuggling, missile and gun manufacturing and distribution, mercenary work, child trading, pornography, so on and so forth.

࿇ ֍ ✳ ❀ ✖ ❀ ✳ ֎ ࿇

Product

"In my youth I stressed freedom, and in my old age I stress order. I have made the great discovery that liberty is a product of order."
—Will Durant (1885-1981)
American Writer and Historian, collaborator of his wife, Ariel Durant

We live in a society where every aspect of our existence is dictated by the laws of exchange. From the products or services (such as food, electricity, water, etc.) that we consume on a daily basis, we can immediately see that their existence alone signifies that someone must be producing them for our consumption. Therefore, it is necessary for us to understand what we mean by a product.

Let us now define exactly what we mean by a "product." It is defined to be *something produced by nature or made by human industry or art that has exchange value.*

If the product is well designed and produced with high quality materials and parts, then it can be marketed and exchanged effortlessly to consumers who will willingly pay for all of the costs of its research, development and production. In other words, it has an exchange value.

The product is something (an object, a service, etc.) or someone (a person with a certain skill, knowledge, etc.) that has been brought into existence. It is the end result of a creative activity, first at the thought level and then at the physical level, sitting at the bottom of a pyramid which has an idea at its apex.

The quality of the product determines its worth and exchange value. Exchange is an important part of the product creation cycle, without which no one would be inclined to spend time and effort to create.

Obviously, an exchangeless product when created is something useless, which no one is willing to pay anything for it, causing no enhancement of the creation process and in fact causing the opposite—a creation cessation.

The Essence of Money

"Rather than love, than money, than fame, give me truth."
—Henry David Thoreau (1817-1862)
American Essayist, Poet and Philosopher

If one examines the flow of money, at first glance one may think that in order to make money, you may have to get a bunch of people together and then have them create a product, which can then be exchanged for money. This is a very cursory and perhaps shallow look at how money can be obtained.

The essence of money can only be understood when the concept of exchange and its generalized form (The generalized exchange principle) is fully grasped. Life is based upon exchange and money is just a subproduct of this process.

In other words, money should not be one's primary focus and goal in life, since it is secondary in its basic nature and comes about after one has engaged in an outflow. Focus on money is the wrong area of emphasis and could completely derail one's creative power and future survival. This is no idle statement as any thief will tell you that every time he steals, he is selling his soul to the devil!

In simple terms, money is an *inflow* of a certain quantity of monetary particles, whether be it dollars, euros, pounds, rials, or dinars. The inflow occurs usually after an outflow of products (goods, or services) has occurred. The reverse seldom or almost never happens.

In fact, the most successful and wealthiest people on the planet work primarily on their true passion and joy of creation becomes their primary focus. They get paid huge sums of money for their production and high quality work, to a point that they actually never have a money problem in life!

"Time is more valuable than money. You can get more money, but you cannot get more time."

—Jim Rohn (1930-)
American Speaker and Author.

Ꮟ Ꮽ ✴ ❀ ✖ ❀ ✴ Ꮳ Ꮟ

Marketing

"We have to choose between a global market driven only by calculations of short-term profit, and one which has a human face."
—Kofi Annan (Ghanaian diplomat, seventh secretary-general of the United Nations, 2001 Nobel Peace Prize.)

To engage in exchange, one must learn how to sell his products through a process called marketing. The English dictionary defines **marketing** as *"all business activities involved in the moving of goods and products from the producer to the consumer, including advertising, selling, packaging, etc."*

By **market,** we mean *the field encompassed by buyers and sellers for the trading of goods and services. It is the medium where a specific product is exchanged. That product is either an application mass or a service.*

Marketing takes a product created as a result of a science and through mass advertisement narrows the range to a few specific specialized particles and through negotiation and objection handling process sells it to a suitable customer and finally collects the money as an end result as shown in the double-pyramid diagram on the next page.

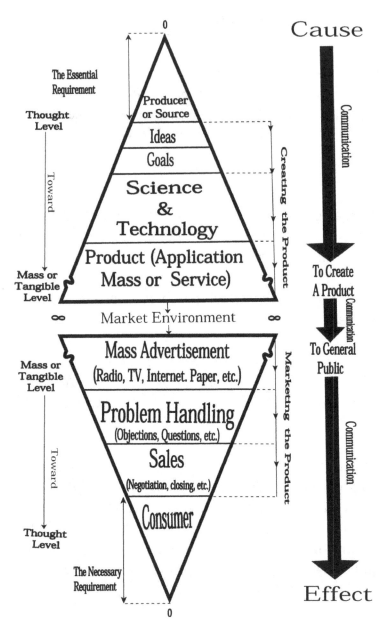

The Double Pyramid of production and marketing: From the producer, to the product, finally to the consumer.

From this diagram, we can see that the production cycle forms the top pyramid and the consumption cycle forms the second inverted pyramid.

The end result of this action (Producer-Product-Consumer) is survival as a keynote of operation. Both the producer and consumer alike will benefit from this action and their lives are equally enriched thereafter.

It should be pointed out that production is much holier than consumption, since the producer is at cause and achieving cause is the highest purpose in this world.

On a final note, it is rather easy to see from the double pyramid diagram that all things begin with an idea, the right idea! Thus, ideas are the source of products and are much more superior to the masses that embody them!

Quizzes #10

Quiz 10.1

What is meant by "**Exchange**?" Give an example.

Can you explain "**How Supply and Demand Determine Prices**?" Give an example.

What are the "**Many Ways to Exchange**?" Give an example.

What are the "**Failures in Exchange**?" Give an example.

What is there a connection between "**Exchange and Prosperity**?" Give an example.

What is the inexorable fundamental rule pervading the "**Exchange Principle**?" Give an example.

Quiz 10.2

What is meant by "**The Generalized Exchange Principle**?" Give an example.

What is meant by "**The Two Major Categories of Exchange**?" Give an example.

What is meant by "**Product**?" Give an example.

What is meant by "**The Essence of Money**?" Give an example.

What is meant by "**Marketing**?" Give an example.

PART 11

Key 9
Do You Know The Trends in Your Marketplace?

The Concept of Trends

"If you paint in your mind a picture of bright and happy expectations, you put yourself into a condition conducive to your goal."

—Norman Vincent Peale quotes (American Protestant Clergyman and Writer, 1898-1993)

The concept of trends is not new but using them in business is. In fact, it is one of the main concepts utilized in the stock and commodity markets. It is an essential tool that most technical analysts of the financial markets emphasize.

Trends are the basic tools used to get and keep any business prospering and keeping it successful. Every individual, group of people or company has a trend associated with its activities. That trend can be up, down or sideways.

Considering the three possibilities of trends, we need to establish which trend an activity or an organization as a whole is in. This forms an important part of the correct estimation of effort in order to fix the problems or enhance the business activity or a sector under consideration. Proper observation and establishment of the correct trend will bring about stability, expansion, and future prosperity.

We should understand that trends exist in everything that we do in life or business and recognition of this fact alone brings about a tremendous amount of simplicity and stability to the business environment.

Any individual, or a company at any given moment, is operating in one of these three possible trends and is therefore subject to the momentum in that trend. This concept can be further expanded and successfully applied to things outside the business world, such as one's family, groups one belongs to, one's existence as a human being, one's physical possessions, etc.

Everything we see around us has a trend. Trends have *momentum* and unless changed by exterior forces, the trend's direction persists. A non-recognition of this factor alone is what leads most entities such as business groups and business operations make wrong decisions and actions and choose wrong policies. In fact, if the trends of such business activities were correctly known by the executives, then the obvious actions would have been just the opposites as the orders of the day!

To understand trends, we need to step back and study graphs of activities (such as price of a stock, a commodity, net income of a company, etc.). These graphs are usually generated by collecting data points obtained over a period of time and are generally referred to as statistics (or stats for short). In the next article, we take up this topic first and then we will continue with our study of trends.

❦ ৪০ ✴ ❀ ✖ ❀ ✴ ৫৪ ❧

Statistics

"Statistics are no substitute for judgment"
—Henry Clay (American Statesman, US congressman, 1777-1852)

The English dictionary defines statistics as *"facts or data of numerical kind associated with an activity, which is assembled, classified and tabulated over a period of time so as to present factual information about that activity."* This numerical information is usually shown as an x-y plot (or graph), and thus is drawn on a two dimensional surface.

A graph or plot of data, as a mathematical tool, shows relative values versus time. In the business world, one value or one data point concerning an activity does not mean anything unless we know what its prior values were. Then and only then can we understand what is going on in that business activity! In other words, there is no absolute value (i.e., a single data point all by itself) in the business world.

Therefore, a graph shows the concept of prior-ness of values and furthermore how present time value compares with the earlier ones. In mathematics, positive and negative values are allowed but in most businesses, accountants use only a positive numerical value to represent any and all activities, whether that activity is positive or negative. For example, a gross income of a business is always a positive number, so when we plot it we place the zero line at the bottom of the chart and infinity (∞) at the top. However, the amount of liabilities (such as loans, bonds, etc.) of any business is obviously a negative number but we plot it as a positive number with zero line at the top of the plot and the graph extending toward infinity (∞) at the bottom! Examples of positive and negative stats are shown below.

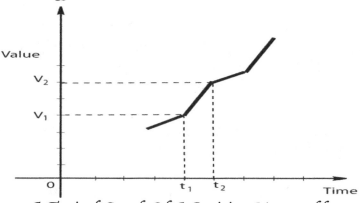

A Typical Graph Of A Positive Measurable Quantity (e.g., Income, Stock Price, etc.)

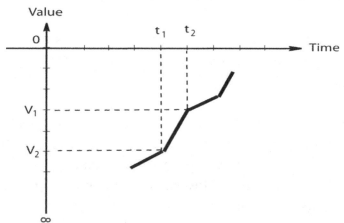

A Typical Graph Of A Negative Measurable Quantity (e.g., loan balance, vacancy, etc.)

A graph measures at each moment of time how right or how wrong a business activity is relative to its past performance. Moreover, based on the trend line, it also clearly delineates how healthy and successful a business activity is operating at the present moment. It also shows how well it is employing the exchange principle in its daily dealings with its customers and environment.

If graphs are prepared with a high degree of accuracy, then they represent facts and thus provide a true picture of a company's performance over time. They dispel rumors and innuendos and are actually the only true measure of a company's performance.

For example, a positive slope (i.e., an uptrend) along with its angle can be used to conclude to what degree the business activity is right or healthy. On the other hand, a negative slope (i.e., downtrend) shows a diseased and dying business and depending on the angle of the slope of the trend line, a greater or lesser degree of wrong decisions are being made by the company executives!

In every company, a specific post called the "Stat-Man or Stat-Person" has to be designated and a fully trained person must be placed in charge of this important aspect of running a business. Not using stats and trend lines has painful consequences and is too grim to face, but if one wants to see examples of it then a cursory look at the headline on the front page of any newspaper will put this matter to rest!

Analyzing the graph or stat is commonly referred to as the technical analysis in the stock or commodity markets and there are volumes upon volumes of books written about different methods of analysis. However, without getting too complicated we will present a simple approach to analyzing the collected data (drawn in the form of a graph) and present a method of approach that is simple and yet very powerful!

The whole idea about graph analysis is to use the results and the conclusions in a systematic way to pinpoint and handle the business activity more effectively, particularly the problematic areas.

Therefore, the chart analysis has the following steps:

a) Establishment of a measurable quantity.

b) Collection of a series of accurate data points.

c) Tabulation and organization of data in the form of a graph (also called a plot or stats).

d) Establishment of the trend and drawing the trend line,

e) Analysis of the trend line in terms of the steepness of its ascent or descent accurately measured by its angle with the horizontal line.

f) Establishing a course of action to strengthen (if uptrend) or handle (if downtrend).

━ ℘ ✳ ❀ ✄ ❀ ✳ ℘ ━

What Is a Trend?

When dealing with statistics over a certain period of time, usually a pattern of behavior emerges, which we call a trend. We define a **trend** as "*The general or prevailing tendency or course of things happening in a period of time such as events, discussions, prices, etc.*"

The trend is the emerging pattern of the graph of activities studied over a period of time. The graph of activities is also referred to as the plot or the statistics (or stats for short). In general, the pattern of stats *or the trend* can be an uptrend, a downtrend or a range-bound trend (i.e., more or less a level or flat trend).

Once the prevailing pattern has been established in terms of the trend, one can then draw a trend line to provide a more precise method of representing the trend. The trend line is a mathematical tool to help us understand exactly what is going on in a set of collected data.

From a simple observation of any graph of activities, one can establish the trend of that graph, which becomes invaluable in the management of that activity. Oftentimes, poor decisions and management blunders stem from a lack of recognition of the trend of the activity, which is vital survival knowledge in the business jungle for any business CEO (Chief Operating Officer), operations manager or head of a company.

The mathematics of any variable quantity tells one that it can assume three possible values if compared to its previous value—up, down or same. And so it is with graphs, by a simple observation of any graph we can see that a graph (such as the price of a stock or commodity, the gross income of a company, etc.) can be in an uptrend (i.e., the trend line has a positive slope), a downtrend (i.e., the trend line has a negative slope) or a range-bound trend (i.e., the trend line has more or less a zero slope or a very shallow angle with the horizontal line).

The **trend line** is generally defined as *"The line connecting the highs in an uptrend on the graph, or the line connecting the lows in a downtrend. For a range-bound trend either of highs or lows can be connected to create the trend line."*

A more convenient method of noting the trend is through the observation of the chart in the selected time frame, and noticing visually if it is up, sideways or down purely by its tendency of direction of motion. This is a fast and reliable method as shown below.

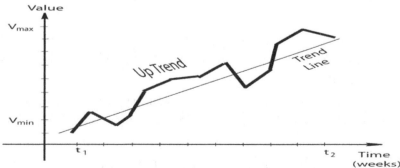

An example of a trend and its corresponding trend line.

Understanding Trends

"The genius of investing is recognizing the direction of a trend - not catching highs and lows"

—Unknown

We have already defined **trend** as **"The general or prevailing tendency or course of things happening in a period of time such as events, activities, prices, etc."**

A trend can also be interpreted as the tendency of statistics to drift in a certain direction over a period of time. The period of time depends upon the scope of operation. If one is day trading a certain stock then the period of time is measured in minutes. If one is swing trading the stocks then the period of time is measured in days or weeks. On the other hand, if one is investing in stocks the period of time is in months or years! Therefore, the period of time for the stats is never fixed but is relative and variable depending on the activity under consideration.

An upward trend for a business activity, even if only slightly upward, shows that people are trying and making progress. On the other hand, a range-bound (or relatively level) or downward shows that the activity is in trouble. Trend is the overall measure of expansion or contraction and is the most valuable of statistic messages.

We also defined a **trend line** earlier as, *"A line drawn connecting the average of highs and lows on the trend."*

Thus, there are three possible cases we need to consider:
1) Up trend with an up-sloping trend line.
2) Range-bound trend, with a relatively level trend line, which has a zero (or close to zero) slope.
3) Down trend with a down-sloping trend line.

These three possible cases are shown below.

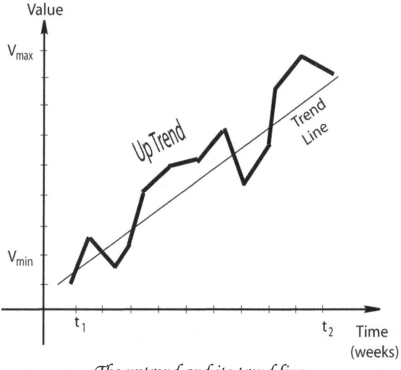

The uptrend and its trend line.

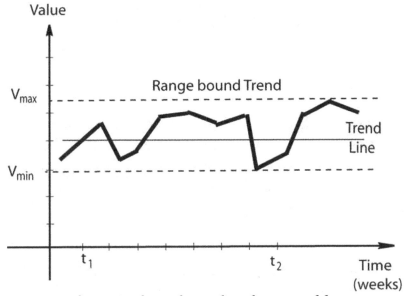

The range-bound trend and its trend line.

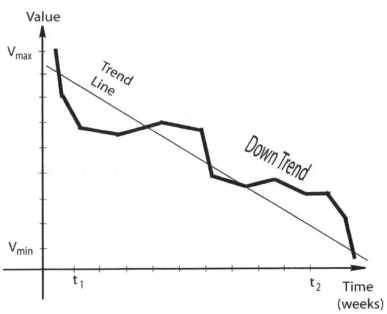

The downtrend and its trend line.

Momentum of Trends

Any individual, or a company at any given moment, is operating in one of three possible trends and is therefore subject to the momentum in that trend. The momentum concept can also be expanded to include one's family, groups one is in, one's physical existence and possessions, etc.

Everything we see around us has a trend and a trend line for their existence and operation. All Trends have *momentum* and follow a law similar to Newton's First law of motion (Law of Inertia), which states that *a particle not subjected to external forces will remain at rest (if not moving) or keep moving (if already in motion).*

This concept seems to apply to the trends and their pattern. That is to say, all trends remain in their existing pattern and the trend line continues at the same slope unless changed by **exterior forces**. For example if a stock has an uptrend, then that uptrend continues until some external force such as bad earning news or an unexpected litigation develops around the company's products, etc.

Therefore, one must be constantly on the watch for forces that may affect the pattern of an activity, the income of an organization or the price pattern of a stock or commodity.

A non-recognition of the trend momentum alone is what leads most groups of people such as investors and business executives make wrong decisions and actions and implement wrong policies where the opposite would have been the appropriate ones.

Some people even go so far as to hope and pray for a change in the trend despite all indicators as to the contrary. These people end up with devastating losses because they do not see how trends and investing are directly correlated and thus ignorance of trends can be an expensive and terribly awakening lesson.

Positioning the Business with the Trend

There is a definite connection between the trend pattern (characterized by the slope of the trend line) and the degree that the exchange is implemented in one's life or business activity, and the degree one is surviving upwards.

When a sector of the market is in demand, it will be in an uptrending market condition. One should consider engaging his business activities in one of the sub-industries of that sector. For example, if real estate is strong, one should consider strongly getting into buying quality buildings at the beginning of the uptrend and consider selling it when the reversal of the uptrend is at hand.

Another example is considering a leading company that is doing well by producing viable and exchangeable products, which have a healthy demand. This company is respecting the exchange process by keeping the customers happy, thus its stock will be in an uptrending pattern, and one should strongly consider investing in such a company at the very beginning of the trend and ride it to enormous profits.

Therefore, identifying the trend of one's own special market is essential to one's survival and prosperity. Without knowing the trend, one is operating with a great handicap in any arena and is liable to engage in many harmful and time-consuming actions, which could be contrary to what the trend dictates.

For example, if one is in an uptrend of any kind he should know that in that area he is selling and exchanging well with the society. On the hand, a downtrend indicates that exchange process is in trouble and needs to be corrected very quickly. Therefore, if one's actions are not geared up toward selling products and getting exchange in, then one potentially could find himself at the brink of total insolvency one day!

The sideways trend is a clear red flag indicating that exchange is going out. It is the boundary line separating two important regions of operation:
    a) Exchange region (uptrend), and
    b) No-exchange region (downtrend).

Therefore, the moral of the story is that one needs:

a) To know the trend one's business is in.

b) To take only those actions that support an uptrend.

c) To correct a downtrend by removing all those obstacles that push the trend down, particularly those people who have a vested interest to enrich their own pockets by keeping one ignorant or use one as a patsy.

d) To be vigilant and constantly alert to guard his business when in an uptrend.

e) To be willing to take quick and immediate actions when the uptrend turns sour!

The above steps (a-e) form a sound business plan and one that should be employed fully in any business activity. Otherwise, one could enter many uncharted territories that would be tantamount to being swallowed up in a quicksand!

Quizzes #11

Quiz 11.1

What is meant by **"The Concept of Trends?"** Give an example.

What is meant by **"Statistics?"** Give an example.

Can you explain **"What a Trend is?"** Give an example.

Why do we need to have a good **"Understanding of Trends?"** Give an example.

Quiz 11.2

What is meant by **"Momentum of Trends?"** Give an example.

Why does one who is in business need to answer this question constantly, **"What Is the Trend that I am in?"** Give an example.

How can you use the concept of **"Positioning the Business with the Trend"** in your own life or business? Give an example.

PART 12

Key 10
Do You Know the Laws
of Your Business?

The Laws of the Land

"A man without ethics is a wild beast loosed upon this world."
—Albert Camus (French Novelist, Essayist and Playwright, 1957 Nobel Prize for Literature, 1913-1960)

In a sane business world, most difficulties and problems could easily be solved through the power of pure and positive communication, on a face-to-face basis, reaching an amicable and workable solution in the process. Both parties mutually trust each other and work toward solving the problem in good faith with full trust.

This ideal scene is totally absent in the today's dangerous environment of the business world. Without knowing the laws of the land, one is putting oneself at great risk, operating in a world of many unknowns filled with enormous vengeance unleashed upon one by the greedy loafer, the poverty-stricken unholy victim who sees one as the answer to one's prayer for wealth! This is the one who wishes to obtain one's hard-earned wealth through a legal system, which easily accepts fabricated web of untruths and untold emotional distress incidents as facts.

One's sanity and health can easily be jeopardized by such unscrupulous characters. Most often in these cases, one is advised and actually can easily be coaxed by the involved attorneys to settle for tidy sums of money to prevent further cost of litigation and losses. This is truly a dangerous environment for any businessman to engage in or for one who aims high and aspires for great grandeur and desires to achieve his intended lofty goals.

One must have a legal team handy and in place for immediate action or attack by such dangerous and money grabbing characters and use the law effectively to combat them at its inception.

Stay Legal for Longevity

In conducting any form of business, one is required:

a) To know the law, or to consult with the legal profession in order to employ all of the pertinent laws of the land.

b) To use a sound logic to implement the pertinent laws. This means, avoiding to use arbitrary policies, rules or codes of conduct when not based on facts, research or actual laws.

c) To develop a system and a set of criteria to identify the specialized particles and filter out the unqualified or the trouble-makers.

One's business, by not following the above three rules, will eventually wind up in disaster and will be pushed toward the brink of extinction, no matter how far-flung one's goals were at the start.

One's activities also need to be recognized by the city, state and federal governments for proper taxation and recognition if one plans to stay in business for a long haul. Tax evasion will not lead to a stable or viable state of affairs.

One also needs to have a legal team on hire or on the payroll for any attacks, disputes or infringements that may occur during the day-to-day actions and in different business transactions.

Part of staying legal is to have proper insurance for each aspect of existence to protect one against extreme and dire circumstances, which are totally unforeseen. There are many types of insurance policies, which could assist one, amongst which health insurance, business employee practices insurance, malpractice insurance, real estate insurance, fire insurance and a general umbrella insurance could be of significant use in business.   /

Having a proper and legally recognized business activity by the governments and related agencies will go a long way in ensuring one's survival in the business arena as well as in keeping the ethics key totally in!

In conclusion, the only reason we use these two rules in business is survival at the highest level. This activity should be engaged with a great deal of fervent, regardless of any associated cost, whether in its design, implementation or carry through. Deviation from these two rules is actually considered to be a fatal activity in any business enterprise. Thus, we can see the truth in the following:

Laws of the land infused into a series of logical and correct policies form the cornerstone of a business, which would truly ensure longevity. One cannot exist without the other.

"Never in this world can hatred be stilled by hatred; it will be stilled by non-hatred -- this is the law Eternal"
Buddha (Hindu Prince Gautama Siddharta, the founder of
Buddhism, 563-483 B.C.)

⊷ ຣ◯ ✳ ❀ ✿ ❀ ✳ ଔ ⊷

Asset Protection

"Don't wait. The time will never be just right."
Napoleon Hill (American author, 1883-1970)

There is a considerable amount of confusion and turmoil in the society at this time to necessitate one to consider a fair degree of asset protection. This could be accomplished by using a combination of Limited Partnerships (LPs), Limited Liability Corporations (LLCs), Family Revocable Living Trust (FRLT), etc. A competent attorney could be of tremendous help and should be consulted in setting up a proper structure for maximum protection.

Some people operate under the false notion that if a high enough insurance coverage is purchased, then any unforeseen circumstance is automatically covered. Even though it is a good assumption, this is a very lazy way to leave hard-won assets open to unscrupulous attacks by the people who are looking for the slightest mistake on your part so that they can utilize a legal system, which is prone to many falsities and pitfalls, all to the detriment of the business owner.

"Every company's greatest assets are its customers, because without customers there is no company."
Michael Leboeuf

Most insurance companies commonly deny coverage at the most crucial time when one is most vulnerable. They look for loopholes and owner's actions to the slightest degree in order to deny coverage. So depending upon the insurance company is an ill-conceived notion and should not be relied upon heavily in lieu of a properly organized and interrelated series of entities to create an almost impenetrable line of defense.

"Time and health are two precious assets that we don't recognize and appreciate until they have been depleted."
Denis Waitley
(American motivational Speaker and Author of self-help books, 1933)

For example, it would be a grave error to hold rental or investment real estate in one's own name rather than established legal entities, since otherwise one then is exposed to a whole gamut of liabilities, which could potentially damage one's financial status to a large extent, should a lawsuit occur.

The assistance of a highly skilled Certified Public Accountant (CPA) as well as a knowledgeable advisor and a competent attorney is indispensable to a successful entity setup for effective asset protection.

"Never walk away from failure. On the contrary, study it carefully and imaginatively for its hidden assets."
Michael Korda

Quiz #12

Quiz 12.1

What is meant by **"The Laws of the Land**?" Explain why it is important to know the laws? Give an example.

Describe how logical and correct series of policies are related to longevity? Give an example.

Describe how longevity and **"The Laws of the Land"** are inseparable?

Quiz 12.2

What is meant by **"Stay Legal for Longevity**?" Explain why? Give an example.

What is meant by **"Asset Protection**?" Give an example.

What are the best ways to protect one's assets? Give an example.

PART 13

Lifelong Selling

Own or Borrow?

"Integrity is the essence of everything successful."
—Richard Buckminster Fuller (US engineer and architect,
1895-1983)

To operate an extremely successful business, one with enormous longevity, **one must own the business fully**. This means all aspects of the operational facilities, including the equipment, tools, land and the buildings.

Even if initially, one has to rent an equipment or the building, **your goal should be to own it outright at some point in the future**. The reason for this is very clear-cut, and that is you achieve total control of the operation and thus dictate or impose your mandates on the environment by not allowing it to interfere with your intentions.

If you rent something, you are borrowing it or getting it as a loan. Imagine if you had a landlord who constantly raised your rent on your building, or decided to terminate your lease, etc., soon your overhead would be so high and your certainty in the future so low that your business survival becomes a question mark.

It should be noted that borrowing to buy something (e.g., a house, etc.) is not necessarily and truly ownership because you are still renting the money, so you are not the owner yet but you are working toward it!

Borrowing money only makes sense if the cash flow from the asset will pay for the cost of borrowing the money (i.e., the interest amount). Otherwise, borrowing to buy a depreciating asset (such as a fancy car or a boat that does not produce income) is not going to pay off in the long run and will bring the stats down.

The idea here is **to own the means and tools of production**, not just to own something for the sake of owning!

Therefore, rule one in establishing the business for long-term longevity is owner-ship and not loaner-ship!

᠆᠊ ℘ ✳ ❀✄❀ ✳ ℃ ᠊᠆

Ownership

"The instinct of ownership is fundamental in man's nature"
—William James (American Philosopher, leader of the philosophical movement of Pragmatism, 1842-1910)

We need to understand the concept of ownership as our society is very ownership happy and a great many people are confused about its many facets.

The concept of ownership can be subdivided into good ownership and bad ownership:

I. Good Ownership: means owning an asset, which has three advantages as follows:

a) A net positive cash flow (i.e., the income from the asset pays for all expenses and then some).

b) An inherent or built-in equity (i.e. the asset is bought under market value).

c) Appreciating in time (i.e., a growing equity as time goes on).

THIS IS CALLED A TRIPLE PLAY[†].

[†]**Note:** A fourth element could be added to the above list for real estate assets and that is tax deductions, which by some is considered to be an added bonus.

An example is an apartment building in a medium to good location (i.e., appreciating) bought under market (i.e., having built-in equity) with current positive cash flow and good rental upside (i.e., having an existing net positive cash flow with future higher rents and potential appreciation).

II. Bad Ownership: means owning something, which does not have a triple advantage of a) a net cash flow, b) an inherent equity, and c) appreciating in time (i.e., growing equity).

An example would be buying an expensive car from a dealer and on credit. Pulling the car out of the dealer's car lot would drop its price by about $5000 to $10,000, depending on the make and model of the car (a negative equity). Then there are monthly interest payments and general car maintenance and upkeep, which produce a negative cash flow. Then as time goes on it starts depreciating and not appreciating (i.e., a vanishing equity).

Another example is to buy raw land in the outskirts of town (in the suburbs) in an un-incorporated part of town with the hope of it going up in value. This is a very speculative type of ownership and is not left to amateurs but only to very savvy professionals. If incorrectly done, this is one of the bad investments or ownership moves one can make. Because it only has a hope factor built into it!

In general, raw land may be appreciating in time (i.e., gaining equity) only if it is in close proximity to a town, city, or civilization which creates a demand for it.

Furthermore, most banks and lenders do not provide loans on unimproved land, which makes it truly a dead asset! This type of ownership is valid on a long time frame but on a short term basis will drain the vital funds, which could otherwise be used for a triple play!

Also, a lot of sales representatives try to cover up their selling intentions by telling the buyer "buy product X because it is a good investment." Therefore, they confuse the actuality (ownership) with a watered-down term (investment) to evade this issue and mislead the buyer into signing the agreement.

The fact of the matter is, **the moment you buy something, you are the owner first** and then maybe an investor, an entrepreneur, a trader, etc. It is not the other way around! So do not let someone confuse you on this important issue and walk away with your hard-earned money and leaving you behind with a false hope.

Therefore, if an asset does not qualify or does not measure up to the triple play criteria it is not worth buying.

Therefore, the rule on ownership of something is, to have a triple play of positive cash flow, equity and appreciation present, before we consider buying it.

Cash Reserve

The English dictionary defines **reserve** as *"cash or assets (readily turned into cash), held out of use by a business to meet expected or unexpected demands."*

It seems to be a good policy that when one is in a high production phase and income, and thus in an uptrending mode, one should put aside somewhere from 5% to 10% of the gross income in a reserve account and keep it untouched indefinitely as a cushion to fall back on in case there is a sudden turn of events in the business operation.

Such an occurrence is very common in the business world because we are in an up-and-down type of economy and every few years we have an economic upheaval of some kind. Feast or famine is the new order of our current society and every one is subject to it. Therefore, to smooth out the ride one needs to have a reserve in his business!

Other than the up-and-down economic picture, we also get occasional business emergencies, which need to be met with unusual sums of cash. If one's operation always breaks even, it is operating well below optimum level that it could.

The optimum level of any operation should be such that it generates a healthy return on investment. In real estate, it is about 5% to 7% in capitalization rate (cap rate) and in stock market, it is about 25%-30% in the return on investment (ROI).

Setting aside a small portion of the income as reserve is a very sensible and healthy action in the operation of any business and should be diligently followed. *It promotes a higher level of survival, adds more longevity and stabilizes the rough edges of an otherwise thriving business activity.*

Goals

"A goal is a dream with a deadline."
Napoleon Hill (American author, 1883-1970)

Goals are an essential part of survival in the long term. Therefore, one must actively set goals and create plans to achieve them.

To achieve a goal, one needs to know how to get things organized and managed properly. One needs to be able to organize his thoughts and intentions as the very first step of this process and then channel them properly in the correct direction so that success is guaranteed.

Now at this point one may realize that the goal and the plan may be too large to be done in one fell swoop. So a more practical approach is utilizing the standard analytical engineering principle where we subdivide this goal into its components (called sub-goals), and then develop a series of sub-plans to achieve each of the sub-goals.

In the process of carrying out the sub-plans, we need to make a series of clear-cut targets to bring them to fruition on a more realistic length of time. Thus setting targets takes away the time-indefiniteness connected with a plan and brings the major goal's deadline more within reach and in the realm of reality!

Of course, in the process of carrying out the sub-plans and achieving the targets, one enters a battle zone of activities, and as a result, one may have to do several things, including but not limited to:

a) Making projects within the framework of a sub-goal that accomplish a part of it.

b) Issuing orders to one's juniors.

c) Keeping track of the work's progress by generating a series of data points for the work accomplished (we may call it statistics or stats).

d) Creating a series of policy to keep the work on track and maintain the wasted efforts to a minimum, to prevent confusion and mistakes and to create harmony in the work environment.

"Most great people have attained their greatest success just one step beyond their greatest failure."
—Napoleon Hill (American author, 1883-1970)

Targets

"Set your target and keep trying until you reach it."
—Napoleon Hill (American author, 1883-1970)

A goal may have many sub-goals within it. To achieve the sub-goals one may have to shoot for targets that are within reach. A target by definition *is a mark in the physical universe for shooting at.*

Broadening and applying this concept to the realm of the business world, particularly the achievement of goals, we obtain a more general definition. A target is defined to be *an objective, which one can shoot for and should be reached on the way to the accomplishment of the overall goal.*

Knowing the concepts of targets well will help one achieve one's goals much faster, provided one applies them with diligence.

Plan of Action

"Reduce your plan to writing. The moment you complete this, you will have definitely given concrete form to the intangible desire."

Confucius (China's most famous teacher, philosopher, and political theorist, 551-479 BC)

Any well-run company will develop a business plan of action when planning to implement a goal. A business plan is a plan of actions in a coordinated and organized fashion. It coordinates the necessary actions and prepares strategy and tactics concerning the accomplishment of the goal and its consequences.

In the process of achieving the goal, there could be many planned meetings between the company executives. These meetings are essential to coordinate actions between different teams and examine the progress of active projects and achievement of the set quotas and targets.

In these meeting such things as, what areas are on target, what areas are off target and are having problems, a discussion of accomplished targets and what are upcoming projects and targets, etc., all based on proper documented and proven facts and data points (as represented in graphs and statistics) are discussed and specific handlings are established to be implemented in the near future.

One can expand the use of a business plan to encompass a lot more than just meetings but contain a detailed financial budget, which lays out a systematic plan for the needed funds in the different activities, such as targets, projects, operations bonuses for ahead of time completions, etc.

Moreover, another important aspect of a well-written business plan opens another door. It can be used in getting proper funding and loans from financial institutions for the various projects that need vital support. Most banks and financial lenders always require the borrower to present a detailed business plan outlining the various reasons of why and where the funds are going to be used and what type of collateral is available to back up the loan. Financing the various projects is essential in one's survival in the business jungle and unless one has a good business plan, his chance of survival would diminish considerably!

Business plans are a sure way to coordinate the performance of the teams within the company, to fund and obtain loans for different activities properly, to acknowledge the real players who are helping and to enhance the overall morale of the involved people about the progress made so far.

"Failure is nature's plan to prepare you for great responsibilities"
—Napoleon Hill (American author, 1883-1970)

☞ ℘ ✳ ❀✖❀ ✳ ℘ ☞

Happiness at Work

"Morale is a state of mind. It is steadfastness and courage and hope."

—Louis L. Mann

The English dictionary defines **"Morale"** as, *"moral or mental condition with respect to courage, discipline, confidence, enthusiasm, and willingness to endure hardship within a group or within an individual."*

It also defines **"Happiness"** as *a condition of great pleasure, contentment and joy.*

"Thousands of candles can be lit from a single candle, and the life of the candle will not be shortened. Happiness never decreases by being shared."

—Buddha (Hindu Prince Gautama Siddharta, the founder of Buddhism, 563-483 B.C.)

With these two definitions in mind, we can instantly see that if one is making good progress toward the achievement of the intended goals and sub-goals then one should find his own and the morale of the group high and full of enthusiasm.

The opposite case is doom, gloom and depression, which indicates that the person is moving further and further away from the goals set in his life. He is drifting away from his goal(s) day by day, and the group is not actively supporting him in his cause by not making it a shared ideal. There is dissonance and divergence in the group and the group is not acting as a single unit in the daily combat against problems and handling of the onslaught of life demands.

From this simple observation, one can quickly see that the success is assured if one can reverse the tide of losses and negative news that can surround any business. One should be able to counteract these negatives with correct actions swiftly (as discussed in the trends key) and move with ferocity and alertness to inform the rest of the group so that the team as a whole will reverse the tide and maintain its morale.

Handling negatives that life hands one in the business world is a science at its foundation and in fact has an exact methodology as dictated by the scientific principles. However, the application and implementation of the corrections that sciences hand out, is an art and depends on the individual's perseverance and his dedication to the goals and ideals and that he is pursuing!

"A smile is the lighting system of the face, the cooling system of the head and the heating system of the heart."

—Unknown

Positivity

"I can live for two months on a good compliment."
—Mark Twain (American Humorist, Writer and Lecturer,
1835-1910)

To understand positive activities in a business environment, we need to visualize a growing and viable activity where energetic, trained and positive people are dedicated to running that business.

From this wealth of positive energy, we inevitably get many positive byproducts including but not limited to:

1. Positive Communication, and
2. Positive Training.

These two factors breed:
    a. Positive Worker.
    b. Positive Executive.
    c. Positive Leadership.
    d. Positive Management.
    e. Positive Policy.

Having 1 and 2 above along with the accompanying factors (a-e above) as the main input to the system, leads us to generate several desirable products as the output:
    A. Positive service.
    B. Positive statistics condition.
    C. Positive cash reserve.
    D. High group morale.
    E. Personal sense of accomplishment and inner happiness.

Knowing the concept of positive activities and applying them on a constant basis in the work environment, will assure a higher degree of success, much to one's pleasure!

❧ ❧ ✳ ❀ ✖ ❀ ✳ ☙ ❧

Negativity

"All the great speakers were bad speakers at first"
—Ralph Waldo Emerson (American Poet, Lecturer and Essayist, 1803-1882)

To understand negative activities in a business environment, we need to visualize a downsizing and shrinking activity where lethargic, untrained and negative people are ruining that business.

From a negative and defeated attitude toward business and life, we inevitably get many negative byproducts including but not limited to:

1. Negative (or criticizing type of) Communication, and
2. Negative (or destructive type of) Training.

These two factors breed a:
  a. Negative Worker, who is very disorganized, is a time-waster and a non-producer.
  b. Negative Executive, who does not order his people and does not get things done.
  c. Negative Leadership, which applies to a leader who attacks his juniors and wants to make them wrong.
  d. Negative Management, which applies to a manager who does not want customers and dodges customer service.
  e. Negative Policy, which is counter-productive to the survival of the business.

Having 1 and 2 above along with the accompanying actions (a-e above) as the main input to the system, leads to the generation of several undesirable products as the output as follows:

A. **Negative service,** i.e., no or poor service and Products.

B. **Negative statistics condition,** i.e., things are getting worse than before.

C. **Negative cash reserve,** i.e., the business is getting into more debts.

D. **Low group morale,** i.e., the overall morale of the company is low and is accompanied by an attitude of doom and gloom.

E. **Personal sense of failure and no inner self-confidence,** i.e., the employees feel defeated with no future to live for because all is lost!

Knowing the concepts of negative activities and implementing methods to detect and eradicate them and then supplanting them with positive activities in the work environment, will assure a higher degree of success and longevity, to everyone's much delight!

Quizzes #13

Quiz 13.1

What is meant by **"Own or Borrow?"** Give an example.

What is meant by **"Ownership?"** Give an example for good and bad ownership.

What is meant by **"Cash Reserve?"** Give an example.

What is meant by **"Goals?"** Give an example.

What is meant by **"Targets?"** Give an example.

Quiz 13.2

What is meant by **"Plan of Action?"** Give an example.

What is meant by **"Happiness at Work?"** Give an example.

What is meant by **"Positivity?"** Give an example.

What is meant by **"Negativity?"** Give an example.

PART 14

The Timeless Principles of Business

The Sell-First Principle

"Procrastination is the thief of time."
Joseph Heller (1923 –1999), American satirical novelist

Before we proceed into specific actions and decisions on particular markets, let us briefly review the foundation of the Sell-First principle, which consists of the following five steps:

1. Use the *Ten Ultimate Keys* to create an organization, which
   a) Can produce a product.
   b) Do a quality assurance on the product to make sure it is exchangeable.
   c) Market the product to get a customer.
   d) Sell the product and obtain money in what is normally referred to as an equal exchange process.
   e) Collect the money and bank it.
   f) Make accurate records of the sales.
   g) Keep vital statistics related to production, sales, backlog, etc. for troubleshooting and improvements when needed.

These steps are not necessarily done in this order but the organization must be able to do all of these functions well and skillfully (this is **the Organization step**).

2. Having an organization in place, one needs to have a specific product in sight and make a few prototypes for demonstration and marketing purposes, but certainly

nothing in massive quantities yet (this is the **product in sight step**).

3. One needs to market and promote the product and find a suitable and qualified consumer who wants that specific product and makes a commitment to buy it (this is **the marketing and promotion step**).

4. Now and only now, we go ahead and produce the product in mass quantities, having already gotten the reassurance that there is a need for the product and that there is a commitment on the line (this is **the production step**).

5. The final step is to exchange the product and obtain the money and wherewithal to remain in business, pay the bills and salaries, improve the quality of the product, etc. (this is **the exchange step**).

If one only focuses on the exchange step and worry about the money aspects of the process and neglect the other four steps, one will surely go under in a short period of time and will fail utterly in the business. This is the mistake most failed businesses commit and never really make it big.

These five steps are all one needs to master and implement and he will be a howling success to the degree that he does employ these five principles in the sequence. His income will be so large where, humorously, he is forced to hire people to throw it overboard so as to make room for more, because there is so much of it coming in!

✻ 🙟 ✳ ❀ ✖ ❀ ✳ 🙞 ✻

The ABCD Principle of Investment

"The instinct of ownership is fundamental in man's nature"
—William James (American Philosopher, leader of the philosophical movement of Pragmatism, 1842-1910)

We need to understand the concept of investment as our society is very disoriented on its fundamental principles and a great many people are confused about its many facets.

The subject of investment has four main fundamental principles, which means that before we buy any asset we need to understand these four principles:

Principle #1 (A): Appreciating in time, that is to say the intended asset must have a growing equity as time goes on.

Principle #2 (B): Built-in Equity, that is to say that the asset must have an inherent or built-in equity, which in simple terms means that the asset should be bought below its market value. This really signifies that the *Book Value* (symbol: **BV**, the actual value of the asset as shown in account books and accurately represented by its net worth) is greater than its *Market Value* (symbol: **MV**, the current or prevailing price of the asset). Therefore, we can write:

BV > MV

Built-in Equity = BV - MV

For example, let us say a rental house is worth $200,000 in a normal market condition, that is to say, it takes $200,000 to build the house from scratch, using the current building materials price and the usual cost of labor. If there is a $40,000 tax lien against it (the liability component), then its book value (or net worth) is $160,000 (BV). However, its market value (the current price that you can purchase it) could be $100,000 (MV) due to temporary market downturn or bad economic conditions. Therefore, this asset has a $60,000 built-in equity, which makes it a 25% candidate for investment (1 out of 4 factors in the ABCD principle being present).

Principle #3 (C): Cash Flow, that is to say that the asset must produce a net positive cash flow, which in simple terms means that the gross income from the asset pays for all expenses plus a healthy profit. This gives one the ultimate staying power to outlast any economic cloud!

Principle #4 (D): Deductions & Depreciations, is the fourth element, which could be added to the above list for real estate assets or business assets for taxation purposes. This is considered to be definitely an added bonus, which can sweeten the investment pie greatly.

Conclusion: The most important element in investment is cash flow (C) and it is where we get the old maxim: *"Cash is King."* This is followed by the built-in equity (B), appreciation (A), and deduction/depreciation (D) factors, in that order, forming the CBAD sequence of importance!

ᵇ⁻ ℘ ✱ ✿ ✖ ✿ ✱ ℘ ᵇ⁻

The Ideal Investment Principle

"The art and science of asking questions is the source of all knowledge."   —Thomas Berger (1924-)
American Novelist

One can classify any investment into five possible categories based upon the ABCD principle:

I. The Ideal Investment, by definition, is an investment, which has all four components of the ABCD principle fully in.

An example is an apartment building:
a) Located in a medium to good location (i.e., appreciating).
b) Bought under market (i.e., having built-in equity).
c) Generating a positive cash flow and good rental upside (i.e., having a bright future of higher rents and potential appreciation due to the rent increases).
d) Having a great tax advantage, which creates good deductions and years of depreciation if managed and maintained well.

Definitely, such an investment has long-term connotations and should not be mismanaged or unloaded for short-term profit reasons.

II. The next tier down from an ideal investment would be **"An Excellent Investment,"** which is defined to be one that has at least three out of four in and the fourth one can be gotten in later or is not as crucial to the operation. This is an investment for medium to long-term holdings.

III. The next tier down from an excellent investment would be "**A Good Investment**," which is one that has at least two out of four in and the other two are not as crucial for the duration of investment. This is a definite short-term hold.

IV. The next tier down from a good investment would be "**A Poor Investment**," which is an investment that has only one out of the four and is missing the other three factors. It does not have all quadruple advantages of a) appreciating in time (i.e., growing equity), b) built-in Equity, c) cash flow, a net cash flow that is, and d) tax deduction and depreciation advantage.

The next tier down from a poor investment would be "**A Horrible Investment**," which is an investment that has none of the four and is missing on all cylinders. It does not have any of the quadruple advantages of the ABCD principle.

An example would be buying an expensive car from a dealer and on credit. Pulling the car out of the dealer's car lot would drop its price by about $5000 to $10,000, depending on the make and model of the car (a negative equity). Then there are monthly interest payments and general car maintenance and upkeep, which produce a negative cash flow. Then as time goes on it starts depreciating in value and not appreciating (i.e., a vanishing equity). Furthermore, it produces no tax advantages of any kind.

Another example is to buy raw land in the outskirts of town (in the suburbs) in an unincorporated part of town with the hope of it going up in value. This is a very speculative type of investment and is not left to amateurs but only to very savvy professionals. If incorrectly done, this is one of the bad investments or ownership moves one can make. Because it only has a hope factor built into it!

In general, raw land may be appreciating in time (i.e., gaining equity) only if it is in close proximity to a town, city, or civilization which creates a demand for it.

Furthermore, most banks and lenders do not provide loans on unimproved land, which makes it truly a dead asset! This type of investment is valid on a very long time frame but on a short term basis will drain the vital funds, which could otherwise be used for a triple play!

Also, a lot of salesmen, brokers, etc., try to cover up their selling intentions by telling the buyer "buy product X because it is a good investment." They present no facts of any kind, only rumors and innuendos and if one does not have his ABCDs of investment mastered, he would become easily a patsy in their hands and will be milked for every penny he has got!

The fact of the matter is that the moment you buy something, if you have not learned your ABCDs and the sell-first principle, you are going to expose yourself to major liabilities, maybe unknown to you at that moment, but surely present and waiting for its moment to pounce at you, your bank account and your life. It would be a time bomb ticking below the radar of your observation and someday will explode much to your chagrin!

Therefore, if an asset does not qualify or does not measure up to the quadruple play criteria, it is not worth buying into or investing in under any circumstances.

Therefore, the "Ideal Principle of Investment" is to have all or most of the four factors present before we even consider investing or buying:

a) Appreciation.

b) Built-in Equity.

c) Cash Flow (Positive).

d) Deduction.

The Sweet Spot Principle

By **"sweet spot,"** we mean *the zone of profitability and benefit in an activity.* Every investment has a "sweet spot" or a "profit zone," which must be kept in mind at all times while one is involved in that investment.

Identifying the sweet spot of an investment (or any activity) is essential and must be understood well before getting into that activity.

The sweet spot is intimately connected with an extremely important arena called the "sour spot" or "risk zone" of an activity. The risk zone must be accurately identified and defensive walls must be erected to prevent one from sliding into this zone. Along with that, definite precautionary measures must be installed to warn one well in advance of its occurrence or entrance.

Therefore, the **sweet spot principle** states that *to succeed in any business activity or investment, one must identify the "sweet spot" as well as "the sour spot" or the "the risk zone" well in advance and long before engaging in that activity. Furthermore, one must always operate the business in the sweet spot and never enter the risk zone.*

If the business conditions worsen, despite all of one's efforts and planning, to a point that one's asset is forced into the risk zone, then one must quickly reorganize and regroup and adjust his business activities so that it goes back into a new sweet spot.

Example #1: In the real estate world, the sweet spot is having a fully insured, well-maintained building in a good location, well managed with all paying tenants, which generates a healthy monthly income. If a tenant is delinquent, or if the building has deferred maintenance, then one is entering the risk zone. One should immediately handle the tenant and repair the building to put it back into the sweet spot.

Example #2: In the stock market, the sweet spot is owning a high-liquidity, uptrending and option-able stock. All of the stock shares should be fully insured by a long-term put option (a static). By selling, an out of the money call option (a kinetic), one generates a good monthly income as long as one stays in the sweet spot (please see below).

Example #3: If one is employed in a very thriving industry and there is much demand for his products, then one must identify the sweet spot of his business. This would be: a) one remains healthy and enthusiastic, b) one increases his knowledge base on a regular basis, c) one moves up in ranks and expands his sphere of influence, which is accompanied by d) an increase in one's salary as a result.

The risk zones are also there if one carefully looks at the scene. First, he can get sick and lose his physical or mental health in an accident. Then there are certain people who could dampen his spirits and take him down the unholy road and in the process either milk him through shady investments, lead him into unthinkable things such as taking drugs (medical or street, etc.), alcohol, etc. Then there are massive layoff threats and economic recessions that one could safely add to the list of risk zones.

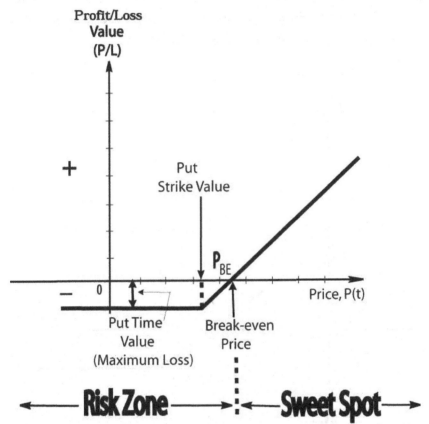

The Two Main Regions To Consider In Any Investment: A) Sweet Spot, B) Risk Zone.

If the stock experiences a severe correction or counter-trend and slides into the risk zone, one should be able to detect this shift in trend and do an "adjustment" by two possible ways:

a) move the put option lower and sell another call above the put's strike price, or

b) Create an active stop-loss order from the beginning and automatically sell the stock and thus disconnect from its negative force. However, one now keeps the existing put to create a new sweet spot as shown below.

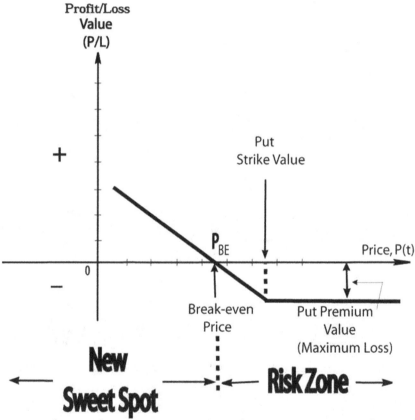

As the Market Moves Against One's Position, One Needs To Adjust and Establish A "New Sweet Spot" For Profitability.

☞~ℰᴆ✴❀✿❀✴ℭᴙ~☜

The Dynamic Investment Principle

The concepts of sweet spots and risk zones and constant adjustment of one's business or assets for profit as well as managing its affairs for maximum efficiency brings forth a whole new concept into view: "dynamic investment."

"Dynamic investment" is a new concept and is defined as *"vigorous and energetic management of one's business activities or investments, based upon one's expert knowledge and training and knowing a) how to constantly remain in the sweet spot, and b) how to shun entering the risk zone."*

This principle requires an investor to display constant alertness and watchfulness of his business activities and investments to a point that it is fully integrated into his day-to-day operation. This is done simply by either:
a) Correctly managing it for trend control-able assets, or
b) Making adjustments to his equity position for trend-controlled assets.

The Static-Kinetic Principle of Business

To come up with the ultimate principle of business in a logical fashion, we need to examine the scientific arena briefly for the underlying foundation.

Through a close observation of the physical universe we can see that every physical object or entity is composed of two parts:

a) *The consideration component, which is a "static" and unchanging.*

b) *The actual physical component, which is a "kinetic," meaning that it is moving constantly microscopically (on an atomic level), even if not macroscopically (on a large scale).*

Thus we see that "***Static and Kinetic***" form a neat pair in dichotomy in any existing physical object or entity.

In sciences, by static we mean something that is truly without motion or change, such as truth or a postulate. In physics, one may consider a very distant star (a physical universe object) a static on a short term basis, however, this is not totally correct because the distant star moves over a long period of time, thus is not truly a static in the strictest sense of the word, but only an approximation or a physical analogue of a true static in the thought universe.

By kinetic we mean a moving particle existing in a space, which is created by the static. However, *to have a kinetic we need to have a static first to set up the goal for the kinetic as well as the required space to place the energy particle (kinetic) in it.*

Therefore, we can conclude in a mathematical fashion *that a static is an independent variable, whereas a kinetic is a dependent variable deriving its existence wholly from the static that caused it.*

Borrowing this concept from the sciences, we define **static** in the business world as something, which is timeless and has a high degree of longevity, such as a stock, land, a well-structured building or a flourishing corporation, etc. In the same vein, we define a **kinetic** as something that its existence or value has temporal dependency and constantly changes with time, such as an option's premium (derived from the stock as the static), monthly payments for rental units (derived from the apartment complex), etc.

Employing these two newly defined concepts of static and kinetic, we can see that the following fundamental principle emerges in any viable business activity:

The *static-kinetic principle* in business involves the proper utilization of a static in conjunction with a kinetic to generate profit, much like an electric motor uses voltage (a static) and current (a kinetic) to generate power. The proper combination of static (the potential difference) and kinetic (the current flow) generates a large output power and consequently a profitable and solvent operation.

Therefore, we can see that the ultimate business principle consists of two steps:

1) *First, we have to create or establish a static.*

2) *Then and only then by bringing about a flow of particles and time sensitive actions (a kinetic) within the confines of the created static we can create a business activity that will generate power and profit. The static forms the centerpiece, the hub, or the stable datum around which all other time dependent activities revolve.*

"In the end, we will remember not the words of our enemies, but the silence of our friends."

—Martin Luther King, Jr. (1929-1968)
American Baptist Minister and Civil-Rights Leader

The Base of the Motor Principle

It is a well-known principle in electrical engineering that to generate *energy or power* we need to cause two factors:

a) Create an electrical potential or pressure (called voltage) between two opposite poles (positive and negative terminals).

b) Create a flow of electricity (called an electrical current) between the two poles by connecting them to the electrical load by wires.

What is seldom (or almost never) talked about is the positioning of the two opposite electrical poles and fixing or fastening them in space in such a way that they never move relative to each other or the surrounding wires, which connect them to the load. This is an absolute requirement that very few scientists have paid attention to and up to now have actually taken it for granted.

Positioning of these two opposite terminals at a certain fixed distance on a platform (the base of the motor) requires an exterior force, the designer of the machine who forces this initial requirement and mandates it without question, right at the outset. Without this initial and deliberate act of setting up the base of the motor in place, there would be no two fixed terminals, no voltage, no current and consequently no power generated.

This observation is extremely important, since it tells us that to create power we need first a stable and fixed structure (the base of the motor). Then and only then, we can place and affix two opposite terminals in close proximity to each other on the base, in such a way as to let them discharge against each other in the form of a current and a subsequent release of energy.

This concept is so essential in life that without it nothing seems to work at all. Let us take a car, the engine is fixed solidly to the chassis, which then allows the spark plugs at fixed locations create a spark and move the pistons up and down and thus generate power.

This concept is so pervasive that it applies to all appliances, motors, batteries, pumps, etc. Even a human body (a kinetic) needs to be at the command of a very highly stable personality (a static), one with huge personal space, in order to thrive and generate power through the motion of its organs. Hostile forces shake up the moment the space of the being inhabiting the body, and then the body unstabilizes, gets sick and quickly loses power.

We can apply this principle with great benefit in the business arena. By a simple observation, we can see that in the business world, the two opposite terminals in the above electrical analogy are: the consumer (negative terminal) and the producer (positive terminal). These two need to be put near each other (as done in the market place) in order for them to go into exchange of goods and services for money and thus generate financial power and wealth.

The base of the motor of course is the organization, which with the **"product in sight"** (prototyped but not mass produced) gets into marketing and promotion of it, procures a paying customer thus places the first terminal (the consumer) near the proximity of the producer (the second opposite terminal). Then another arm of the organization gets engaged in the production of the product, which closes the gap between the producer and the consumer, thus allowing the exchange process to be completed. All along, the organization as a whole, acting as the base of the motor, is aiding and abetting the vital flow of goods, services and money to take place.

Without the organization acting as "the base of the motor" there would never be any generated power, because it engages in the following vital steps that only an organization can perform:

a) First, searches and finds a qualified consumer through marketing and promotion (this requires an organization).

b) Second, creates and trains a producer into existence who can produce the advertised product, creating a potential difference of opposite polarity to that of the consumer (this also requires an organization).

c) Third, allows the exchange process (product out the door and money coming in) to take place and thus create a sensible economy and enormous prosperity for the group (this also requires an organization). This is shown on the next page.

Any violations of these three vital steps or any alteration of the sequence of the actions in these steps would be disastrous and would bring about a lowered exchange rate, a reduced prosperity and a lack of viability for the group as a whole.

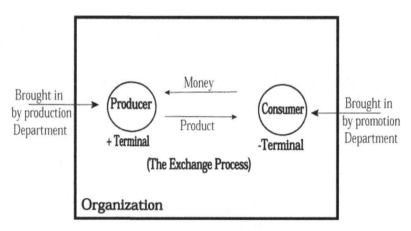

The Base Of The Motor Principle.

Prime the Pump Principle

"Determine never to be idle. No person will have occasion to complain of the want of time, who never loses any. It is wonderful how much may be done, if we are always doing."

— Thomas Jefferson

To **prime** means *to supply water to a pump*. A pump is a device used to move fluids and gases such as water, oil, etc. The pump is a suction valve that had to be primed with water so that the pump would function properly. The term "priming the pump" is derived from the operation of older pumps positioned on a well opening, wherein one had to pour water into it initially, and then by expending effort such as by moving the handle up and down, one could extract water. In other words, one had to put water into the pump first before one could extract a stream of water through the pumping process.

If we take this simple concept into investing, we start seeing the panoramic view of life, that is to say, one must supply knowledge, enthusiasm and vitality (initial supplied water) into the pump of life plus effort and energy (up and down motion of the handle) before one can expect any return in terms of prosperity and financial affluence.

This is a far more important concept that anyone has ever conceived before, far beyond the old cliché, "no pain, no gain!"

Priming the pump, as a fundamental life principle, is such an encompassing and essential concept that most people are vaguely familiar with its deep roots; even those who know it, they do not know it good enough to apply it in their lives and investments.

Let us take a few examples at this juncture, to clarify the utter importance of this underlying principle in all of life actions.

For example, if one is in a relationship with his spouse or close friends, then obviously he expects to be treated nice and friendly by the other party. Such an expectation is often met by a lot of disappointments, primarily because one is not applying this principle well. He has to start priming the pump of life, be nice and courteous, and show respect toward all people including one's spouse. Sooner than later, the pump of life will start flowing the water of respect and kindness toward one in many ways and on many unforeseen levels.

Another example is in the investment arena. This is where an investor's first encounter in the stock market is perhaps with a broker who promises him wealth and riches if one opens an account in the broker's firm and follow his recommendations. One's natural expectation is to learn from the broker and become an expert trader in the process. His high aspirations and hopes are dashed in no time after heavy losses and revelations that the broker is just a pseudo-mentor, an order-taker, posing as a teacher and is using one as a patsy to line his own pocket. One would soon find out that the broker is actually a failed investor and his knowledge in the investment arena is no more than a bean counter's abacus, far below what is needed to survive the investment arena!

At first glance, one's rude introduction to the investment arena may seem very unfair, however, upon close observation one finds out that it is all based upon the violation of the "prime the pump principle."

If one wants to be truly an investor, one simply has to prime the pump in several ways:

a) Learn the fundamental principles of investment, which are: the *sell-first principle, the ABCD principle, the sweet spot principle, the dynamic investment principle, the static-kinetic principle, prime the pump principle, fly with the eagles principle*, etc.

b) Have an adequate initial investment capital to start an account with sufficient money so that one is not forced to make irrational and panicky actions.

c) Learn the mechanics of trading by paper trading first.

d) Learn to read charts and indicators well.

e) Learn and develop sound trading strategies that incorporates the principles outlined in part (a).

f) Learn to become one's own consultant and thus bypass the use of any broker's advice in your trading plan.

g) Know the ten ultimate keys in this book well enough to establish self as a business professional with good communication lines, good trend reading ability, good ethics presence and a good organization to support one adequately.

h) Trade only one-lot trades (100 shares of stock or one contract of options) until he can handle larger number of shares of stock or option contracts with confidence.

i) Master steps (a-h) above extremely well, so that one can enter the trading or investment arena with a sound foundation to extract investment water from the pump of the markets, and without being used as a patsy in the hands of others.

The Patsy Principle

"Only the educated are free."

—Epictetus (55 – 135 AD)
Greek Philosopher

A *patsy* by definition *is someone who is naive and gullible and thus can easily be deceived, cheated and victimized.*

The world of investment is run on the shoulders of many of the gullible investors who are brought into the playing field by brokers, investment seminars, cold callers, etc. and turned into patsies for the benefit of many financial predators, for a limited time until their money runs out.

There are professional investors, market makers, speculators and patsies. It could be said that patsies finance the livelihood and lifestyle of the bigger and more savy investors.

The concept of patsy is well explored by the slave master and the unscrupulous individual who is willing to sell your soul to the devil to make his living and he does not even care about what happens to you as a patsy. The fact that you lost all of your money by getting mixed up with him and his business proposition is totally accidental and besides the point! He chalks it up to your bad judgment and figures that it was your decision for all of these bad financial moves anyhow that led you to lose all of your capitals.

When the patsy loses, the financial manipulator (or the patsy consultant) heavily discounts the fact that he supplied the method and all the information that led one to make all those bad decisions. Obviously, it appears so but in actuality it was one's decisions based upon the consultant's bad information and one's own naiveté and gullibility that led one to trust him and think that he is working in one's best interest, while he was being milked one all the way and they did not even care!

The consultant is only worried about himself. He is truly a self-centered individual who will sacrifice anything and anyone on his way to make the financial wealth that he so desires. He is looking for a starry-eyed patsy to supply the cash.

If we understand this simple concept and pour it into the investing arena, we start seeing the panoramic view of financial markets more clearly: the markets, the charlatan consultant or broker, and the patsy. It should not be like this at all, but mostly it is so in this modern day and age of sophisticated thievery!

The cure for this unfortunate condition is relatively simple but not easy. One needs to:

1. Never use brokers as consultants, because they are mostly failed investors.

2. Learn the basics and fundamentals of the business from a knowledgeable and expert person who acts as one's coach and has no vested interest in his teachings.

3. Develop a high understanding of the subject and know all of the precise definitions of all relevant terminology by consulting a dictionary and clearing up all areas of misunderstandings.

4. Find a niche in the market and apply the data to that niche market.

5. Practice under close supervision of a coach who can provide constructive and positive corrections.

6. Continue to practice daily, drill amply and learn until one is an expert.

7. Achieve such an expert knowledge through drills and practice that one becomes his own consultant and never again a patsy.

Therefore, the moral of the story is: "Become educated so that you will never be a patsy!"

⊶ ℘ ✶ ✿✗✿ ✶ ℃ ⊶

Know Thy People Principle

"Don't waste your time with explanations; people only hear what they want to hear."

— Paulo Coelho Brazilian (1947-), lyricist and novelist.

To be successful in life or business, one needs to know the people that surround him in any life situation, work condition or business scenario. People involved in any activity are important and knowing who they are, and what their basic traits and characteristics are, is an essential tool for survival.

To simplify our analysis, we resort to an analogy in the world of birds. As will be seen this will help us greatly to simplify and understand this complicated subject better.

Just to name a few of the more significant birds, we note that there are several that play a big role in our day to day activity and are very relevant to our work, as follows:

a) **Vultures.**

b) **Vampire bats.**

c) **Hawks.**

d) **Owls.**

e) **Turkeys.**

f) **Eagles.**

Vultures are birds of prey that eat the flesh of dead animals. This type of bird could easily represent the characteristics of someone who is greedy and ruthless. Someone who would prey upon one's misfortune and would be happy and actually benefit when one fails in life or business.

Vampire bats are flying nocturnal mammals that drink the blood of other live animals in order to survive. This class of animals does not quite fit the definition of a bird but since they fly we use them to illustrate our point further. These animals represent people that take lifeblood out of another's hopes, dreams and make nothing out of one's aspirations and leave one in a total chaos, shambles, mental apathy and in an invalidated state.

Then there are **hawks**, which are birds of prey that have keen sights and hunt during the daytime. If a hawk would be representing a type of personality, it would be someone who preys on others and has a warlike and hostile attitude when resolving problems.

Owls are nocturnal birds of prey that hunt at night. They are famous for being quiet and noiseless when flying. They stay up at night and sleep during the day. It would represent someone who stays up late at night habitually to do work, to finish a project, read a book, etc. However, more importantly, it could be the kind of predatory people such as thieves and robbers as well as gang members who attack at night and act very quietly to victimize their preys.

Then there are **turkeys**, which are mostly domesticated birds and are raised and used for food. If turkey would be representing a class of personalities, it would be people who usually fail, have low persistence level, and are ignorant and very defenseless.

Finally, there are **eagle**s, which are birds of prey noted for their large size, great strength, great powers of flight and vision. An eagle type personality would be a strong-willed individual who is a great visionary and has a tremendous power of leadership coupled with a great strength to guide his group in any chosen field of endeavor.

This principle states *that to survive in any activity in the business world, one must know the people involved in that activity to such a great extent that he knows their motives and intentions well in advance of the display of their actual actions.*

Therefore, the moral of the story is to know your people well in advance of doing business with them.

Fly With the Eagles Principle

There is an old saying that expresses the powerful fact that "If one wants to fly like an eagle, then one needs to hang around the eagles."

This statement at first glance appears to be more like a worn-out cliché, however, if one explores it further its truth becomes evident. One soon finds out that it is one of the best principles that one can follow in business or life.

Part of the problem is that one's awareness must encompass many other types of birds that exist and need to be avoided. Therefore, one needs to be highly trained to identify such birds and needs to raise his awareness tremendously in this arena before one is considered a savvy businessman.

Considering the classes of birds studied so far, one can see that eagles and turkeys are diametrically opposite to each, a form of duality in their nature, decision-making power and lifestyle.

Exploring this duality concept would allow us further to examine life and the business world in more depth. This means that one has to know where the turkey's habitats are to stay away from and never mingle with, so that their contagious bad habits never have a chance to transfer over to one's life!

The obvious reasons of staying away from turkeys are three folds:

a) First, turkeys can't fly,

b) Second, they have this self-created and yet erroneous notion of "how they know it all" as well as "how they know best how to survive in life," which makes them totally unteachable, and

c) Third, they are usually somebody else's meal.

To survive this world's many camouflaged traps, one needs to be an eagle. Period. So one needs to develop oneself into an eagle in a short order of time before one gets gobbled up by other birds of prey!

Furthermore, one needs to recognize that *"he is sitting on a gold mine,"* but his unawareness of it causes him to look elsewhere for gold!" One needs to develop or learn the tools he needs to use in order to first survey the mine and then using proper tools tap into the gold vein and create enormous wealth for self and others in the process, without ever consulting the uninformed turkeys of this world for advice or guidance!

One needs to develop habits and a personality style, which is based upon the following observations:
a) Eagles have a great size and strength,
b) They have a great power of perception, and
c) More importantly, they can fly high, and be in a position well above it all and as a result have a better view of things and thus make better decisions!

This principle if used correctly in one's life would prove invaluable. The following examples are applicable here:

a) If one wants to be a millionaire (an eagle), he would not try to learn from almost-solvent people much less seek their mentorship. The list of such people could include such people as his financially challenged parents, teachers, counselors, or even his needy friends and peers. Instead, he should talk to and associate with millionaires and other successful people.

b) If one desires to be prosperous and affluent (an eagle), then one needs not to hang around or associate with people who constantly invalidate and make him wrong for having high dreams (vampire bats). He should cut these vampires loose and seek educators and the best experts to guide him toward affluence.

c) If one wants to become the best in his field of study or a desired sport, then he should stop listening to people who have a vested interest in his failure such as a jealous neighbor or an envious associate (vultures). He should seek and hire high quality coaches and good counselors who have his best interest at heart.

d) If one aspires to achieve great heights in life, then one should pay no attention to or seek a gang member's blog or advice on the internet or a thief's latest adventure or scoop in ragtag magazines or rumor lines (Owls). Instead, he should steer his ship to positive dreamers who are achieving their goals every day and have a plan of action.

This principle states *that to succeed in life only hang around and associate with the eagles of life for maximum leverage and benefit and do not allow any other birds to come nearby in order to poison one's thinking well, thus saving oneself plenty of future grief*!

Therefore, this work is intended for the eagles of this world and intends to turn them into super eagles; a new species of birds that is more intelligent and much superior to any existing breed!

Therefore, the moral of the story is to fly with the eagles and neither scratch with the turkeys of this world, nor associate with or seek advice from vampire bats, vultures, hawks or owls of life or the business world .

Shun the Negative Principle

"As if you could kill time without injuring eternity"
— Henry David Thoreau

To *shun* means, *"to deliberately avoid."* This concept heavily leans toward an intentional act on one's part not wanting actively to go near something, like intentionally avoiding a contagious disease.

Today, we live in a world with many communication channels, which are capable of enormous information transfer at a rapid rate. Use of satellite communication systems, fiber optics telecommunication systems along with RF (Radio Frequency) and microwave communication towers and links have created an interwoven information network that can transmit, relay and receive high quantities of information extremely fast. They can transfer video or voice from any point on the globe to another at practically a blink of an eye.

With the advent of internet and rapid availability of information in many ways and form (such as video, audio, data, etc.), we as a species of Homo sapiens (modern man) have emerged into uncharted territory.

The speed of transfer of information has put us at the threshold of extremely new problems, which has totally changed the scope and dimensions of the game of life. What this means is that we could potentially be bombarded with an avalanche of bad news at such a great speed, primarily of an alarming and threatening nature, get zapped by its vicious negative mental force, and experience an enormous stress in a short order of time, and never really know what happened.

So it should not be any great surprise for any one of us to find our lives and sanity at the mercy of such highly sensationalized wicked information that can traverse large distances, thanks to father of modern wave theory, James Clerk Maxwell!

Even though Maxwell never imagined his mathematics and brilliance in proposing the wave theory be put to such an abhorring purpose, yet here we are and can't help it but be rained on everyday with the bad news pouring out of the news media which have taken our communication system hostage for their own unholy purposes. We are the targets of this unpleasant and wicked information outpour that is endlessly generated by the merchants of chaos.

Therefore, in this modern age, it becomes one's urgent duty to guard against this torrent of the most sordid and gruesome acts and completely shun the arrival of such data through any and all news outlets, such as newspapers, internet, TV, radio, magazines, etc. Even if one stumbles upon such data by total accident, he should immediately shut off the source.

To think that one needs to be curious and receive information of any kind, especially bad, is pure folly! Just to allow any set of unpalatable information to arrive at one's mental doorstep is a pure act of treason toward one's sanity and future welfare. It is equivalent to drinking from a water well, which is poisoned with radioactive waste materials. Extremely toxic! The result is a slow but sure death of sanity and consciousness.

There is no real truth in the bloody car accidents, terrorist attacks, piles of train wrecks and tales of gruesome mayhem and murder. These all sap your mental power and dull your wits.

There is no actual truth to the heavily jazzed up news that someone miscontrolled his car and fell off a bridge. It is just an instance of bad or no control over his car and environment. Alternatively, the news that someone had a fight with his neighbor, pulled a gun, shot him, and then killed himself. This is just a datum about someone's inability to communicate. It simply shows his lack of ability to conduct a healthy level of communication with another person and now to focus on this inability and make news out of it is quite destructive of the society's morale as a whole. There are millions of such instances of bad and negative communications that are constantly pumped into the society. The road to truth does not travel through negativity.

The road to truth strictly lies in the realm of positivity, in the ability to communicate, in the firm and decisive control of one's tools of work, in one's honesty and sincerity toward his friends, in all of the positive traits of a human being usually called virtues. That is where we find truth. In other words, there is no truth in untruth, so one should stop looking where there is none!

One will never find it in the trash heap of accidents and negativity of life, where up to now, we have been misguidedly directed to look, much to our chagrin and at the expense of our future prosperity.

Therefore, **"Shun the Negative Principle"** *consists of three parts:*
  a) *Handle the negatives and problems of life by actively helping those who are in dire need and actually seek one's advice and want assistance to resolve their problems.*

  b) *Do not actively search for and receive negative information of any kind. This really means that one should really shun all types of negative information about a "so and so crime" or a "such and such accident" or the latest "belittling rumor or scandal" about a star or political figure or anyone else!*

  c) *Do not actively transmit or relay negative information of any kind to anyone else. This really means that one should not make a big production of negative things that happens to one and play the victim's role, rather try to resolve problems amicably with the other party.*

Using this principle one completely filters out the negative and allows only the positive to be received. This is an active filtering process and should never be forgotten as job one, which is usually left out of the equation of life and livingness!

Therefore, always shun the negative side of life and never relay it to anyone else either as a point of interest; because at that moment one has strayed away from the truth into the labyrinth of toxic waste!

This opens the door to one main thing: *dwell upon the positive side of life, on solutions, on positive control, on good communication, honesty, kindness, compassion, love, admiration, dignity and respect.*

Therefore, the moral of the story is three-folds:
a) Handle own life's problems effectively and assist those who need and ask for help,
b) Seek or receive no toxic waste, and
c) Generate or relay no negativity.

Sell to Survive
or
Create to Sell?

There is an enigma and a considerable amount of confusion in life as well as the business world as to which course of action is best to follow:

a) Sell to survive , or

b) Create to sell.

Even though most businessmen tend to go into sales because it seems easier and more lucrative, however, it is an apparency. If one is not well-versed in the ten keys of this work and does not have a well of enthusiasm, he will soon find himself burnt out and ending up disliking the profession and his lifestyle altogether.

Obviously, one cannot survive just selling things on a robotic and mechanical basis, hoping that he will earn a huge salary as some top salesman do. If money is the objective, he is in the wrong profession as selling is far different than earning a paycheck.

Truth be told, one must be a lifelong salesman and cultivate strong traits of a genius in himself to start seeing success and prosperity.

If one realizes that:

a) Every time he talks to someone as a teacher or friend, he is selling his ideas; or

b) Every time he is engaging in an activity with another human being he is selling and buying at the same time; or

c) Every time he makes a decision to do something, he has to sell himself on it first and then his team, or

d) Every time he recommends a product, represents a company he is selling self and the company to the client, or

e) Every time he convinces a customer to buy product "X," he is putting his credibility on the line and is actually selling his knowledge of the marketplace to the client, then it should be amply evident that the business of selling is not limited to just the salesman but to every living thing on the planet, whether plants, animals or human beings.

To keep a plant in a healthy and thriving condition, it must be fertilized and irrigated regularly. However, it must sell itself to its owner first before any of this happens. The selling action on part of the plant is actually a creative activity and takes place in terms of producing new flowers, new leaf growths or providing shade for the owner.

Similarly, for someone to keep an animal as a pet, it must sell itself in terms of its usefulness and companionship to its keeper first; otherwise, it will find itself in the homeless animal shelter. Again, the selling action is in terms of creation such as home protection, loyalty, carrying loads, producing dairy or meat, or cute acts of entertainment for the owner.

This concept easily extends to the human affairs and can be easily observed in the business world.

Therefore, the business of life requires us to be a salesman at the core of our existence. Whatever we do in life or business is a creation at its basic foundation, whether as a buyer, a talker, a doer, a motivator, etc., which needs to be sold to others successfully.

It is interesting to note that we need to have the intention to sell really well on many levels in order to be prosperous. This is important to understand because our created actions, sayings and emanations are constantly being sold to the world around us willy-nilly with quite a bit of ramifications on other people, so it is best that we make it good and positive.

In the final analysis, the degree of our success in the business of life or commerce alike depends upon:

a) The degree other people believe in us and buy our products (i.e., ideas, actions, persuasions, decisions, etc.).

b) The degree others see a benefit in their own lives through using our products.

c) The degree that one is sold on his products in the first place and believes in its rightness with such a high level of self-convinced-ness that spurs him to continue creating it.

Therefore, the moral of the story is: **"do not sell just to survive, but be so self-convinced, credible** and knowledgeable about the product you are selling, whether it is an idea, an object or a project, that people can't help but to buy you first and along with that your created product"

⊷ℰ✳❀✳❀✳ℜ⊷

Quizzes #14

Quiz 14.1

What is meant by "**The Sell-First Principle?**" Give an example.

What is meant by "**The ABCD Principle of Investment?**" Give an example.

What is meant by "**The Ideal Investment?**" Give an example.

What is meant by "**The Static-Kinetic Principle of Business?**" Give an example.

What is meant by "**The Base of the Motor Principle?**" Give an example.

Quiz 14.2

What is meant by "**Prime the Pump Principle?**" Give an example.

What is meant by "**The Patsy Principle?**" Give an example.

What is meant by "**Know Thy People Principle?**" Give an example.

What is meant by "**Fly with the Eagles Principle?**" Give an example.

What is meant by "**Shun the Negative Principle?**" Give an example.

Which one is more important "**Sell to Survive or Create to Sell?**" Why? Give an example.

PART 15

Advanced Business Principles

The Bright Phases Shining on the Business Radar

"What men want is not knowledge, but certainty."

— Bertrand Russell (1872-1970)
English Logician and Philosopher

There are certain patterns of existence (or Phases) in a business activity, which shows health along the road to success and therefore knowing them well will put it on the business radar.

More precisely by "phase" we mean *a pattern of existence or a state of occurrence or beingness, which is one of the changing states or stages of development of something such as a business entity's income, a factory's production level, etc.*

These phases or patterns of existence form a subset in the bigger arena of trends of the market one is involved in intimately. When properly identified and exactly followed according to its handling method, one will create expansion and viability and will lead a company out of the quagmire of confusion and ultimate demise, which is so common in the small business arena!

The **bright or positive phases** or patterns of existence in a business activity will start one's company or activity from the ground floor up and on the road to success. These **positive phases** are all in the uptrending pattern and can have many angles for their trend line starting from a low positive angle (around 5 degrees) to a high positive angle (80 degrees)

Even though these patterns are primarily applied to a business organization in this work, they could equally be applied to any other entity such as *an individual's life, a government's activity, a nation's production, etc.*

The Dim Phases Fading from the Business Radar

"If I have lost confidence in myself, I have the universe against me."

—Ralph Waldo Emerson (1803-1882)
American Essayist

There are dim phases or patterns of existence (or **Negative Phases**) in a business activity, which are fading from the business radar and if not handled properly, one will soon find his business enterprise below the ground floor of existence. These dim phases must be climbed out rather quickly before one can be considered to be a viable activity by the society.

Thus, the road to success does not always start at the ground floor but sometimes in the basement; knowing these unhealthy phases well will put an organization, eventually, on the business radar.

These patterns of existence, as will be seen shortly, are dim or negative Phases and when properly identified and exactly followed according to its formula will pull one out of the lower dredges of existence and will gradually put one at the doorstep of the first viable and bright phase on the business radar!

Following the pattern's formulas will pull one's company or activity out of the basement into the ground floor and on the road to success. These **negative phases**, are all in the downtrending pattern and can have many negative angles for their trend line starting from a low negative angle (around -5 degrees) to a high negative angle (around -80 degrees)

Even though these phases are primarily applied to a business organization in this work, they could equally be applied to any other entity such as an individual, a relationship, a marriage, a government, a nation, etc.

The Black Phases Submerged Below the Business Radar

"All religions, arts and sciences are branches of the same tree. All these aspirations are directed toward ennobling man's life, lifting it from the sphere of mere physical existence and leading the individual towards freedom."

—Albert Einstein (1879-1955)
German Born American Physicist, Nobel Prize in 1921

If one does not stop the slide in one's business stats and it keeps fading from the business radar, it will eventually disappear from the radar altogether and one's company will be nonexistent but completely. This is where one potentially can enter a whole new underground world below the business radar if one is not quite vigilant about his operations and his ultimate role in life!

Failing the negative phases, one enters the **black phases** of a business. Even though such black phases are hard to visualize for most logical and savvy business-oriented people, however, it is relatively easy to grasp that there are certain business activities, which have aligned themselves quite opposite to life.

These activities are created by groups, which form a minority in our society (about 20%) but engage in very dangerous activities and are quite destructive of the moral fiber of the remaining 80% of the society. Examples of such groups are: terrorist groups, thieves, human traffickers, drug dealers and pushers, gun smugglers, war

452   Advanced Principles of Success & Prosperity

mongers, white-collar criminals, pornographers, prostitutes, slave masters, psychiatrists, so on and so forth. These can have the same patterns of existence in terms of trends and trend lines as discussed earlier. However, we need to alter the definition and the concept of "business activity," dramatically in order to consider their work as production; because what they are doing is truly not business in the strictest sense of the word. Even though they may have a different think on their production, but we know that their product is extremely subpar and not worthy of exchange even though they are getting paid for their products and services!

"Great ideas often receive violent opposition from mediocre minds."

—Albert Einstein (1879-1955)
German Born American Physicist, Nobel Prize in 1921

These undesirable **black phases** can be roughly subdivided into four general echelons:

1. **Small-Scale Destruction (SSD) Phase:** This is a low to mild level of betrayal to mankind and life, done randomly and not affecting many such as pick-pocketing, shoplifting, prostitution, etc.

2. **Medium-Scale Destruction (MSD) Phase**: This is a medium level of betrayal to mankind and life; the organized and planned actions (no longer random) are done against specific groups with the intention of destroying the intended groups (defined as enemies from their viewpoint). These actions include terrorism, white-collar crimes destroying a major firm from inside, computer hacking stealing vital information, creating computer viruses that paralyzes a business sector or a

whole company, organized mobs trafficking illegal goods, etc.

3. **Large-Scale Destruction (LSD) Phase:** This is a high level of betrayal to mankind and life; the general actions are done on a massive level toward the destruction of specific races, certain religions, or nations with the intention of eliminating a large class of people. Examples are many but a few would serve: American psychiatrists mass drugging the children of a whole nation in the name of "curing" some invented disease, German psychiatrists who incited Hitler into destroying millions of Jews in the late 30's to mid 40's, war-mongering politicians tumbling down nations and destroying millions of lives in the process, genocide promoters, so on and so forth.

4. **Very Large-Scale Destruction (VLSD) Phase:** This is the highest level and the ultimate betrayal to man and life; the general actions done against mankind include extremely large sectors of life and large chunks of the physical universe. Examples include such things as nuclear bombing of a whole country or continent, blowing up a whole planet, contaminating the water supply of a whole nation, biological warfare on a global level, etc.

Thus, the road to success does not always start at the ground floor or even the basement but sometimes in the depth of a dungeon 50 feet deep below the basement!

Knowing these unhealthy phases well and following the keys laid out in this book, if followed diligently, will eventually put an organization on the business radar and align it toward prosperity.

Even though these phases of existence are primarily applied to a business organization in this work, it could

454 Advanced Principles of Success & Prosperity

equally be applied to any other entity such as an individual, a relationship, a marriage, a government, a nation, etc.

To sum, there are five positive phases, five negative phases and four black or betrayal phases in the entire existence. It is rather obvious that morality is out in the four betrayal types of activities and the business model is upside own in a major way as the involved group members are being guided by a false mentor or an evil-intentioned leader, and therefore are operating in an inverted pyramid mode, which exists below the zero line.

The Figure on the next page depicts these phases of existence more accurately in a nutshell.

"It has become appallingly obvious that our technology has exceeded our humanity."

—Albert Einstein (1879-1955)
German Born American Physicist, Nobel Prize in 1921

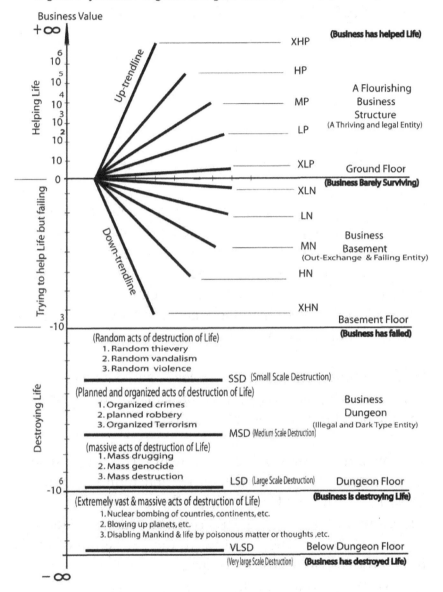

The panoramic view of types of business relative to Life.

Positive Energy

"Always laugh when you can. It is cheap medicine."

—Lord Byron (1788-1824)
English Romantic Poet and Satirist

One of the best ways to excel in life is to surround oneself with people who exhibit and exude positive energy.

By positive energy environment, we mean an environment where one is constantly validated without any hint of negativity or criticism. It is an environment of deep respect, acknowledgement and validation for one's presence and existence as a spiritual being. As it turns out, one's general state of happiness and mental well-being is a direct outcome of such an environment.

In such a state, one will grow by leaps and bounds and will start to develop and create extraordinary products beyond one's wildest dreams and imaginations.

This would be an ideal environment, like a microwave oven, where the energy will grow and multiply quickly, creating a bonfire of enthusiasm. An environment where any correction is no longer a criticism or an invalidation, but a positive learning step toward the perfection of one's final product, a necessary ingredient in the process of achievement of one's goal.

One's self-confidence grows enormously and one becomes such a powerhouse that nothing can stop its forward momentum.

☞ ℘ ✳ ✿ ✖ ✿ ✳ ℜ ☜

Negative Energy

"Our limitations and success will be based, most often, on our own expectations for ourselves. What the mind dwells upon, the body acts upon."

—Denis Waitley (1933-)
American Motivational Speaker and Author of Self-Help Books

In the process of survival on a daily basis on earth, one often finds oneself the target of much criticism and censure toward which one soon develops much resistance and sensitivity.

Truth be told, this type of activity is the byproduct of a negative environment and negative energy, where one is dealing with people who are so stressed out and unhappy in their own lives that they will burst into anger at the drop of a pin!

The basic components creating a negative environment generating lots of negative energy are a few, but can be summarized as:

1. Unhappy, out-ethics, belligerent and destructive individuals infiltrating the group and taking on key executive posts.

2. Production stats crashing at an alarming rate due to no or worse yet false reports.

3. The activity's fabric is decaying and falling apart due to poor management decisions, along with irresponsible and criminal leaders.

4. The morale of the group, as a whole, is down and group members are blaming each other, denying their own causation in activities, which should be under their control.

5. People in the group cannot trust each other and are not honest in their communications or actions. This means that lots of criminals are running around in the group committing crimes, terrorizing and destroying the remainder of the group. These unsavory and foul activities happen on a daily basis without anyone reporting or claiming responsibility for any of them.

6. One of the symptoms of negative environments is the use of drugs of all types and forms, legal or illegal drugs! It quickly becomes quite rampant and soon becomes the panacea for all problems: physical, mental and spiritual!

A perfect example is in the mental health industry, where the patient walks in and complains about a certain problem; the psychiatrist's solution is immediate invalidation of "it is only in your mind," or "you are imagining it," so on and so forth, followed by a strong mental drug "to cure" the problem. This acts as a further invalidation of the patient's reality and drives him further into apathy. He will soon find himself addicted to the drug with the original problem numbed out of existence, and now replaced with a new one, i.e., the drug dependency. The psychiatrist's "solution" leaves the patient in physical disarray and makes him feel negated and usually regretful for having talked to "the doctor." This is a *legalized negative environment* created and based upon false authority, totally designed to ruin the person's reality and sanity!

In such an environment, lots of backstabbing and dirty tricks are played on the group members to a point of jeopardizing one's sanity and endangering one's ethical standards. One's nerves are constantly on edge, and one's character is usually sabotaged and humored. One's actions are constantly criticized, invalidated and corrected harshly!

In such an environment, one usually shrinks in size and his personal ability is reduced to a point of utter disbelief in self as a being, and eventually one loses his self-confidence altogether in a short period of time!

Macroeconomics

"Only the educated are free."

—Epictetus (55 – 135 AD)
Greek Philosopher

We know **economics** is the *science of production, distribution and consumption of goods and services produced. As a science, it perforce deals with the material aspects of life and studies the problems of capital, labor, wages, prices, taxes, etc.* It is derived from Greek *"oikos"* (house), *"nomos"* (managing), which adds up to *"management of a house."*

The English dictionary defines **macroeconomics** as a *branch of economics dealing with the broad and general aspects of an economy, or all the forces on a large scale at work in an economy, or with the interrelationship of large sectors, as in total employment, investment or income of a country as a whole. In other words, economics dealing with the controlling factors in the economy as a whole.*

We have to modify and further refine this concept of macroeconomics, to make it more understandable for our work. This can be done by realizing that there are visible things that one can detect and see with the naked eye and these things when exchanged whether on a household scale, a national or global scale could be called **macroeconomic**s or the economy *on a macroscopic scale!*

Therefore, in this work we have broadened the definition of **macroeconomics** to mean *the exchange of goods and services on a visible level, done in the macroscopic universe.*

For example, one sees a car created and sold, a fruit produced and consumed, a haircut done and exchanged for money, a nation drilling and selling oil to another country, so on and so forth. These are all visible things and one can directly see and experience them. The exchange principle is visibly at work on a visible or macro-scale!

There is another complementary and yet extremely essential aspect to macroeconomics, which has to be understood in its purity before this subject can make sense. This subject, of course, is **microeconomics** and will be discussed next.

Microeconomics

"Begin to see yourself as a soul with a body rather than a body with a soul."

—Wayne Dyer (1940-)
American Motivational Speaker and Author

We now deal with an invisible factor, which is constantly at work but seldom gets noted and worse yet, hardly is given any proper credit for its contribution to the macro-level of existence; and that subject is **microeconomics.**

The English dictionary defines **microeconomics** as the *branch of economics dealing with specific or particular aspects of an economy, such as the price of a stock, the costs associated with running a company, the price of production of oil, so on and so forth.*

Upon further examination of this subject, it becomes rather obvious that this definition needs to be further expanded in order to become more practical.

Microeconomics is the *production of micro-particles in any living entity (such as a body, a company, a nation, etc.) that is essential and needed for the exchange on a microscopic scale (invisible to the naked eye) in order for the larger organism continue survival on a larger scale. The Generalized Exchange Principle (GEP) is at the heart of this subject!*

Let us take a simple example of microeconomics for the physical body. On a microscopic level, we can see that there is a constant and unending flow of micronutrients and food particles at each instant of time at the cellular sites of the body. This action brings about a constant level of cell maintenance and procreation and thus allows the whole body to exist on a macroscopic level!

Through trillions years of evolution, cells have specialized themselves into performing very specific actions to bring about certain micro-products (This means that cells have learned early in the evolution process to niche themselves as a method of greater level of survival!) The creation of many micro-products lead to a macro-product, which becomes a visible function of the body. That is to say, to get one specific bodily function, many cells have to contribute at a micro-scale to make it a visible reality! For example, many specialized cells create a kidney, which specializes in one specific function and that is filtering poisonous and harmful particles (created by cell waste products, etc.) out of the blood stream. Many cells contribute to this action and the final product is a cleaned and purified blood.

Then there are a number of other cells that by creating a duct system (such as blood vessels, veins, etc.), first carry these poisonous particles and waste products to the kidneys and then out of the body system in the form of urine, etc. Thus they create a transportation system, where a constant stream of cell waste-products leave the cell sites and are transported to the kidneys and then out of the system by very elaborate filtering system and waste disposal mechanisms. Therefore, on a micro-scale we are back to the exchange principle and its generalized version!

As a result, there is a constant give and take between different organs of the body and the cells within it with the environment. Cut this exchange process for an unusual length of time and we will severely limit the operation of this complex machine, if not injuring it in the process.

Therefore, GEP is visibly at work for all life organisms and not understanding it or following it will jeopardize the operation and future survival of this biological machine and life itself on a microscopic or macroscopic level!

Therefore, when we see someone's body, we are looking at the product of microeconomics at work, and when the body starts dying on a macroscopic scale we immediately know that exchange on a microscopic scale is not taking place! Knowing this is only half of the battle, the other half of the problem could be called the diagnosis stage, which is understanding the reasons why the exchange is not taking place and then fixing it.

For instance in the body example above, the microeconomics of the body is disrupted, maybe because one is eating food void of nutrients, vitamins and minerals (e.g., white bread, coffee, donuts, sodas, etc.); or maybe the person is under some major stress and serious suppression that does not allow him to get proper rest and allow nutrition to flow properly to the body.

"It is far better to grasp the Universe as it really is than to persist in delusion, however satisfying and reassuring."

— Dr. Carl Edward Sagan (1934-1996)
American Astronomer, Searching for Intelligent Life in the Cosmos

The same analogy can be used to any macro-scale entity regardless of its size. For example, let us take a nation and study its microeconomics. On a micro-scale, the basic unit of the society (or the cell) becomes the individual! That is to say, each person is actually a group member and needs to get a proper education of fundamentals of life and existence as discussed in the ten keys in this book. Receipt of this education is the give and take of the micro-nutrient to each cell of the macro-organism (called a nation or society) and is essential in order to have a macroeconomics. Then and only then we can have a system that can function orderly on a level that can sustain large-scale expansion on a visible level.

When the source of this vital information for survival is faulty and toxic and its "give and take" is not checked for accuracy, then and only then we get many ills in the society. The list of ills of a society is endless but they are all based upon the "unhealthy cell concept." We get such ills as recession, unemployment, depression, poverty, economic implosion, wars, embezzlement, theft and robbery, so on and so forth.

A society's ill economics and the disruption of the microeconomics go hand and glove together! It all goes back to the individual who is the cell of the society and who is not producing and yet has to eat and consume to survive. Therein lies the enigma and the bold truth that is hard to confront.

Currently, our society has no solution for the illiterate individual who has all or most of these ten keys out and can never get them in because he cannot be communicated to on any level!

Everyone seems to be looking for the magic key that will open the doors to prosperity and happier economic times, but no one seems to have noticed that when you have many individuals (cells of a body) out of communication and exchange with the rest of the cells (other individuals and groups) through mis-education, mis-information and neglect then perforce that society is doomed to failure; just like a sick body that withers and dies from a severe lack of internal and organic communication, and exchange of nutrients!

Therefore, based upon this logic it is not hard to visualize the illness that caused the demise of the Roman empire, the Greek civilization, the Persian empire, the British empire, the Egyptian civilization, so on and so forth.

"It is the mark of an educated mind to be able to entertain a thought without accepting it."

—Aristotle (384 – 322 BC)
Greek Philosopher, Scientist and Physician

Moreover, it is interesting to note that the American society is currently under a major illness bordering on becoming a terminal disease. In fact, it has been going downhill since the 1950's and 1960's and recently the descent has accelerated by the introduction of widespread psychiatric mind-bending drugs into schools and its forced usage upon unsuspecting victims (children), and further drugging of the masses to the hilt by the psychiatrists through the inventing of artificial mental diseases, which have no basis in facts. The current use of these drugs by the unsuspecting victims, believing in the drug panacea and having the "doctor knows best" mentality, has crippled the beings in our society mentally and spiritually!

These victims are the cells of the society and have been turned into robots without any volition or power of choice, and through non-productivity, have been made to look like a small cogwheel of an economic system with no role in it. In short, the microeconomics of the society has been disrupted because one cannot educate a drugged zombie, who cannot focus on any subject for any length of time and has no attention span worth a nickel!

Without this action on a micro-scale, then we have no macroeconomics on any level but a constant economic upheaval, exchange disruption and social violence coupled with economic mayhem in our a) financial systems, b) stock markets, c) production cycles of goods, d) job employment rates and many other economic aspects!

Most government leaders are not truly scientists in the truest sense of the word and do not know the ten keys discussed in this book, therefore, their solution to macro-economic problems are usually short term and creates many other unforeseen problems!

"Happiness is the meaning and the purpose of life, the whole aim and end of human existence."

—Aristotle (384 - 322 BC)
Greek Philosopher, Scientist and Physician

Therefore, the moral of the story is, in order to fix the economy of a nation one must realize that he is trying to fix the macroeconomics of that society. In order to fix that, one must fix the microeconomics, which eventually leads to the individuals (i.e. the cells) of that society, whose physical and mental health ultimately determines the health of the economy and the society at large!

Quizzes #15

Quiz 15.1

What is meant by "**The Bright Phases Shining on the Business Radar?**" Give an example.

What is meant by "**The Dim Phases Fading from the Business Radar?**" Give an example.

What is meant by "**The Black Phases Submerged Below the Business Radar?**" Give an example.

What is meant by "**Building Confidence?**" Give an example.

Quiz 15.2

What is meant by "**Positive Energy?**" Give an example.

What is meant by "**Negative Energy?**" Give an example.

What is meant by "**Macroeconomics?**" Give an example.

What is meant by "**Microeconomics?**" Give an example.

What is "**The Most Powerful Ingredient to Success?**" Give an example.

PART 16

Unlimited Income Strategies

Now what...

"Great things are not done by impulse, but by a series of small things brought together."
—Vincent van Gogh (Dutch Painter, one of the greatest of the Post-Impressionists, 1853-1890)

If you have persevered through this book so far, congratulations!

Now we are going to combine the genius traits with the ten ultimate keys to create a business plan, no matter what the activity, will make you extremely prosperous.

At the core of the business plan lies long-term goals based upon sell-first principle. That is to say, *before you even consider buying anything, you must consider when and how you are going to sell it.*

The Sell-first principle is such an essential and powerful concept that 99.9% of people out in the business world either:
a) Do not know about it.
b) Have a complete misunderstanding on it by doing confusing things and making contradictory decisions and actions.
c) Misapply it completely by using high-risk methods and end up losing the house.
d) Believe quite the opposite and think buying is the most important.

e) Know about it but do not know how to apply it correctly, so stand on the business sidelines.

The 0.1% who know this principle are filthy rich beyond belief and would not even consider revealing their secrets.

The moral of the story is that *one must **investigate** the sale price of the asset before one **invests** in it!*

There is an old maxim in the business world that sums up the sell-first principle in a nutshell:

"Buying a financially sound asset at a discount is practically half sold!"

How to Buy an Existing Business

"Cash can buy, but it takes enthusiasm to sell"
—Unknown

If you are going to buy an existing business from someone, we need to do several steps, which are essential:

1. Develop a **mental system** of what is the greatest thing in demand in the society. This in essence is a cookie cutter system that can be repeated over and over without change.

2. Establish a **rate of return** that is acceptable. In the Real Estate market, it is about 5%-8%. Anything lower than this is not acceptable, as it becomes a burden and not a cash flow system. In the stock market, a good rate of return is between 20%-30%.

3. Choose a **good location (or a good company)** and examine the prospective business's physicality, portfolio, profit and loss, cash flow, viability, etc.

4. Analyze the operating business's **books and records** and determine how much upside in equity and income exists.

5. We need to have a **quadruple play**:
   a) **Appreciation** (good location),
   b) **Built-in Equity** (i.e., under-market value),
   c) **Cash flow** (5%-8% in Real Estate and 20%-30% in stock market), and

d) **Deductions**.

6. If all or most is present, it is a good deal, **buy** it.

7. Apply the **trends concepts**, i.e., make it possible for a successful transition to take place, when you take over the job your predecessor has left behind. Thus, there are two possibilities!

> **A. The Very Successful One-** If you find yourself buying a successful business, it means that it is in an up trending pattern. You just keep the trend going up; keep watchful for hostile forces, and try to find out any existing problems and handle them immediately. Keep exchange in and do everything possible to add to the up trending pattern by expanding the positive angle of the trend line. Focus on that particular business and the jobs at hand and do not get distracted by other business propositions and other attractions. For example, if one is in the real estate business, then no attention should be given to or be persuaded to start a full time job trading stocks and commodities.

> **B. The Very Unsuccessful One-** On the other hand if you get a business that is not operating well and is in terrible shape, recognize that the previous owner has left it in disorder, which needs to be handled. Therefore, you need to apply the downtrend pattern concepts to it and turn the trend around by using an external force to lift it up. Then apply the exchange formula and put the business back in exchange by using proper

outflows in response to the demands and inflows.

8. Then continue using the **trends** concepts and gradually move it into a slight up trend. Once the operation goes into a small up trend, expand its angle of the trend line by doing positive actions to build up the business, avoid unrelated activities and increase public support by expanding the communication lines, and in the process make yourself a small fortune!

9. Use the next article on "**How to Run a Business**" to manage the business and to further expand your business operation.

How to Run a Business

"Either you run the day or the day runs you."
— Jim Rohn (American Speaker and Author. He is famous for motivational audio programs for Business and Life, 1930-)

If we are going to run an established business, the steps to follow are completely different than setting one up.

The steps can be outlined as follows:
1. Create a company command chart showing all **functioning posts and duties,** with all names current and accurately marked.

2. Have a **duty write-up** for every post so that all of the duties of that post are clearly identified.

3. Have the **policies and rules** clearly known to all staff.

4. Have a **reward system** in place and have it be well known to all staff.

5. Develop a series of clear-cut goals with a master plan of how to achieve them. Subdivide the goal into sub-goals, sub-plans and **targets**, which are realistic.

6. Develop a series of measurable quantities (for each division of the company), which become the **stats.**

7. Train the person in charge of a department to prepare weekly stats for each division. He should establish the trend of each activity or area of production each week (This person is called the

stat-man or stat-person and is a post all by itself usually carried out by the head of a division).

8. Create a **business plan** and have weekly executive meetings to discuss the upcoming week's activities based on the trends provided by the stat man, so that progress toward the goals and targets are made.

9. Keep **a watchful eye** on the production trends and encourage staff to report accurately all down trend areas.

10. Be aware of **risks and problems** lurking around the work place and train staff to recognize and handle it properly.

Two Distinct Classes of Assets

There are two distinct classes of assets, which should be understood well in the game of business, if one intends to stay above water for a long haul. These are:

I. Trend-Controllable Assets

Trend-controllable assets consist of a whole class of assets whose activities and trends are, to a large extent, under the owner's or executive's direct control. Examples of such assets are: a family-owned restaurant, an apartment complex, a gas station, any type of privately-owned enterprise, etc.

In essence, the owner or the executive is in the driver's seat and makes all of the vital decisions. He runs the show on many levels and has a say on what goes on.

In this type of assets, the trend of operations (e.g., cash flow, loan balances, production rate, etc.) are directly established by the owner and the team of executives.

Because of this factor, this class of assets is very management-oriented and labor-intensive. Moreover, it requires hands-on and constant work to maintain and produce the intended products.

II. Trend-Controlled Assets

Trend controlled assets are those assets whose trends and activities are completely outside of one's control and one is only a passenger in the trend-ride (up, down or flat). Example of such assets are all publicly owned companies and their stock shares, Exchange Traded Funds (ETFs), option markets, future commodities, bonds, etc.

Due to this enormous lack of control, one's focus should be on available data from these asset classes either on a fundamental or technical level. One of the most valuable pieces of information that could be used for one's investment purpose as well as the correct decision to buy or not, is the price chart.

One needs to get trained and develop *chart reading skills* as one of the first and foremost essential tools of the business. It is an absolutely necessary step, which would enable one to know the trend and thus invest with it.

Because the chart reading skill is the cornerstone of one's investment methodology, then one needs to know how to use it for exchange purposes, which is finding where the supply and demand prices are. This requires proper identification of where the support (demand price) and where the resistance (the supply price) are located on the chart clearly as shown on the next page.

Therefore, for proper investment in trend-controlled assets, one needs to get trained and become skillful in the following areas:
A. Chart reading.

Stock price

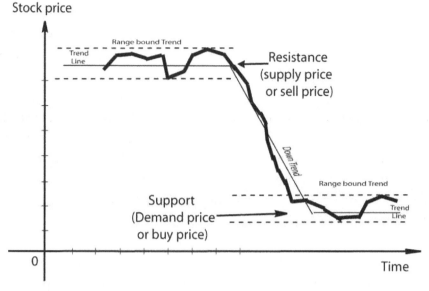

Location of the areas of support and resistance on the price chart, where one can get into exchanging the asset for maximum profit.

B. Correct determination of the trend of a particular stock both, short-term (ST) and long-term (LT) trends.

C. Correct determination of the direction of the trend for the general market.

D. Accurate establishment of the location of support and resistance prices on the chart.

E. Correct placement of a buy order (if both trends, ST and LT, are up).

F. Proper assessment of the risk amount and correctly insuring the stock with a put option.

G. Proper modeling of the stock position on a profit/loss chart and correctly identifying the sweet and sour spots.

H. Keeping a watchful eye on the trend angle and get ready to act if major counter trends or corrections start developing.

I. Adjust the position as needed to keep the trade profitable.

J. Liquidate the complete position (stock and option) if the trend reverses or if the profit objective is met.

The Preferred Investment Strategies

I. Stock Market

In stock market, one must think long term and use the business principles in this book really well to become a howling success. Understanding that one needs to be well-capitalized ($20k to $100k) is essential, because then and only then one can start the business properly. The preferred method is the *married put strategy* as follows:

a) Buying a highly liquid stock (preferably a dividend-paying stock) in an uptrend on the weekly and monthly charts. The asset forms an appreciating (growing) static, which is being assisted by the momentum of the uptrend acting as a tailwind.

b) Buying a deep-in-the-money long term "put option" to protect and insure the asset (a semi-static, the insurance leverage).

c) The combination of "the stock and the put" is called "*the married put strategy*" and forms a solid foundation upon which we can nest all of our future trades. This acts as the base of the motor, as discussed earlier. It also employs the law of leverage (LOL) and the law of operating time (LOT).

d) Selling an out of the money call, preferably at the put strike price to generate a monthly income (a kinetic). This employs the law of money (LOM).

e) Using risk management principles, we limit the total risk to single digits of the position itself or the entire portfolio value. This means that one should allocate a maximum of 5-8% risk value for each stock (this is called the "At Risk" value), which should not be more than a 1-2% risk of one's entire capital value. This is the insurance leverage at work, which allows one to take on positions without much worry or fear of loss. *Limiting the loss to a known single-digit value* is the most important facet of this strategy, making it superior to all other forms of trading.

f) The entire stock portfolio investment should take no more than 50% cash from the account. The other 50% cash is essential for adjustments and unforeseen circumstances.

g) The married put strategy forms the core of our trade and acts as the base of the motor, the principle essential to long-term success. Now depending on what the stock does we can carry out two possible actions:

   i. If stock goes up, then we can move the put option up to lock profits further (the ratchet principle), or sell a call at the put-strike to generate income (renting the stock out), or a combination of both.

   ii. If stock goes down, keep moving the put down one strike at a time, and sell calls at the put strike price to generate a cash profit. This also allows us to start buying the stock itself at a lowered price using the generated profit (a form of reinvesting the profits, which is the compounding principle at work).

The married put strategy as the base of the motor is shown on the next page. From this Figure, we can see that we are in a protected stock-ownership position, which allows us to engage in and benefit from the exchange opportunities that the up and down motion of the stock provides.

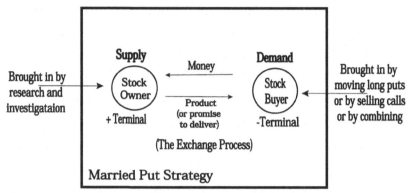

The Married Put Strategy As The Base Of The Motor, Enabling us To Benefit From The Exchange Process.

The Advantages of the *Married Put* strategy are:

a) Use of the *Sell-First* principle.

b) Use of the *Static-Kinetic* principle.

c) Use of the *Prime the Pump* principle.

d) Use of the *Law of Leverage* (LOL), by using the insurance, option, and automation levers.

e) Use of the *Law of Operating Space* (LOS).

f) Use of the *Law of Operating Time* (LOT).

g) Use of the *Law of Money* (LOM).

h) Use of the *Ratchet* principle.

i) Use of the *Compounding* principle.

j) Use of the *Long-Term Solution* principle.

k) Use of the *Duality* principle.

l) Unlimited profit potential with limited loss.

m) A stress-free trading environment rule.

n) Noise filtering rule (removing stock's daily price noise).

II. Real Estate

We need to employ the following methodology:

a) Buy recession-proof assets such as rental houses or multi-family apartment complexes in good locations (a static forming the base of the motor).

b) Calculate the gross rents and the market rents (pro forma rents). This provides the cash flow factor needed to assure us that there is a good upside in rents, which could lead to future potential appreciation in value.

c) Find the mix of the apartment complex; make sure it is a healthy mix of one-, two-, and three-bedrooms with a few single units (less than 10% singles or bachelors).

d) A great indicator is the price per square foot (psf) which is the paramount parameter in one's search for ideal investment assets. Currently, it is around $100-$150 for apartments in the Greater Los Angeles area.

e) Another indicator is the building price divided by the gross rents, which yields the "Gross Rent Multiplier, or GRM," which is currently a number between 7 and 10 in the Greater Los Angeles area.

f) One also needs to pay attention to the upside in rents, which is based upon the market rents (pro forma rents) and thus calculate the future building value (appreciation factor from rent alone). Appreciation could also come from desirability of location due to its proximity to shopping or job centers, transportation hubs and other factors.

g) One should buy the asset below current market value (the built-in equity factor) as a final element to guarantee further success!

The Business Principles & Stocks

"There is always plenty of capital for those who can create practical plans for using it"
—Napoleon Hill (American author, 1883-1970)

To apply the sell-first principle successfully to the stock market, we need to understand and implement the following **rudiments** at all times:

1. All positions we take on must have long-term connotations using high volume and liquid assets.

2. Any position we take on must have a tolerable and predefined risk associated with it, i.e., less than 5%-8% of the position itself and no more than 1% of the total portfolio value.

3. Never assume unlimited risk positions to make a limited profit. This is referred to as naked position trading and should be shunned as it is highly dangerous.

4. Always assume positions with limited risks but unlimited profits. This is the reverse action to #3 above and is referred to as "hockey stick trading," because of the shape of its graph when we plot the "profit-loss" vs. "price," as shown on the next page.

5. Make adjustments to any position as time goes on, in such a way as to reduce the initial risk even further and making it even more riskless or bulletproof.

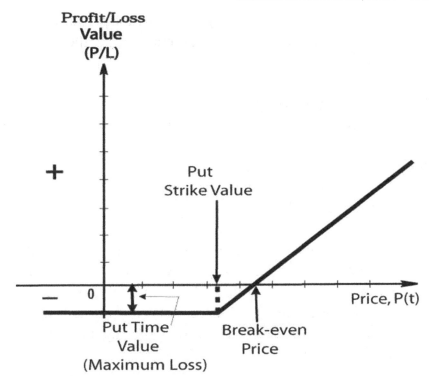

Hockey stick Risk Graph suitable for ideal trading strategy.

Note: *The term "position" refers to the combination of stock shares and the put option contracts taken collectively. This combination as a whole establishes the "sweet spot" zone on "the profit and the loss chart (P/L)," which is above the "break-even price" on the P/L vs. the stock price chart.*

With these five rudiments in, one can then and only then approach the markets and produce a stream of income on a regular basis.

The specifics of how we apply the sell-first principle and how we implement it can be summarized in the stages below:

Step 0 –Rudiment stage:
Master the five rudiments above well,

Step 1 – Organization stage:
1A. We need to establish a brokerage account and learn their platform really well.

1B. One must learn how to read charts and identify the prevailing trend accurately in the time frame specified (such as hourly, daily, monthly, or weekly charts). One must learn the popular indicators such as moving averages (MAs), Bollinger Bands, stochastics, etc.

1C. one must learn how to do a risk graph for any position and then learn a software that graphs it. Risk graph is a profit and loss diagram, (P/L plot) drawn vs. stock price.

Step 2 –Product in sight stage:
2A. Perform a stock search on the broker's platform using the following criteria:
a. Price range: $10 - $100
b. Daily volume ≥ 1 million shares
c. Option volume ≥ 10-20 contracts and healthy premiums
d. Weekly and monthly price in an uptrend (longer time frame). This ensures an appreciating asset (A of ABC principle) due to its continuing uptrend!

e. Daily price near 8-period MA or 20-period MA and in the lower part of the Bollinger band (shorter time frame). This is buying in an uptrending stock below the market value, which is the average in the Bollinger band (B of ABC principle).

Step 3 –Marketing and promotion stage:

From step 2, one finds a suitable stock that meets our uptrend criteria and is well in demand by its daily volume and option contracts. There are a lot of interests in the chosen stock due to its high volume and uptrend.

Step 4 –Production stage:

One must buy the stock as identified in step 3 (e.g. 1000 shares) and then buy appropriate number of long-term or LEAP put options (e.g. 10 contracts) preferably deep in the money to completely protect the asset. This should cap the risk to less than 5-8% of the purchase price.

Step 5 –Exchange stage:

Either at the beginning or shortly thereafter, one sells an appropriate number of out of the money short-term calls (e.g. 10 contracts) near the put strike price to generate a healthy profit. This brings in the cash (C of the ABC principle) on a monthly basis for the next few years. This cash flow is based on the sell-first as well as the ABC principles and creates it without much risk or worry.

⊷ ℘ ✶ ❀ ❇ ❀ ✶ ℘ ⊷

Model Case Studies

The case studies below form model methods for proper investments in real estate and stock market arenas. These case studies elucidate some of the principles we have discussed in this work and should be followed for successful investment results.

Case 1- Stock Market- Covered Call

Buy an uptrending stock (a static), which is a timeless entity, and then selling a deep in the money (DITM) call against it. This is called a covered call trade.

For example, buy 100 shares of Caterpillar, Inc. (symbol: CAT) stock at $30 and sell a one contract of 15-25% DITM call 30 days out (e.g., $25 strike price) for $6. Here one collects $1 if the stock goes up, sideways or down (by $5 or 16%) in one month. If one repeats this process relentlessly for twelve consecutive months without being called out, then one gains about $12 in one period (12/30=40% gain).

In effect, this makes a monthly cash flow as well as stock ownership within reach. One will own the stock free and clear in 2.5 years, in addition to its potential price increase (capital gain) and the stock's profit distribution to shareholders (dividend) in this period!

The selling of the DITM and its percentage in the money depends greatly on the pattern of the stock and its trend line slope. If the stock is bullish, then using a 15% DITM call is justifiable. However, if stock is flat, one should sell the 25% DITM call to provide better protection.

Case 2- Stock Market- Collar

Buy an uptrending stock, a timeless entity and thus a business static, and then selling an out of the money (OTM) call against it. Then use some of the proceeds of the sold call to buy an OTM put in the same month for protection. If the put is longer term then it would be called a married put with a covered call component. The put is the insurance policy that adds a blanket of security and stability to our stock ownership.

For example, buy 100 shares of Wells Fargo Corporation (symbol: WFC) stock at $20 (when 20-40 days Moving Average (MA) crosses over to the upside) and sell the next strike call 30 days out (e.g., $22.5 strike price) for $1 and then buy a $17.50 put for $0.40 in the same moth. Here one collects $0.60 upfront, however, if the stock goes up above $22.50 in 30 days, one can collect another $2.50, for a total of $3.60 profit (18% profit). If the stock remains the same or moves sideways, one still collects $0.60 (3% profit). If the stock moves down, one only can lose ($2.50-$0.60=$1.90) or 9.5% in one month. As long as the trend remains up, one should repeat this process relentlessly for twelve consecutive months (without being called out), which on the average brings in ($0.60+$3.60-$1.9) =$2.30 every three months, or $9.20 in a year (46% gain). This is called a "Collar" trade.

In effect, this makes a monthly cash flow as well as stock ownership within reach. One will own the stock free and clear in about two years; this is in addition to its potential price increase (capital gain) and the stock's profit distribution to shareholders (dividend) in this period!

The selling of the OTM and its percentage out of the money depends greatly on the pattern of the stock and its trend line slope. If the stock is bullish then using a one- or two-strike out OTM call is justifiable. However, if stock is flat or range-bound, one should sell ideally the At-The-Money (or ATM), or one-strike out OTM call to provide better income.

Case 3- Stock Market- LEAPS
For expensive and yet uptrending stocks (price>$60), buy a DITM LEAPS call (a static) with the least time value. This would simulate an almost timeless entity, which can be used to sell then a deep in the money (DITM) or ATM call against it. This is a simulated covered call trade but technically speaking is a call debit spread trade.

For example, Apple company (AAPL) is currently trading at $127 in May 2009; buy 1 contact of Jan 2011 $75 call (about 20 months out) for a premium of $60 ($8 time value) and then sell a one contract of 15-25% DITM call (e.g., July $115 strike price) for $17. Here one collects $5 time value, if the stock goes up, or sideways. If it goes down no more than 9.5% (12/127= 9.5%) in 2.5 months, one would break even. However, even in this case one can lower the call's strike price and reduce losses. If one repeats this process relentlessly 8 times in a 20 months period without being called out, then one gains about (8x$5=$40) in 20 month period (40/60=67% gain).

The disadvantages of this trade is a) lack of the stock's profit distribution to shareholders (dividend) in this period, and b) the inverted hockey-stick P/L graph, which would limit the upside potential for large gains.

The selling of the DITM and its percentage in the money depends greatly on the pattern of the stock and its trend line slope. If the stock is bullish, then using a 15% DITM call is justifiable. However, if stock is flat, one should sell the 25% DITM call to provide a better protection against downside slides.

Case 4- Real Estate Market

Real estate is another vehicle for investment and the basic concept consists of buying a piece of real estate such as an apartment complex, a retail center or office building in an uptrending neighborhood as a business static, properly insure it against unknown events, and then collect a healthy monthly rent (a business kinetic). This is a controlable asset, which requires spot-on management skills and generally is maintenance-intensive. If managed properly, this type of asset could create a positive cash flow on a long-term basis and become one of the best investment avenues in which one can get engaged.

There are many factors that go into real estate investments and one needs to master them all early on for making the correct decisions and acquiring quality real estate assets. These are:

a) Price per square foot (psf).
b) Gross rent multiplier (GRM).
c) Upside in rents.
d) Built-in equity.
e) Location of the asset.
f) Price per unit.
g) Capitalization rate (cap rate).
h) Net operating income (NOI).
i) Return on investment (ROI).
j) Unit mix (i.e., type of units: singles, 1 bedroom, etc.).
k) Pro forma rents (also called market rents).
l) Future of the asset as a whole.

An important caveat here is the concept of buying land in general, which even though a static, should be avoided as a general rule of thumb, since usually no kinetic (i.e., income, rent, etc.) can be generated around it to lead to any actual power or profit.

Risk Management

An important caveat in any kind of investment is to have risk management always implemented in all of the trades regardless of its probability of occurrence. The trading strategies discussed here all have risk management firmly in place, however, prudent choice of strategy as well as managing the trade is essential for ultimate success. Just like an apartment building that needs a manager to maintain and report problems, so do we need to manage our trading structure, and thus any current trade that we are involved!

When one is running a business or company, the trend is usually under his control, whereas for trading assets such as stocks or commodities, the trend is established by many external forces behind the scene, which are totally beyond one's control.

Some of these forces are huge to such an extent that they change the pattern of the stock to a large extent without one's consent. If one does not have proper risk management already in place, he is liable to lose quite a bit of money.

Therefore, when trading stocks, commodities, or futures markets, one must install in advance proper risk management measures and circuit breaker rules so that when catastrophe happens and the market moves against one in an unpredictable shift of pattern (e.g., from an uptrend to a down trend, or vice versa), then one is automatically disconnected from the excessive forces in the market and his trading "house' does not burn to the ground!

In other words, installing *risk management as an essential part of the trading strategy* automatically forces the trader out of the market with a small loss. Giving a small loss to the markets is the correct approach, when the trend shifts against one due to sudden or unknown exterior forces.

Getting out of a bad position keeps one's confidence intact and prevents a major blow to one's sanity in case of a major move against one's position.

Therefore, one should take the small losses rather than being faced with a painful and emotional decision, which could potentially cost not only his *sanity* but also his bank account and severe debt if the trade is not managed carefully!

Applications of Logic in Business

The concept of logic is intimately related to survival and long-term existence and viability. Utilizing the logic's principle in any business is essential to its survival at the highest level, and investing is no exception!

Therefore, in the game of investment, one needs to employ the principles of logics with great fervor and to the fullest extent, if one is planning for a long haul in this business activity.

The application of the principles of logic to investing breaks down into the following series of governing guidelines:

1. Diversify all positions held in one's account. This means holding shares of different stocks each from different sectors, industries, or sub-industries. If one is trading commodities, this means holding long (or short) positions in different commodity groups such as some contracts in grains, some in metals, some in financials, etc.

2. For accounts under $100,000, allocate no more than one-tenth (10%) of one's total investment capital to each stock or commodity position. This is an important point to implement, because if the position goes south for any reason, then the ensuing losses will not completely wipe one out. The losses

are small and manageable and will not destroy one's sanity or self-confidence in one's judgment, decision power and ability to trade!

3. Always use the trend key as the ultimate guiding principle to make a sound trading decision. *The trend is clearly established by the crossover between the 40-day and 80-day exponential moving averages (MAs) on a daily chart. It is a safety switch that puts one on the correct side of the force and momentum of the trend and lights up one's path to make a number of correct decisions and choose the correct strategy: Bullish, Bearish or sideways!*

4. Never use rumors, hunches, gut feelings (i.e. do not ignore charts). Never team up with or worse yet seek advice or listen to ignorant or uninformed individuals (such as green brokers, drinking buddies, etc.) to make important trading decisions. Never allow such individuals monitor or advise one about what to buy and what to avoid. Be cold and calculated in your decisions at all times by using the trends key as your mantra for successful trades (This is a corollary to guideline #3 above).

5. Never use unlimited risk strategies (such as naked selling, etc.) in your trading no matter how enticing or delightful the circumstances are or present themselves in the trading world.

6. Make risk management the core and the cornerstone of one's trading business and take small losses when things seem to go against one. This means that not

fighting the trend if it has reversed and clearly is opposite to what one's trading strategy is dictating.

7. Keep the communication key implemented at all times for any position one is in. That is to say, keep in touch with the markets one has an active position in, either through alert signals from the brokerage house, automatic emails, or having access to live quotes throughout the day or on an end-of-day basis.

8. Keep the principles of risk management fluid in your mind and never allow anyone or any peculiar circumstance cloud the risk management in any business.

9. Implement the risk management principles from the start to the end of any transaction and never leave it out of the equation. Life becomes stress-free and decisions are made much more easily if one has implemented it early on

10. Never become a patsy in the hands of a more savvy player who wants to transfer his risks to you and make the deal to go through at your cost! This particularly applies to brokers who have a vested interest in getting their commission check funded by the patsy!

The Moving Parts of an Investment

All investments are one way or another about one's ability to handle the motions of the market and all entities connected with it.

As an example, let us consider the stock market and see the motions connected with it as outlined below:

Example 1 - Stock Market
1. Market price.
2. Volatility.
3. Economic conditions.
4. Earnings reports.
5. Terrorist attacks.
6. Interest rate.
7. Supply and demand.
8. Time ticking.

As another example, let us consider the real estate market and realize what motions are connected with it as outlined below:

Example 2- Real Estate Market
1. Market price.
2. Lenders.
3. Code Enforcement. Health Department, Building and Safety Department.
4. Pests, rodents, roaches, termite, etc.
5. Tenants.
6. Incoming rents.

7. Price of materials.
8. Economic conditions.
9. Brokers.
10. Earthquake, tornado, flood, rain, and wind.
11. Vendors.
12. Bank loans.
13. Cash reserves.
14. Repairs and maintenance.
15. Gangs and the neighborhood decline.
16. Liability and lawsuits.
17. Permits and registration.
18. Taxes--property and business.
19. Interest rate.
20. Time (gnawing at the foundation and structure of the building).

The Categories of Investors

There are several levels that one can invest in the stock or commodities market. These levels can be briefly summarized as:

I. Expert Level
The expert uses trading strategies that can handle any motion of the market. He has a full use of software and employs very scientific approach to trading. He has a high understanding toward markets and always looks at them to learn and modify his own perception of them. He has no fixed ideas about them. He sees and decides with no uncertainty and has a complete understanding of the subject. *He has risk management at the heart of his trading plan and gives it the highest priority in all of his trades.* For this reason, the married put strategy is the cornerstone of many of his trades.

II. Master Level
The master uses trades that can handle the motions in the market to a large extent but not totally. He employs technical trading methods that use software to a large extent but he is sometimes out of contact with the markets. He has a normal understanding toward markets and sometimes looks at them to learn and modify his own perception. He has some fixed ideas about them with some confusion and misunderstandings in the subject.

III. Journeyman Level

The journeyman uses trades that hold the motion and dampens it. He tries to predict the markets but ends up fighting the market movements. He uses the software sometimes. He trades by the seat of his pants and displays his understandings as hate toward markets, and resists looking at them. He is filled with a lot of misunderstandings and fixed ideas.

IV. Apprentice Level

An apprentice uses trades that try to equalize with the market and endure its motions. He has occasional and sporadic use of software as a playful thing and not as an observational tool. Pretending to understand and having occasional success but acts emotional toward the general market conditions. He has many false underlying ideas and is riddled with misunderstandings. He is scared of markets but is filled with a false self-confidence that he knows more than the market. His strategies are underhanded and have high inherent risks.

V. Novice Level

A novice uses trades that makes him suffer quite a bit and allows the market to destroy him. He works on beliefs and convictions that are not factual. He has no understanding of the markets. He uses no software of any kind and considers it unimportant, thus has no vision of the market and is mostly out of communication about it. He has no risk management in his strategies and is very emotional toward market movements. He is filled with big misunderstandings about trading and basic concepts and can be classified as a "could've," "should've," and "would've" type of trader, filled with much regret and sorrow! His style of trading is completely risky:

VI. Delusional Novice Level

He uses trades that succumb to market's motion and easily becomes a total effect of it. In other words, when the market moves against his positions he freezes. He acts on beliefs and whims and does not use software of any kind. He has no understanding of the market but pretends he understands them. He constantly writes scripts for the markets he is involved in as a way of predicting market behavior, without even following the news.

He has very poor technical analysis skills but considers himself very knowledgeable. He holds onto short high-Delta options (short Delta>50) hoping that the markets will calm down or will go in his favor—hallucinatory type of trading. He is filled with many misunderstandings and confusions about trading and basic concepts. He does not use any risk management in his trading and is super emotional towards the market movements.

He constantly uses naked positions and is not even aware that he is in *"unlimited loss"* territory. His style of trading is based on praying and hoping. He has many sleepless nights, constantly in anguish about the markets when volatility shoots up, so he has many stressful moments. He has some occasional wins and successes, which is heavily overshadowed by many heavy losses. He usually gets liquidated at the end of a long and losing trading battle; usually loses his trading account and ends up owing money to the brokerage house. His style of trading is completely irrational and has infinite risk built in each one of his trades.

Quizzes #16

Quiz 16.1

What does one need to know in order **"To Buy an Existing Business?"** Give an example.

"How does One Run a Business?" Give an example.

What are **"The Preferred Investment Strategies**?" Give an example.

Why is it important to know **"How to Apply the Business Principles**?" Give an example.

Quiz 16.2

What is meant by **"Application of Concepts**?" Give an example.

What is meant by **"Risk Management**?" Give an example.

What is meant by **"Application of Logic in Business**?" Give an example.

What are the motions connected with **a) Stock market, b) Real Estate Market**? Give an example.

What are the **"The Categories of Investors**?" Give an example.

What should one do to attain **"The Master or Expert Level"** as an investor?

PART 17

The Final Summary of Thoughts

Building Confidence

"Reason and free inquiry are the only effectual agents against error."

—Thomas Jefferson (1762-1825)
American 3rd US President (1801-09).

This work is all about building confidence and the way you achieve a high level of confidence in self or others, and achieving his hidden dreams and tyrn them into reality. The steps are as follows:

1. One begins with oneself as the starting point of one's financial future and through proper training achieves the knowledge required to assume an identity (such as a teacher, a carpenter, a plumber, a pilot, etc.).

2. One needs to gather a pool of workable knowledge that can become one's asset in the business world.

3. One needs to become skilled in the art of leadership and execution of plans and delegation of responsibility, and be able also to oversee them until their completion.

4. Now, he needs to have an edge in the market place to beat out the competion and bring in the desired public that demands his product or service. This edge is primarily the quality of service, honesty and prompt and sincere communication and secondarily the price of his product.

5. The next factor is directly proportional to the number of ways one is connected to the market place, whether, through land-line phone, cell phone, mail, email, internet site, etc. and how expertly he has manned these lines and how fast he responds to any particle that flows on them.

6. The next factor is the niche market one is in and how much demand the society has for the niche market's products or services.

7. The next factor concerns the people one has teamed up with and how organized and how bright and competent they are in handling the business activities such as delivering the product as promised, doing quality check before shipment, collecting the money, marketing and promotion, planning for future expansion, etc.

8. The next factor concerns the number of products and services one can and is delivering in any given period of time. This factor determines the number of ways one is exchanging with the society around him and directly determines the degree of his viability and prosperity in life. If one only has a 9-5 job, and if the economy goes into one of its commonly occuring upheavals, he would be out of a job and into a chaotic world of uncertainty and massive amounts of mental stress and turmoil. This could have easily been avoided if he had another product or service, which he could exchange with the society such as a real estate investment with a positive cash flow. This fact opens the door to the concept of "multiple streams of income," which one should actively seek to employ in his life.

9. The next factor is one's knowledge of the trends in the economy particularly in his own niche market or field of study. These trends are indicators of mega forces that are investing or divesting in certain markets where their footprints can easily be detected by charting the market versus time (e.g. price of a stock, prime interest rate, consumer index, manufacturing index, foreclosure rate, etc.). One should get a mental picture of the whole chart

and establish quickly whether it is in an uptrend, sideways or down trend. Based on this observation, one can quickly buy, hold or sell for each trend, respectively. This is called flowing with the economy and using it one could gain (or save) an enormous wealth. This is contrary to the common investing startegy of "buy and hold," which means stubbornly holding on to one's opinion of the market made some time in the past (a fixed idea) and refusing to change in the face of new information.

10. The final factor is knowing the laws of the land as well as knowing good logic principles such that one ends up making sound and viable decisions that save him from litigation or self confidence erosion. For example, if one is a stock investor, one must learn all of the government rules to set up proper legal entites to protect one's assets, and early on separate brokers as mentors and purely relegate their function as order takers. Then learn a sound trading/investing system from a knowledgeable mentor and using good logic and sound judgemnet, then trade small lots until one is a professional investor. The same applies to working for a company, to being a real estate owner, or to being a business owner.

An important *caveat* is that one should not treat all sources of information with the same level of trust, and early on develop a judgement for separating the wheat from the chaff. He should close the doors to all nonscientific sources of information and those who pose as "pseudo-teachers" as learning from them is not only very expensive but highly poisonous, if not fatal, equivalent to drinking from a toxic well!

Therefore, the moral of the story is that one should examine the sources of information before accepting data from them and detect "false mentors." This takes a great deal of awareness of self and other's motives, as many could pose as one's mentor for their own benefit rather than putting student's progess in mind as the first priority. Such a false mentor is usually based upon an inherent conflict of interest in the make-up of the source. An example would be a stock or commodity broker, who wants the trader to keep buying and selling different stocks or commodities, and actually never intends to be one's mentor but poses as so, only to collect a healthy monthly stream of income!

Thus we can see that the first prerequisite is to have a truly expert mentor or educator, then and only then one can embark upon a high road of expansion in business or science. Having this situation well at hand could be visualized in terms of the mentor shining a light on one's path by imparting his wisdom, and thus light it up so that one can see his whereabouts and the actual road to success ahead of him.

Caveat: *An important caveat worth mentioning here is that there are human beings who get caught up in the day-to-day survival activities and run into either a false or no mentor and thus do not tap into their inner wealth and truly never achieve a higher level of prosperity. These may even sometimes gravitate toward the darker side of life (such as becoming a member of a gangster group, or becoming an employee of a drug dealer, etc.) thinking that they are doing great, never realizing that they have had a false mentor poisoning them all along in their life!*

"The art and science of asking questions is the source of all knowledge."

Thomas Berger (1924-)
American Novelist

๏⁓ ℘ ✳ ❁ ✖ ❁ ✳ ℃ ⁓๏

The Ratchet Principle

"The only thing that interferes with my learning is my education."
—Albert Einstein (1879-1955)
German Born American Physicist, Nobel Prize in 1921

The *ratchet principle* is a natural consequence   or a corollary to the *insurance leverage* concept discussed earlier.

By definition, a *ratchet* is *a mechanical device allowing rotation in only one direction.* It consists of a toothed wheel whose teeth slope in one direction, so as to catch and hold a pawl (a pawl is a hinged tongue, the tip of which engages the notches or teeth of a ratchet wheel), thus preventing backward movement. It is used in certain wrenches, hand drills, etc., to allow motion in only one direction.

Since the beginning of recorded time, we seem to have been in a contest with the physical universe. When it comes to our business world, we seem to be totally inclined in the direction of trying to understand the physical universe with the idea of using the obtained knowledge for improving our own conditions of existence. The ratchet wheel is a borrowed concept from the physical world around us, which wants to destroy every physical structure or gain by bringing it down to its own level of chaos and random disorder of atoms and molecules.

In such a competetive and very dangerous environment, we need to be extra cautious about gains and progress that we make. Thus the ratchet principle is born as follows:

The **Ratchet Principle**: *is the principle, which states that every time we make a positive gain or profit in some direction, we need to immediately consolidate (solidify, firm up and strengthen) the gain, and preserve it by economizing time, effort and money, or by making it extremely difficult and/or impossible to lose.*

The obsession with the ratchet principle may be justifiable because our very survival on the physical plane depends on this point alone and no other.

In our daily existence, we are faced with enormous factors. We are faced with this unthinking and imposing thing called the physical universe, which cannot be dealt with or reasoned with on any level other than force. It only knows force. It is a universe of unintelligent force, which has submerged all living beings within it.

Being confined to a fragile and physical body, which cannot tolerate much force, however, our main tool against the onslaught of the physical universe's demands and mandates is our organized bodies of knowledge, particularly the ratchet principle. This knowledge has been obtained through millennia of postulation and observation of the cause-effect of the observed phenomena in nature using the scientific methodology.

The knowledge about the physical universe, particularly the business world, has been handed down and with the help of the ratchet principle has been preserved and improved from generation to generation relentlessly up until now. It is rightly so, because knowing this precious principle well and applying it effectively to ourselves and our surroundings has meant a higher level of survival for us, our children and all of our codependents.

An example may elucidate this point further. Let us say, that through hard work and diligent application of his business knowledge, an entrepreneur obtains a large sum of money. Using the ratchet principle, he should a) immediately bank the money, b) pay all of his debts, c) continue working hard, d) avoid all work detractors and time wasters, e) avoid going on a buying spree, or f) engage in unproven investments foolishly.

He should further consolidate his gains by:

a) Discovering what caused this sudden increase of fortune, and

b) Strengthening one's discovery as found in (a), by investing time, money and effort wisely in order to enlarge the scope of operations, productivity and profits in that direction only. Achieving this, one will prevent any backward movement (the same principle used in a ratchet wheel).

"Human history becomes more and more a race between education and catastrophe."

—H. G. Wells (1866 - 1946)
English Novelist and Historian

The Compounding Principle

"The most powerful force in the universe is compound interest."
—Albert Einstein (1879-1955)
German Born American Physicist, Nobel Prize in 1921

The English dictionary defines *compounding* as *making something greater by adding something new to it.* It also defines *compounding interest* as *making a sum of money grow larger by adding interest to the sum and letting the new sum gain even more interest.* In other words, we are obtaining interest on the accrued interest as well as the principal itself. Mathematically, if we let:

P_0=Initial Principal, and I= Annual Rate of Interest, then we can write:

$P_1=P_0+IP_0=P_0(1+I)$,   (principal after the 1st year)

$P_2=P_1+IP_1=P_1(1+I)=P_0(1+I)^2$,   (after the 2nd year)

:

$P_n=P_{n-1}+IP_{n-1}=P_{n-1}(1+I)=P_0(1+I)^n$.   (after the nth year)

For example, if we have a principal amount of $1,000 gaining at an interest rate of 10% per annum, after the first year we will have $1,100. Now, we can use $1,100 as our new principal and have a principal of 1,210 after the second year. After the 10th year of compounding, we will have a total principle anount of :

$P_{10}=1,000 (1+0.1)^{10}=\$2,593$

On a linear scale and a noncompounding interest scenario, we would have a principal of $2,000 after ten years. So the money grows much faster with compounding interest program (2.5x). In 30 years, the principal money in a noncompounding program would be $4,000, which is (4.36x) less than the compounding program ($17,449).

Therefore, the rate of growth of the principal in the compounding interest program is in a geometric progression manner, which means that money grows much faster with time than the noncompounding program (linear or fixed rate case).

The key to compounding lies in reinvesting the profits back into the interest-earning system and making the profits work for us, just like adding a new principal would. In engineering terms, this concept is referred to as a *"posistive feedback system."*

From the above, we can see that the definition of compounding primarily applies to money, however, we can generalize this definition into other *types of assets* and obtain a much more workable principle, called the *"Compounding Principle"* as follows:

The **Compounding Principle**: *states that once we establish and own a certain type of asset, then we can compound it by reinvesting the profits back in, to create more of the same type of asset at a much faster pace than normal. This would enable us to accelerate the wealth accumulation process, geometrically or exponentially, depending upon the type of compounding that we employ. This is the cornerstone principle of becoming financially indepenedent in a short order of time!*

For example, let us say that by using the ABCD principle, one buys his first rental house at a below-market price. Now he can tap into 75% of the equity of the asset and use that as a downpayment to buy his next house at a good price. He can then repeat this process over a period of 10 years and accumulate 30 homes with a gross cash flow of $30,000 per month. This is compunding at its best.

Another example in the stock market would elucidate this concept further. Let us say, one invests $10,000 and buys 500 shares of an uptrending and dividend-paying stock plus a proper put insurance for a total of $20 per share. If one does this at the beginning of the stock uptrend and if at the end of the first year the stock value increases to $50 per share, then one has obtained the following stock principal (assume a dividend yield of 6% at an average value of $35):

Dividend=6%x500x(20+50)/2=$1,050

Total stock asset value =$26,050

He can now use this $1050 to buy 21 more shares and so he now has 521 shares and if the stock doubles to $100 over the second year, then he will have (6% at an average value of $75):

Dividend=6%x521x(50+100)/2=$2,345

compounding stock asset value =$52,100+$2,345=$54,445

Noncompounding stock asset value=$53,300

Net Compounding gain=$1,145 (in 2 years)

Thus we have 11.45% increase of asset in two years, due to compounding effect. We can now buy another 23 shares and lct thc 544 shares of stock gain a dividend yield of 6%. Over a ten year period, if we can grow our stock shares by an average of 20 shares per year due to compounding principle, we will have 200 more shares, which corresponds to a total increase in value of $20,000, if stock remains at $100 and there is no further capital gain. Therefore, the compounding principle alone will grow our intial stock shares by 40% (200/500) in 10 years without any effort on our part.

From these two examples, we can clearly see that the compounding principle can do magic for one's business and grow one's wealth and fortunes by leaps and bounds!

The Visualizing Principle

"It's not that I'm so smart, it's just that I stay with problems longer."

—Albert Einstein (1879-1955)
German Born American Physicist, Nobel Prize in 1921

The English dictionary defines **visualizing** as *forming a mental image or a picture of something in the mind.* It is the process of making something perceivable to the mind and thus bringing it into the realm of reality, as far as the mind is concerned. This is the initial step in all of the new designs and novel products.

It is by far the greatest principle that we have encountered so far in this book because it represents life at its basic core. Life progresses to the degree that it can visualize things into existence.

The foundations of life are simple if not easy. First and foremost, we have an individual with a sane mind who has many capbilities and potentialities. Next, we have dreams, which are at the core of the individual's existence, all in a conceptual and ethereal form, not necessarily visualized or verbalized.

Then, we have a series of purposes, which lead to a series of desirable goals. This is where mental action of visualizing comes into play. To implement goals effectively, one is required to have a good mental ability to visualize things such as the final products and the plans of actions to achieve them. With this at hand and the desired final product in full view at the mental level, one is in a very strong and favorable position to start seeing the future mentally, thus propeling himself into action, execution of plans and creation of a new reality.

With this preamble, we can now express the visualizing principle as:

The **Visalizing Principle**: *states that everything worthwhile in life requires, first and foremost, a clear and vivid picture of it at the mental level before its actual materialization at the physical level. This principle is at the core of existence and operation of all successful and prosperous investors and entrepreneurs.*

For example, if one wants to own a house of a certain size or location, he should first visualize it before even looking for one to buy. Now, keeping this visual picture in mind (about the size and location of the house), if he embarks upon getting it in the physical universe, he will usually get it much faster and with less obstacles or stress.

Utilizing this principle, we can see that entering the business or investment world and become greatly successful, is all about visualizing exactly what one wants before acquiring it. This is the incredible power of a sane and rational mind!

Avoid Time Wasters

"As if you could kill time without injuring eternity."
— Henry David Thoreau

One of the most precious assets one possesses is his production time in which he can produce a product. If one's time is utilized effectively by a careful planning and scheduling, one can then achieve any goal his heart desires.

By definition, *time wasters are those activities that do not contribute to the production of a desirable product and the achievement of one's goal!*

Therefore, one must develop a clear-cut system to identify the "time-wasters" and weed them out quickly through a systematic filtering process so that one can achieve his objectives in a timely manner.

The major time-wasters creating major leaks in one's tank of production time are:

1. **Receiving unsolicited phone calls or mail**— These belong usually to cold callers, merchants, brokers, etc. and should be completely ignored.

2. **Receiving job-related or other important phone calls and mails**— These should be routed to an answering machine and a mail bin and be answered at an opportune time.

3. **Reading newspapers and magazines, watching TV news, or taking coffee breaks**—The time for these activities should be relegated to other unproductive times such as during meal times or in the evening during relaxation time.

4. **Being interrupted by people**—These should be disengaged effectively in a hurry. This really requires a great art of dealing with people in a polite and respectful manner as well as a great communication skill so that they leave on their own determinism without feeling hurt or upset.

5. **Not having all tools before one starts the job**—One should gather all tools of production before start. This will help cut one's production time greatly by not looking for a much-needed tool or item frantically during production period.

6. **Not knowing one's job function well**— *This is easily the biggest time waster of all time!* This means that one needs to be hatted really well on his post before he even thinks about production. Otherwise, he will produce a sub-par product that no one really wants. Nevertheless, the many hours of time he spent producing the unwanted product is totally wasted forever and cannot be exchanged for money or be counted as production. The reason is obvious, because it has to be redone correctly by a trained person all over again!

7. **Not knowing exactly what is needed or wanted**—Even when a skilled person who knows his job well does a job without reading the job requirements and specifications, he ends up doing a wrong job producing a wrong product! Therefore, before doing

a job, one needs carefully to read the instructions and make sure one does exactly what is wanted and not some misunderstood action un-looked for by the employer.

8. **Having a number of attention grabbers and mental parasites**—This really means that one needs:
   a) To get plenty of rest for work or sleep well the night before.
   b) To clear his mind from upsets with his associates, spouse, etc.
   c) To disregard the distracting thoughts that occur during the day by writing them down on a notepad and handle after production period.

This step is essential since it eliminates all of the mental parasites that could absorb and substantially reduce one's mental energy output level!

Knowing these time-wasters makes one more at cause over his work environment and life, and gets more done in less time. It allows one to achieve some old dreams that have been put on the back burner due to lack of time. One now truly should have time and know-how to grab hold of his future and make his dreams into a reality!

"Time is a created thing. To say 'I don't have time,' is like saying, 'I don't want to."

— Lao Tzu

The Long-Term Solution Principle

"We can't solve problems by using the same kind of thinking we used when we created them."

—Albert Einstein (1879-1955)
German Born American Physicist, Nobel Prize in 1921

To obtain large-scale success and become wildly prosperous, one must think long-term solutions to life's myriads of problems that are constantly handed down from many sources on a constant basis.

As long as one is alive and has a thrust vector toward certain goals, then he will encounter problems that will intervene and act as obstacles on the road, until handled by one's superior planning and intelligent solutions!

Goals are an essential part of survival in the long term. Therefore, one must actively set goals and create plans to achieve them. To achieve a goal, one needs to know how to get things organized and managed properly. One needs to be able to organize his thoughts and intentions as the very first step of this process and then channel them properly in the correct direction so that success is guaranteed.

Only a dead man who has no goals is problem free, but then he has no life or future either.

At each moment of time, one sits at the center of many of these incoming problems and their related forces. These forces could be divided into three classes:

I. **Body-related forces**, are forces and energy flows, whether external or internal, which can influence and impact the body. These include such things as motion of the blood in the veins, nervous energy in the nerve channels, internal cellular forces, bone growth, air pressure in the lungs, gravitational forces, energy emanations from the sun, galactic and stellar radiations, etc.

II. **Mind-related forces**, are forces that are embedded in a series of past experiences (good or bad) on the physical level or the mental plane, and provide a track record of one's existence from birth to now, which can influence one's present attitude and behavior in business or life.

III. **Spiritual-related forces**, are potential forces and energy flows in the form of abilities and disabilities resident in the individual, and consist of his perception powers, decision power, reasoning power, communication ability, his alertness and awareness of the environment, attention to details, perception of truth, setting goals, making plans, etc.

However, if these three classes of forces are not correctly dealt with on a methodical basis, just like a scientist or an engineer would in dealing with his technical projects, then one can be pushed into many undesirable directions unknowingly.

One day, one looks up and finds himself at the beck and call of the gentleman with the scythe and at that moment of time he may suddenly realize that he has failed to deal with these hidden forces properly and these forces got the best of him!

Let this book be the call to arms and act as a wake-up call to one's own long slumber, created by these huge and invisible forces, which have placed him in an unfavorably low-altitude position relative to the physical universe and his own universe, and have subjugated him to the whims of this unthinking universe.

Therefore, one must never cower from problems or shun them or hope that none come his way; because by doing that he is basically announcing, loud and clear, to the world that he is withdrawing from life and has no further goals to attain. This defeatist attitude will surely invite a total future nonexistence on many levels with a resulting shrinkage of personal ability and vitality.

Instead, he must possess a superior attitude of actively striving toward the achievement of a higher personal altitude so that he can look down upon life with a commanding presence (and not look up to the universe as a slave would) and fully expect that he will succeed despite the odds.

Truth be told, it is really a matter of relative size: if one is such a powerhouse of energy and vitality of presence then most problems presented to him would relatively seem small and have no chance of even having an effect upon him. This really means that he is traveling on a climbing road to the mountain-peak of prosperity, and is becoming larger in presence and positive sphere of influence.

On the other hand, the opposite can also hold valid. That is to say, if one thinks he is just a cog in the huge machinery of the world, then he is going to be bent by the smallest problem that comes up his way. Eventually, he will be crushed under the forces of many such small problems and would not even come near the realm of prosperity, but actually stay in the valley of suffering, misery and poverty.

The main consideration in the business world is to have a going concern, that is to say that it is expanding on a regular basis and has a stable operation guaranteeing long term survival (i.e. it has longevity).

From our earlier discussions, we can see that each of the ten ultimate keys opens a different door, so that when we apply all of them simultaneously in a systematic manner to any business, we will create an avalanche of positive solutions and a high degree of success. This will be accompanied by a large cash flow on a regular basis, which will guarantee long-term survival.

Another aspect of long term success is based upon caring. A caring attitude for self and others is essential and encompasses a) One's watchful attention on the customer's satisfaction, b) One's concersn for own group's well being, c) One's ensuring that all money is collected and d) One's establishment of a high enough monetary exchange value for the product so that longevity of own group is guaranteed.

Furthermore, It is not difficult to see that "*exchange and longevity*" are two direct sub-products of utilization and relentless pursuit of employing the advanced principles presented in this work. Exchange is an inexorable principle in nature that seems never to have been violated on a long term, even if slightly ever so on a short-term basis.

A bright individual starting a new business may ask questions to broaden his point of view in order to learn new information about someone or something. He never assumes that he knows before finding out the facts either through questions, surveys, research or live communications. This is how he succeeds in life day after day (short term) or year after year (long term).

One should also employ the concept of logic intimately in his daily survival or long-term existence and viability. Utilizing the principles of logic in any business is essential to its operation at the highest level.

This could equally be applied to the world of investing as well. Therefore, in the game of investment, one needs to employ the principles of logics with great fervor and to the fullest extent, if one is planning for a long haul in this business activity.

If one can think long term every time he did something then his actions perforce must have long roots of responsibility and planning embedded in them pretty well. Even though, one may not have all the time in the universe at his diposal but one must act as if he does. For example, if one invested long term in any form of asset class whether stocks, real estate, or other commodities such as metals, bonds, etc. and if he also insured them against loss fully, and developed a plan for selling it at the get-go as well as managing it in the interim, then one's intentions could be labled long term and one will survive well in the long run, as many closed doors of life hidden away from plain sight would magically open up.

However, buying an asset without proper or adequate insurance and not being cognizent of its resale value or not knowing how to manage it for effective cash flow, is labeled short-term or myopic thinking and could lead to catastrophe!

The world at large, whether financial, business, marital, or spiritual surrenders to one the moment he starts thinking and developing long-term plans.

Obviously, to make long term plans one needs to know this book really well and implement it within an inch of one's life if one expects to get superior results! This book lays out the milestones one needs to achieve in order to arrive at the final destination: *a life or a business enterprise with unlimited prosperity*!

The journey toward an unlimited prosperity as a worthwhile dream could become a reality if one took proper steps, and is actually well deserved if one follows the path fully blazed in this work!

With the above discussion in mind, *the long-term solution principle comes into its own and* states that *to solve any problem correctly, one should solve it in such a way that the final solution will be workable on a long-term basis and will benefit all of the parties involved.* Such a solution would remove stress and anxiety from ones life and replace it with hope, optimism, and inner satisfaction and happiness.

If this principle is applied to an investment strategy, it should have an unlimited upside profit and a very limited downside risk, which translates into a large sweet spot zone of profit and a very small risk zone (or sour spot).

The long-term solution methodology consists of the following steps:

1. **Establish your purposes, goals, and targets, in that order.**
2. **Devise a methodical plan (strategic and tactical) to attain the goal and targets, and thus the purpose.**
3. **Learn the knowledge and skills to enable one to carry out the plan.**
4. **Organize a competent team to assist one.**
5. **Use "The Fifty Positive Genius Traits," "The Ten Ultimate Keys," and "The twelve Timeless Principles" to implement the steps of the plan.**
6. **Allow ample space (Law of Operating Space, LOS) to operate in and plenty of time (Law of Operating Time, LOT) to work the plan.**
7. **Operate and think primarily in terms of the seven-levers of the law of leverage (LOL), the law of money (LOM) and the law of prosperity (LOP).**
8. **Create an honest feedback system to collect data and review the progress in order to correct the**

plan or method of operation as needed, but never alter the original goal or purpose. *In other words, change the path, never the purpose!*

If one follows this series of steps and adheres to them persistently, the universe will open up in many mysterious ways to flow money, power, good fortune, success and abundance of many pro-survival things. This leads to a unique and incredible situation where one cannot help but be pushed gradually by many friendly forces toward the realm of prosperity of enormous magnitude!

In short, following these eight steps to the letter, will cause one's volume of production and brand name to eventually soar to the top of that particular business sector and one's success will be inevitable, as the sun follows the dawn!

Once the word gets out about one's quality and integrity of operation, there will be people lined up and anxious to buy one's brand of products and services. One will soon find himself rising toward an unlimited profit potential by winning a large percentage of the market share in one's business niche, and thus starting to dominate it.

The old cliché "think big" seems too small to even bother with or utilize in one's long term thinking methodology, in business or life. Instead, one should now substitute this old cliché in his daily endeavors toward prosperity with a more modern and appropriate one: "Think infinite!"

The Duality Principle

"Heart knows neither duality nor the limitations of space and time."

—Sri Sathya Sai Baba (1929-)
Indian Spiritual Leader

An important *principle* is the concept of *"duality,"* which has special significance in the sciences as well as the business world and thus needs to be addressed in depth.

The word *"Dual"* comes from the Latin word *"Duo,"* which means "two." In scientific jargon, the word "dual" is used to mean two concepts or things that are comparable to each other but are opposite in nature and thus act as counterparts to each other.

The items in a pair of dual concepts complement each other and therefore form a complete set. For example, concepts of (positive & negative), (+∞ & −∞), and (buy & sell) are pairs of dual concepts. Furthermore, combining the concept of duality with the principle of relativity of knowledge gives us the whole panoramic view of our physical universe in its entirety and covers all bases as shown on the next page.

On a more general level, we can see that every material item in the physical universe is matched up with its dual, and together they create a locked up standing wave, a sort of equilibrium of forces which has a location but does not allow a real indefinite flow to exist and thus causes the physical universe, as a whole, to float in time.

The concept of **"Dual"** is used extensively and implicitly in the business world and when used in this book we mean specifically, *two concepts, energy forms or physical things that are of comparable magnitudes but of opposite nature, thus becoming counterpart of each other.*

"Act with kindness, but do not expect gratitude"

—Confucius (551-479 BC)
China's Most Famous Teacher, Philosopher, and Political Theorist

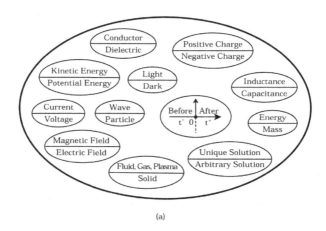

(a)

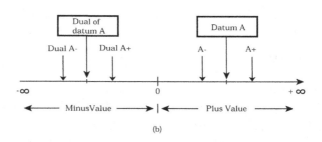

(b)

a) Examples Of Dual Concepts, and b) Duality Combined With The Principle Of Relativity Of Knowledge.

*The concept of "dual" leads to the "**Duality Principle**," (or **The Principle of Duality**) which is a very important concept in the sciences and engineering as well as in the business or life in general.*

*The **Duality Principle** is defined as "The principle that for any known principle or statement of fact there is a dual principle or statement of fact, in which one replaces quantities and operations with their duals. In other words, if a statement is true, it remains true if each quantity and operation is replaced by its dual quantity and operation."*

By observing and understanding one of the items of a pair, the properties of the other item in the pair can be predicted and grasped. Thus one can gain a deeper understanding about each item or the whole pair by this process.

Thus, using the duality principle we have the following **dual statements** of facts at work in the business world:

➤ Static-kinetic principle.

➤ Buy long term vs. sell short term principle.

➤ Buy low volatility vs. sell high volatility options.

➤ Low risk vs. high profit transactions.

➤ Buy low vs. sell high investing.

➤ Sweet spot vs. sour spot principle of trading.

➤ Becoming a buyer vs. a seller.

➤ ABCD principle vs. bankruptcy concept (mentally or physically).

➤ The Dynamic Investment Principle vs. static investment principle (i.e., making no adjustments like buy and hold strategy).

> Prime the pump principle vs. becoming a human vacuum-machine (Operating on inflows).

> Ratchet principle vs. the patsy principle.

> Visualizing principle vs. robotism in life.

> Compounding principle vs. gambling.

> Fly with eagles vs. scratch with the turkeys.

> Shun the negative principle vs. agreeing with the zapping sharks in the society.

> Create to sell vs. sell to survive modality.

There could other dualities but these are the main ones.

"Every explicit duality is an implicit unity."

—Alan Watts (1915-1973)
American Writer

﹃ ℰ✻❀✻ℰ ﹄

Instilling Lifelong Learning

"Intellectual growth should commence at birth and cease only at death"

—Albert Einstein (1879-1955)
German Born American Physicist, Nobel Prize in 1921

If one intends to achieve a high level of prosperity, one needs to instill some very positive habits in his life early on and cultivate new ones as one grows more confident.

One of those positive habits is lifelong learning. One must develop a system in his personal life such that he is constantly exposed to correct information with regard to his profession or areas that he would like to improve. The information could be in the form of;
a) Textbooks.
b) Audio CDs, tapes, etc.
c) Recorded video tapes or DVDs.
d) Live lectures at college or university.
e) Seminars and conferences.
f) Educational shows on TV or radio.
g) Educational internet sites.

If one implements the above system into his life diligently, then he can't help but become superior in his creative powers and start visualizing a prosperous life, which is the beginning of the road.

We know well that prosperity does not happen accidentally. However, we may not be quite sure what the elements of prosperity are on a methodical basis. The elements of prosperity are:

1) A correct plan of actions.

2) A well organized team.

3) A creative and able mind trained in effective problem solving.

4) Knowing the ten keys well.

5) Having a majority (if not all) of the genius traits.

6) Having an avid desire to learn and expand.

7) Thinking long term solutions.

Accomplishing the requirements laid out in steps (a-g) above, requires one to have a strong lifelong learning goal along with a plan for its achievement at the core of his character and existence.

The Most Powerful Ingredient to Success

"Whoever undertakes to set himself up as a judge of Truth and Knowledge is shipwrecked by the laughter of the gods."

—Albert Einstein (1879-1955)
German Born American Physicist, Nobel Prize in 1921

Most people in business believe in a magic formula or an incredible turn of events to make one a success in the business world. As it turns out, the truth is incredibly simple and if one truly grasps what is to follow in this article and in its entirety, then one's success is a surety!

*The **most powerful ingredient to success** is and will always be to have the associates, the workers, the clients and all others, **to have trust and faith in one as an individual**!*

It should be noted that by *trust,* we mean *reliance or dependence on the integrity and honesty of a person,* which translates into staying truthful by not telling lies or doing hidden harmful actions. On the other hand, by *faith* we mean *loyalty and staying bound by a promise,* which connotes absence of betrayal and treason as well as keeping one's words (whether verbal, written, etc.) once given.

This seems to be an unbelievably simple thing but it is the essence of success in the business world. If one can create such an atmosphere of trust and belief in one's character, one's goals and actions, then the wealth of the world starts flowing in one's direction in mysterious and magical ways!

However, to achieve such a state where others can trust one and believe in one, *one must be sold on himself first*! This means that one should have faith and trust in himself as a first pre-requisite. One should have such a high certainty on self as a positive force and helpful person that he can transmit that feeling to others compellingly and convince them to become part of one's team. This will make others push one's cause forward much faster and start tooting the horn favorably to promote one's benevolent intentions, while all along they feel that they are also benefiting from this action. This truly opens the door to enormous prosperity for one because with such a huge team backing one up, two questions arise and get answered rather swiftly:

a) Who could possibly stop one in his pursuit of his goals without being bulldozed over by one's supporting cast?

b) Are there any sufficient reason or unhandled uncertainty that could get one worried about future survival?

The obvious answer to either question is a resounding none!

Those who violate this principle may never get another chance to prove themselves in the business world, because their clients will leave them in droves.

The truth of this statement and its utter simplicity must be accurately tested and grasped well before one can gain certainty in it as an operating principle in life or business!

The Business World
in a Nutshell

"The true sign of intelligence is not knowledge but imagination."
—Albert Einstein (1879-1955)
German Born American Physicist, Nobel Prize in 1921

We can summarize and distill our entire work into the following essential elements:

Element #1- An Alert and Aware Viewpoint: This element lights up the entire business enterprise and is the brain of the operation from inside.

Element #2- Dreams, Purposes, Goals and Plans: This element is essential to give one a direction to flow power to, create menaingful motion and actions.

Element #3- The 50 Genius Traits: This element gives one the blueprint of the ideal traits one needs to possess to not only unfold one's true unlimted potential but also become a powerhouse in the society, a major force to reckon with. It enables one to take on the proper professional identity or role to engage correctly in the business world and get successful results. The list of these traits is shown in the table on the next page.

Table 1- All of the Traits to Achieve Absolute Genius Status

Trait#	Genius Traits
1	Having a Great Drive
2	Having Great Courage
3	Being Highly Devoted to Goals
4	Being Immensely Knowledgeable
5	Having a High Honesty and Integrity Level
6	Having Great Optimism
7	Having a High Ability to Judge
8	Being Highly Enthusiastic
9	Being Highly Willing to Take Calculated Risks
10	Having a Dynamic Energy flow
11	Being Highly Willing to Undertake an Enterprise
12	Being Highly Able to Motivate and Close People
13	Having an Outgoing Personality
14	Having a Great Ability to Communicate Well
15	Being Extremely Patient
16	Having Great Perception Powers
17	Being a Great Perfectionist
18	Having a Great Sense of Humor
19	Being Highly Versatile
20	Being Highly Adaptable
21	Being Highly Curious
22	Being an Excellent Individualist
23	Being a Great Idealist
24	Being Immensely Imaginative
25	Having a High Ability to Grant Beingness
26	Having a Great Balanced Life
27	Being a Great Leader
28	Being an Intelligent Investor

Trait#	Genius Traits (continued)
29	Being an Expert Salesman
30	Being a Great Humanitarian
31	Being a Great Environmentalist
32	Having a Great Spiritual Understanding
33	Being Highly Divine
34	Being a Clever Innovator & Problem Vanisher
35	Being a Superb False Data Detector
36	Being a Master Negotiator
37	Being a Great Futurist
38	Having Unlimited Space
39	Being able to Handle Any Incoming Force or Motion
40	Being a Great Scientist
41	Being able to Stay Exterior Stably
42	Being Able to Select the Correct Game to Play
43	Having a High Self Confidence
44	Having Great Certainty
45	Being a Great Visionary
46	Being a Great Adventurer
47	Being an Excellent Decision Maker
48	Having an Excellent Awareness Level
49	Being Able to Remain Always at Positive Cause
50	Being Able to Assume Any Identity at Will

Element#4- The 10 Ultimate Keys: The element enables one to make correct decisions and do correct actions in the business world. The list is as follows:

1. "Viewpoint Key"
2. "Knowledge Key"

3. "Leadership Key"
4. "Idea Key"
5. "Communication Key,"
6. "Niche Key"
7. "Establishment Key,"
8. "Exchange Key,"
9. "Trends Key"
10. "Legal & Ethics Key"

Element #5- The 12 Timeless and time-tested **Principles**: This element provides the guiding principles that will assist one further on the road to financial solvency. The list is as follows:

1. The Sell-First Principle.

2. The ABCD Principle of Investment.

3. The Ideal Investment Principle.

4. The Sweet Spot Principle.

5. The Dynamic Investment Principle.

6. The Static-Kinetic Principle of Business.

7. The Base of the Motor Principle.

8. Prime the Pump Principle.

9. The Patsy Principle.

10. Know Thy People Principle.

11. Fly with the Eagles Principle.

12. Shun the Negative Principle.

Element #6- The 5 unique and Extraordinary **Principles**: This element provides the extra guiding principles to assist one further on the road to financial solvency. The list is as follows:

1. The Ratchet Principle.

2. The Compounding Principle.

3. The Visualizing Principle.

4. The Duality Principle.

5. The Long-Term Solution Principle.

Element #7- The 5 Laws of Success: This will magnify all of one's efforts greatly and will reduce stress and anxiety in the process of carrying out the intended goals and execution of actions. The list of these laws are as follows:

1. The Law of Leverage (LOL)–The 7 levers are:
   Lever #1- Own Resource Leverage:
   a) *One's Own Knowledge (OOK)*,
   b) *One's Own Time (OOT)*,
   c) *One's Own Work (OOW)*,
   d) *One's Own Money (OOM)*.
   Lever #2- The Network Leverage:
   a) *Other People's Knowledge (OPK)*,
   b) *Other People's Time (OPT)*,
   c) *Other People's Work (OPW)*,
   d) *Other People's Money (OPM)*.
   Lever #3- The Option Leverage.
   Lever #4- The Insurance Leverage.
   Lever #5- The Ten Keys Leverage.
   Lever #6- The Genius Traits Leverage.
   Lever #7- The Automation Leverage.

2. The Law of Operating Space (LOS)

3. The Law of Operating Time (LOT)

4. The Law of Money (LOM)

5. The Law of Prosperity (LOP)

Element #8- The 15 Rules of Operation: These rules will help one to reduce stress, simplify life to a large extent and enable one to achieve his goals. The list of these rules are as follows:

a. **Increasing Decision Power Rule.**
b. **Building a Cash Cushion Rule.**
c. **Creating a Stress-Free Work Environment Rule.**
d. **Setting up a Reward System Rule.**
e. **Having a Postive Mental Attitude (PMA) Rule.**
f. **Removing Negativity Rule.**
g. **Removing Broker Tips Rule.**
h. **Never Arguing Rule.**
i. **Constantly Improving Rule.**
j. **Noise Filtering Rule.**
k. **Outflowing More Than Inflowing Rule.**
l. **Long-term Thinking Rule.**
m. **Winning the War Despite of the Battles Rule.**
n. **Never Giving Up Rule.**
o. **Reinvesting the Profits Rule.**

Element #9- Properly Executing the Plans: There are long-term and short-term plans that one should create and implement properly before one can achieve his dreams and attain his goals. These two types of planning are as follows:

Strategic Planning: This step provides the master plan of actions, allowing one to position all of his financial resources and and manpower in the most advantageous position on a large scale and in the long haul, prior to engaging in the battle zone of activities in the business world.

Tactical Planning: This step allows one to gain a short-term advantage by arranging one's resources skillfully during or beforehand, in order to attain lower-range objectives.

Element #10- The Most Powerful Ingredient To Success: This is the element of *truth, trust and faith*, which provides the ultimate guiding principle to light up one's path to financial solvency, enormous success and sheer abundance. This factor alone will *build enormous confidence* in one's ability to survive the unfriendly economic forces of this universe and enable one to soar to the top no matter what goes on in the economy!

The Realm of Success and Prosperity- By definition, *Success is a favorable outcome or a desirable end to an activity*, whereas *prosperity connotes well-being, wealth, flourishing, being at one's best, thriving, and living in an abundance of all desirable things*. It is the ultimate goal of any living individual: *to be successful and prosperous*, which has now become a possibility with this book!

Utilizing the above ten elements, one can approach this final destination of his journey with confidence. By knowing this work and understanding how to get to this realm, one now has greatly increased his odds of success.

These elements are shown in the form of a series of concentric circles on the next page. From this Figure, we can see that the road map to prosperity is through a guiding viewpoint having a dream and a purpose who can visualize dynamic goals as the first order of priority. By knowing and applying the ten ultimate keys and fully assuming the fifty genius traits one by one, gradually one starts to think in terms of long-term solutions to life's problems. Then, with the help of the twelve timeless and time-tested principles and the five laws of success, one either develops a team of his own (or works in a well-organized group) to implement strategic and tactical plans of actions to achieve his goals and unlimited propserity as the final destination (see below). *This is success and prosperity in a synopsis!*

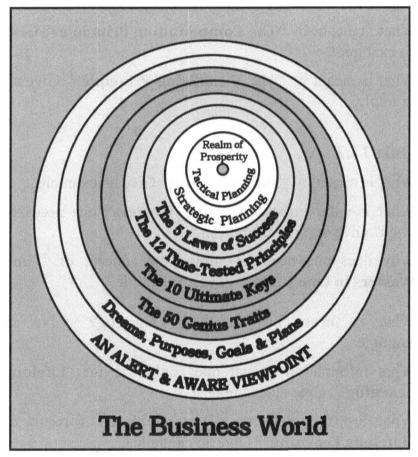

The Components Of Prosperity In The Business World.

Quizzes #17

Quiz 17.1

What is meant by **"Building Confidence?"** Give an example.

What is meant by **"The Ratchet Principle?"** Give an example.

What is meant by **"The Compounding Principle?"** Give an example.

What is meant by **"The Visualizing Principle?"** Give an example.

Quiz 17.2

What is meant by **"Time Wasters?"** Give an example.

What are the important **"Time Wasters"** one needs to avoid? Give several examples.

Why does one need to employ the concept of **"Time Wasters in One's Life?"** Give an example.

What is meant by **"Lifelong Learning?"** Give an example.

What information format one could use for **"Lifelong Learning?"** Give an example.

What are the elements of prosperity as a result of **"Lifelong Learning?"** Give an example.

What is meant by the **"Duality Principle?"** Give an example.

What is **"The Most Powerful Ingredient to Success?"** Give an example.

What are the ten elements in **"The Business World in a Nutshell?"** Give an example for each of the ten elements.

PART 18

The Epilogue

Epilogue

"There are two ways to live: you can live as if nothing is a miracle; you can live as if everything is a miracle."
—Albert Einstein (1879-1955)
German Born American Physicist, Nobel Prize in 1921

To live as a vital and powerful character, one must create in plentiful quantities, and beyond that one must develop great skills in selling one's ideas, products or services successfully.

Therfore, if one a) creates in abundance, and b) sells it with great success, then one will transcend the phrase "mere survival" and will enter a new modality of existence called "prosperous existence."

If one can think long term every time he did something then his actions perforce must have long roots of responsibility and planning embedded in them pretty well. For example, if one invested in any form of asset class whether stocks, real estate, futures and and commodities such as metals, bonds, etc., and if he also insured them against loss fully, and developed a plan for selling it at the get-go as well as managing it in the interim, then one's intention could be labled long term. Utilizing this approach, one will survive well and many hidden and closed doors of life will magically open up.

However, buying an asset without proper or adequate insurance and not being cognizent of its resale value or not knowing how to manage it for effective cash flow, is labeled short-term or myopic thinking and could lead to catastrophe!

In summary, the world at large, whether financial, business, marital, or spiritual surrenders to one the moment he starts thinking and developing long-term plans. Obviously, to make long term plans one needs to know this book really well and implement it within an inch of one's life if one expects to get superior results!

This book lays out the milestones one needs to achieve in order to arrive at the final destination: *a life or a business enterprise with unlimited prosperity*!

The journey toward an unlimited prosperity as a worthwhile dream could become a reality if one took proper steps, and is actually well deserved if one follows the path fully blazed in this work!

The journey to prosperity is worth the travel.
You have just begun. The sun is waiting for you!

The Final Assignment

1. **Sketch:** Draw a diagram showing your total understanding of the path to the realm of prosperity as discussed in this book. Accurately show all of the steps needed to enter this realm.

2. **Essay:** Write an essay on how you could apply the concepts discussed in this book to your own life in order to approach the realm of prosperity. Divide your life into several subsections and see what you could do to improve each subsection as follows:

   a. Personal life.

   b. Family or Marital life.

   c. Business life.

3. Write down your final results and conclusions, obtained from applying the principles in this book while doing this assignment.

Free Gift Offer

Please type in the following link exactly and then download the free gift:

http://www.csun.edu/~matt/ultimatekeys.zip

1. Once a pop up window shows up, click on "open" to unzip the file. Make sure you have the WinZip software to unzip the files properly.

2. After unzipping the files, create a folder called "KRCbooks_Gift" in the C: drive.

4. Save all of the files into this folder.

Glossary of Technical Terms

The following glossary supplements the presented materials in the text, but does not replace the use of an unabridged business dictionary, which is a must for mastery of our business world.

A

Absolute
a) That which is without reference to anything else and thus not comparative or dependent upon external conditions for its existence (opposed to relative), b) That which is free from any limitations or restrictions and is thus unconditionally true at all times.

Application Mass
All of the related masses that are connected and/or obtained as a result of the application of a science. This includes all physical devices, machines, experimental setups, and other physical materials that are directly or indirectly derived from and are a result of the application. In this book when we say application mass, we really mean "technical application mass." See also Generalized application mass, Technical application mass and personalized application mass.

Axiom
A self-evident truth accepted without proof.

B

Bidirectional
Responsive in both directions.

Bilateral
Having a voltage-current characteristic curve that is symmetrical with respect to the origin. If a positive voltage produces a positive current magnitude, then an equal negative voltage produces a negative current of the same magnitude.

C

Communication Principle
A fundamental concept in life and livingness, intertwined throughout the entire field of sciences, that states for communication to take place between two or more entities, three elements must be present: a source point, a receipt point, and an imposed space or distance between the two.

Current
Net transfer of electrical charges across a surface per unit time, usually represented by (I) and measured in Ampere (A). Current density (J) is current per unit area.

D

Dichotomy
Two things or concepts that are sharply or distinguishably opposite to each other.

Discovery
The gaining of knowledge about something previously unknown.

Dual
Two concepts, energy forms or physical things that are of comparable magnitudes but of opposite nature, thus becoming counterpart of each other.

Duality Theorem
States that when a theorem is true, it will remain true if each quantity and operation is replaced by its dual quantity and operation. In circuit theory, the dual quantities are "voltage and current" and "impedance and admittance." The dual operations are "series and parallel" and "meshes and nodes."

E

Electric Charge (or Charge)
(Microscopic) A basic property of elementary particles of matter (e.g., electron, protons, etc.) that is capable of creating a force field in its vicinity. This built-in force field is a result of stored electric energy. (Macroscopic) The charge of an object is the algebraic sum of the charges of

its constituents (such as electrons, protons, etc.), and may be zero, a positive or a negative number.

Electric Current (or Current)
The net transfer of electric charges (Q) across a surface per unit time.

Energy
The capacity or ability of a body to perform work. Energy of a body is either potential motion (called *potential energy*) or due to its actual motion (called *kinetic energy*).

F

Flow
The passage of particles (e.g., electrons, etc.) between two points. Example: electrons moving from one terminal of a battery to the other terminal through a conductor. The direction of flows are from higher to lower potential energy levels.

Force
That form of energy that puts an unmoving object into motion, or alters the motion of a moving object (i.e., its speed, direction or both). Furthermore, it is the agency that accomplishes work.

G

The Generalized Exchange Principle (GEP)

This principle states that every part of life is in constant exchange with every other part of life and nothing can exist without exchange principle being constantly at work on a macroscopic or microscopic level.

Granting Beingness

Imbuing or bestow life to others and things and treating them with a high level of respect and dignity; Allowing others to be who they wish to be and understanding that other people are important and should be communicated with and treated with a high degree of regard for their feelings and opinions.

H

Hypothesis

An unproven theory or proposition tentatively accepted to explain certain facts or to provide a basis for further investigation.

I

Input

The current, voltage, power, or other driving force applied to a circuit or device.

J

K

Kinetic
(*Adjective*) Pertaining to motion or change. (*Noun*) Something which is moving or changing constantly such as a piece of matter.

Kinetic Energy (K.E.)
The energy of a particle in motion. The motion of the particle is caused by a force on the particle.

Knowledge
Is a body of facts, principles, data, and conclusions (aligned or unaligned) on a subject, accumulated through years of research and investigation, that provides answers and solutions in that subject.

L

Law
An exact formulation of the operating principle in nature observed to occur with unvarying uniformity under the same conditions.

M

Man
Homo sapiens (literally, the knowing or intelligent man); mankind.

Mathematics
Mathematics are short-hand methods of stating, analyzing, or resolving real or abstract problems and expressing their solutions by symbolizing data, decisions, conclusions, and assumptions.

Matter
Matter particles are a condensation of energy particles into a very small volume.

Mechanics
The totality of the three categories of application mass: a) Generalized application Mass; b) Technical application mass, and c) Personalized application mass. See also classical mechanics and quantum mechanics.

Model
A physical (e.g., a small working replica), abstract (e.g., a procedure) or a mathematical representation (e.g., a formula) of a process, a device, a circuit, or a system and is employed to facilitate their analysis.

N

Natural Laws
A body of workable principles considered as derived solely from reason and study of nature.

Newton Laws of Motion

Three fundamental principles (called Newton's first, second, and third laws of motion), which form the basis of classical mechanics (also called Newtonian mechanics) and have proved valid for all mechanical problems, not involving speeds comparable with the speed of light and not involving atomic or subatomic particles.

Newton's First Law of Motion

The law that a particle not subjected to external forces remains at rest or moves with constant speed in a straight line.

Newton's Second Law of Motion

The law that the acceleration of a particle is directly proportional to the resultant net external force acting on the particle and is inversely proportional to the mass of the particle.

Newton's Third Law of Motion

The law that, if two particles interact, the force exerted by the first particle on the second particle (called the action force) is equal in magnitude and opposite in direction to the force exerted by the second particle on the first particle (called the reactive force). This is also called the law of action and reaction.

Noise

Random unwanted electrical signals that cause unwanted and false output signals in a circuit.

Nomenclature

The set of names used in a specific activity or branch of learning; terminology.

Nonlinear
Having an output that does not rise and fall in direct proportion to the input.

O

Occam's (or Ockham's) Razor Doctrine
A principle that assumptions introduced to explain a thing must not be multiplied beyond necessity. In simple terms, it is a principle stating that the simplest explanation of a phenomenon, which relates all of the facts, is the most valid one. Thus by using the Occam's razor doctrine a complicated problem can be solved through the use of simple explanations, much like a razor cutting away all undue complexities (after William of Occam, an English philosopher, 1300-1349, who made a great effort to simplify scholasticism).

Output
The current, voltage, power, or driving force delivered by a circuit or device.

P

Particle
Any tiny piece of matter, so small as to be considered theoretically without magnitude (i.e., zero size), though having mass, inertia and the force of attraction. Knowing zero size is an absolute and thus impossible in the physical universe, practical particles range in diameter from a

fraction of angstrom (as with electrons, atoms and molecules) to a few millimeters (as with large rain drops).

Passive
A component that may control but does not create or amplify electrical energy.

Physical Universe (Also Called The Material Universe or The Universe)
Is a universe based upon three ideas, called original ideas (space, energy and change) and has four main components (matter, energy, space and time).

Positivity
Is the state of being in an explicit and question-free condition; certainty; confidence; assuredness; definiteness of purpose and goal.

Postulate
a) (NOUN) is an assumption or assertion set forth and assumed to be true unconditionally and for all times without requiring proof; especially as a basis for reasoning or future scientific development; b) (VERB) To put forth or assume a datum as true or exist without proof.

Potential Energy (P.E.)
Any form of stored energy that has the capability of performing work when released. This energy is due to the position of particles relative to each other.

Principle
A rule or law illustrating a natural phenomenon, operation of a machine, the working of a system, etc.

Pyramid of Knowledge
Workable knowledge forms a pyramid, where from a handful of common denominators efficiently expressed by a series of basic ideas, axioms and natural laws, which form the foundation of a science, an almost innumerable number of devices, circuits and systems can be thought up and developed. The plethora of the mass of devices, circuits and systems generated is known as the "application mass," which practically approaches infinity in sheer number.

Q

R

Radio Frequency (RF)
Any wave in the frequency range of a few kHz to 300 MHz, at which coherent electromagnetic radiation of energy is possible.

S

Science
A branch of study concerned with establishing, systematizing, and aligning laws, facts, principles, and methods that are derived from hypothesis, observation, study and experiments.

Space (Also Called Created Space)
The continuous three-dimensional expanse extending in all directions, within which all things under consideration exist.

Static
(*Adjective*) Pertaining to no-motion or no-change. (*Noun*) Something which is without motion or change such as truth (an abstract concept). In physics, one may consider a very distant star (a physical universe object) a static on a short term basis, but it is not totally correct because the distant star is moving over a long period of time, thus is not truly a static but only an approximation, or a physical analogue of a true static.

Subjective Time
Is the consideration of time in one's mind, which can be a nonlinear or linear quantity depending on one's viewpoint.

Symbiont
An organism living in a state of association and interdependence with another kind of organism, especially where such association is of mutual advantage, such as a pet. Such a state of mutual interdependence is called "symbiosis."

T

Technical Application Mass (T.A.M.)
Is the category of man-made application mass that is produced directly as a result of application of a science using its scientific ideas, axioms, laws and other technical data. Examples include such things as a television set, a

computer, an automobile, a power generator, a telephone system, a rocket, etc. See also Application mass, Personalized application mass, and Generalized application mass.

Technology
The application of a science for practical ends.

Theory
An explanation based on observation and reasoning, which explains the operation and mechanics of a certain phenomenon. It is a generalization reached by inference from observed particulars and implies a larger body of tested evidence and thus a greater degree of probability. It uses a hypothesis as a basis or guide for its observation and further development.

Time (Also Called Mechanical Time or Objective Time)
That characteristic of the physical universe at a given location that orders the sequence of events on a microscopic or macroscopic level. It proceeds from the interaction of matter and energy and is merely an "index of change," used to keep track of a particle's location. The fundamental unit of time measurement is supplied by the earth's rotation on its axis while orbiting around the sun. It can also alternately be defined as the co-motion and co-action of moving particles relative to one another in space. See also subjective time.

U

Unidirectional
Flowing in only one direction (e.g., direct current).

Unilateral
Flowing or acting in one direction only causing a non-reciprocal characteristic.

Universal Communication Principle (Also Called Communication Principle)
A fundamental concept in life and livingness that is intertwined throughout the entire field of sciences that states for communication to take place between two or more entities, three elements must be present: a source point, a receipt point, and an imposed space or distance between the two.

Universe (Derived From Latin Meaning "Turned Into One", "A Whole)
Is the totality or the set of all things that exist in an area under consideration, at any one time. In simple terms, it is an area consisting of things (such as ideas, masses, symbols, etc.) that can be classified under one heading and be regarded as one whole thing.

V

Viewpoint
Is a point on a mental plane from which one creates (called creative viewpoint) or observes (called observing viewpoint) an idea, an intended subject or a physical object.

Voltage
Voltage or potential difference between two points is defined to be the amount of work done against an electric field in order to move a unit charge from one point to the other.

Voltage Source
The device or generator connected to the input of a network or circuit.

W

Wave
A disturbance that propagates from one point in a medium to other points without giving the medium as a whole any permanent displacement.

Wave Propagation
The travel of waves (e.g., electromagnetic waves) through a medium.

Wavelength
The physical distance between two points having the same phase in two consecutive cycles of a periodic wave along a line in the direction of propagation.

Recommended Resources

1. Bauar, Gail, *Engineering Ethics: An industrial perspective*, Elsevier Press, 2006.

2. Baxter, William F., *People or Penguins: The Case for Optimal Pollution*, New York: Columbia University Press, 1974.

3. Bonine, John E., *The Law Of Environmental Protection: Cases -- Legislation -- Policy*, St. Paul: West Publications, 1984.

4. Catalano, George, "*Engineering Ethics: Peace, Justice and the Earth*," Prentice Hall, 2006.

5. Frankenberg, Kurt and Zerenner Ernie, *The Blueprint, Limited Risk Investing*, Wilmington: Power Financials Group, 2010.

6. Goodpaster, Kenneth E., *The Concept of Corporate Responsibility*, New York: Random House, 1984.

7. Harris, Charles and Michael Pritchard, and Michael Rabins, *Engineering Ethics: Concepts and Cases*, Wiley, 2004.

8. Martin, Mike, *Ethics in Engineering*, McGraw Hill, 2004.

9. Moriarty, Gene, *The Engineering Project: Its Nature, Ethics, and Promise*, Prentice Hall, 2006.

10. Merman, Stephen K. and John E. Mclaughlin *Out-Interviewing the Interviewer*, New York, Prentice Hall, 1983.

11. Mitton, Jay W. *The Asset Protection Bible*, The Legal Protection Group, LLC, 2005.

12. Petulla, Joseph M., *Environmental Management in Industry* in Albert Flores, ed., *Ethics and Risk Management in Engineering*, Lanham, Md: University Press of America, 1989.

13. Radmanesh, M. M. *The Ultimate Keys to Success in Business and Science*, Bloomington: AuthorHouse, 2008.

14. Radmanesh, M. M. *Cracking the Code of Our Physical Universe*, Bloomington: AuthorHouse, 2006.

15. Radmanesh, M. M. *The Gateway to Understanding: Electrons to Waves and Beyond*, Bloomington: AuthorHouse, 2005.

16. Radmanesh, M. M., *The Million Dollar Concepts in Business Series*, 2-CD pack audiobook, Los Angeles: KRCBooks, 2010.

17. Radmanesh, M. M. *The Gateway to Understanding: Electrons to Waves and Beyond WORKBOOK*, Bloomington: Author-House, 2005.

18. Radmanesh, M. M. *The Eight Keys to the Treasure Vault Series*, 4-CD pack audiobook, Los Angeles: KRCBooks, 2010.

19. Radmanesh, M. M. *The Mechanics Series*, 4-CD pack audiobook, Los Angeles: KRCBooks, 2008.

20. Radmanesh, M. M. *The Science Series*, 4-CD pack audiobook, Los Angeles: KRCBooks, 2008.

21. Radmanesh, M. M. *The Insight Series*, 4-CD pack audiobook, Los Angeles: KRCBooks, 2008.

22. Robinson, Simon, Engineering, Business & Professional Ethics, Elsevier Press, 2007.

23. Schwartz, G., and P. W. Bishop. *Moments of Discovery*, New York: Basic Books, 1962.

24. Taton, R. *History of Science*, Vols. I-IV. New York: Basic Books, 1964.

25. Wightman, W.P.D. *The Growth of Scientific Ideas*, Yale University press, New Haven, Conn., 1969.

Index

About the Author

Matthew M. Radmanesh received his BSEE degree from Pahlavi University in electrical engineering in 1978, his MSEE and Ph.D. degrees from the University of Michigan, Ann Arbor, in Microwave Electronics and Electro-Optics in 1980 and 1984, respectively.

He has worked in academia for Kettering University (formerly GMI Engineering & Management) and in industry for Hughes Aircraft Co., Maury Microwave Corp. and Boeing Aircraft Co. He is currently a faculty member in the electrical and computer engineering department at California State University, Northridge, CA.

Dr. Radmanesh is a senior member of IEEE, Eta Kappa Nu, and Tau Beta Pi Honor societies and a past president (three years) of the SFV Chapter of the IEEE Microwave Theory and Technique (MTT) society. His many years of experience in both microwave industry and academia have led to over 40 technical papers in national and international journals and several design handbooks in microwave engineering and in solid state devices and integrated circuit engineering.

His current research interests include design of RF and Microwave devices and circuits, millimeter-wave circuit applications, photonic engineering as well as engineering education. He received the distinguished lecturer award at the 1994 IEEE international Microwave Symposium and was awarded twice by IEEE LA council for his contributions to the MTT society (1994, 1995). He also received two awards for commitment and dedication to education from IEEE in 2002 and 2003.

Dr. Radmanesh won the MPD divisional award while at Hughes Aircraft Co. for his pioneering work in the development and design of solid state millimeter wave noise sources in Ka-band as well as V-band, and a similar award for his outstanding contributions to the HERF project from Boeing Aircraft Co. He holds two patents for his pioneering work and novel designs of two millimeter-wave noise sources.

Dr. Radmanesh has authored several popular books including *"Electronic Waves & Transmission Line Circuit Design,"* in 2011, *"Advanced RF & Microwave Circuit Design,"* in 2009, *"The Ultimate Keys to Success in Business & Science,"* in 2008, *"RF & Microwave Design Essentials,"* in 2007, *"Cracking the Code of Our Physical*

Universe," in 2006, and another *"The Gateway to Understanding: Electrons to Waves and Beyond,"* accompanied by a comprehensive WORKBOOK in 2005, all published by AuthorHouse; as well as another textbook entitled *"Radio Frequency and Microwave Electronics Illustrated"* published by Prentice Hall in 2001, with its Chinese edition (ISBN 7-5053-7628-4) published in 2002, and the Korean language translation (ISBN 89-7283-264-2) in 2005. He has also created and produced seven multi-CD audiobooks on education, engineering sciences and business. His hobbies include chess, philosophy, soccer and tennis.

Dr. Radmanesh has created a wealth of technical information in electronics, engineering, sciences, education and the business world using time-tested principles and the scientific methodology. He intends to bring about a higher level of understanding in the business and scientific communities across the Globe and the society as a whole, about the basic principles of life and livingness of which the knowledge about business, science and engineering is but a subset.

Quick Order Form

Telephone orders: Call 1(888) 280-7715 toll free. Have your credit card ready.
Email orders: mattradman@yahoo.com,
Postal Orders: KRC, Matthew Radmanesh
　　　　　　　　PO Box 280188, Northridge, CA 91328-0188,

Please send the following books, disks or reports. I understand that I may return any of them in the *original condition* for a full refund—for any reason, no questions asked.

_____

_____

_____

_____

Please send more FREE information on:
o Other Books　　o Consulting　o Speaking/Seminars

Name:_____

　　　Address:_____

　　　City: _____State: _____Zip: _____

　　　Telephone:_____

　　　Email address:_____

Sales tax: Please add 8.25% for products shipped to California addresses.

Shipping by air:
U.S. only: $4.00 for first book or disk and $2.00 for each additional product.

Payment: o　Check　　o Money order
Make the check or money order payable to: KRC

Other Books By The Author

The Gateway to Understanding: Electrons to
Waves and Beyond, AuthorHouse, 2005.

The Gateway to Understanding: Electrons to
Waves and Beyond WORKBOOK,
AuthorHouse, 2005.

Cracking The Code of Our Physical Universe
Waves and Beyond, AuthorHouse, 2006.

 Radio Frequency and Microwave Electronics
Illustrated, Prentice Hall, 2001.

 RF& Microwave Design Essentials, AuthorHouse,
2007.

 The Ultimate Keys to Success in Business &
Science, AuthorHouse, 2008.

Printed in the United States
by Baker & Taylor Publisher Services